QUICK
ESCAPES

from San Francisco

Second Edition

Q U I C K
ESCAPES

from
San Francisco
30 Weekend Trips from the Bay Area

by

Karen Misuraca

A Voyager Book

The Globe Pequot Press

Old Saybrook, Connecticut

Photo Credits

Pp. 1, 3, 13, 23, 65, 74, 82: courtesy Sonoma County Convention and Visitors Bureau; p. 34: courtesy Napa Valley Visitors Bureau; p. 45: courtesy The Fetzer Winery; p. 54: courtesy The Gingerbread Mansion; p. 89: courtesy Joshua Grindle Inn; p. 101: courtesy Diane Smith; pp. 112, 221, 279: courtesy National Park Service; p. 120: courtesy Marin County Visitors Bureau; pp. 127, 136: courtesy Santa Cruz Convention and Visitors Bureau; p. 129: courtesy California Office of Tourism; p. 148: courtesy Richard G. Averitt; p. 157: courtesy Carmel Visitors Bureau; p. 170: courtesy Carmel Valley Ranch Resort; pp. 183, 185: courtesy Sacramento Convention and Visitors Bureau; p. 194: courtesy Nevada City Chamber of Commerce; p. 210: courtesy Bear Valley Lodge; pp. 223, 233: courtesy Lake Tahoe Visitors Authority; p. 243: courtesy Incline Village Visitors Bureau; p. 253: courtesy Trinity County Chamber of Commerce; pp. 261, 269: courtesy Shasta Cascade Wonderland Association; p. 289 courtesy Yosemite Park and Curry Company. All other photos are by the author.

Library of Congress Cataloging-in-Publication Data

Misuraca, Karen.
Quick escapes from San Francisco : 30 weekend trips from the Bay
    area / by Karen Misuraca. — 2nd ed.
        p. cm. — (Quick escapes series)
    "A Voyager book."
    ISBN 1-56440-890-6
    1. San Francisco Bay Area (Calif.)—Tours. I. Title. II. Series.
F868. S156M63 1996
917.94'60453—dc20   96-7374
                                                              CIP

Manufactured in the United States of America
Second Edition/First Printing

Acknowledgments

Thanks to the generous innkeepers of Northern California and to Michael and my girls for sailing steadfastly along with me.

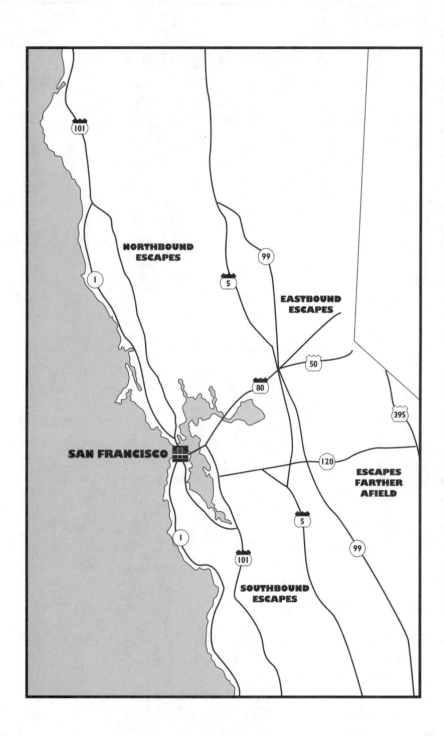

Contents

Introduction

When Horace Greeley traveled overland from New York to San Francisco in 1859, he mused, "As we neared the California trail, the white coverings of many emigrant wagons dotted the landscape, giving the trail the appearance of a river running between great meadows, with many ships sailing on its bosom."

Today's travelers still sail along Northern California's highways, their hearts set on enjoying the natural beauty and historic richness waiting to be discovered in this part of the state.

Those of us who live in or visit the Bay Area are within easy distance of wine country, gold country, redwood country—villages by the sea, cabins in the mountains, houseboats on the delta. It's hard to avoid clichés when describing the wide variety of destinations accessible within a few hours. From the missions of the Salinas Valley to the historic mansions of Lake Tahoe, honky-tonk beach towns, country roads, hiking trails under the pines, seafood cafes beside a bay—you can escape every weekend for a year and still have a hundred places to see.

At a loss for what to do this weekend? These detailed itineraries provide everything you need to know for a getaway from the city. Every escape is a driving tour, with sightseeing, recreation, restaurants, and lodgings located and described. To give you a variety of activities from which to choose, days are lively, packed with sights and sidetrips. Annual **Special Events** are listed, as are **Other Recommended Restaurants and Lodgings. There's More** gives you a reason to return another time. And for advance planning, maps, and local visitor's bureaus, there's **More Information**.

If you favor weekends tucked away in one peaceful spot, use the chapters to book your hotels, choose restaurants, and read about what all the other tourists are doing.

For maximum enjoyment of your short, sweet sojurns, take care to avoid heavy traffic times—Friday and Sunday afternoons and commuting hours. Keeping California's microclimates in mind, be prepared for weather changes throughout the year, particularly in the coastal and mountain regions. Fog and rain, or even snow, may not be what you expected, but discoveries made on a wintry weekend could turn you into a California lover, in more ways than one.

If you're looking forward to a particular bed-and-breakfast inn or a restaurant, be sure to call well in advance. And remember that in some resort communities, businesses may not be open every month of the year.

Most restaurants and lodgings listed are in the midrange pricewise;

a few special places are expensive. Rates and prices are not noted, because they can be counted on to change.

When you come across a memorable place that would be an appropriate addition to this book, or if you have comments on how the escapes worked out for you, please drop me a note. Thanks is due to the travelers who made useful suggestions and contributions to this second edition of *Quick Escapes from San Francisco*.

It's a good idea to include the following items in your getaway bag:

Jacket, long pants, and walking shoes for trail hiking and beach-combing in any weather

Binoculars (so as not to miss bald eagles circling and whales spouting)

Corkscrew, a California necessity

Daypack or basket with picnic gear

Maps: The directions and maps provided herein are meant for general information—you'll want to obtain your own maps.

California State Park Pass: Most state parks charge a day fee of several dollars. Frequent visitors to the state parks will save money by purchasing an annual car pass and/or boat launching pass (discounts are available for seniors and those with a limited income).

For more information on Northern and Central California destinations, write or call the California Office of Tourism, P.O. Box 9278, Van Nuys, CA 91409; (800) 862–2543.

The information in this guidebook was confirmed at press time. We recommend, however, that you call establishments before traveling to obtain current information.

Northbound Escapes

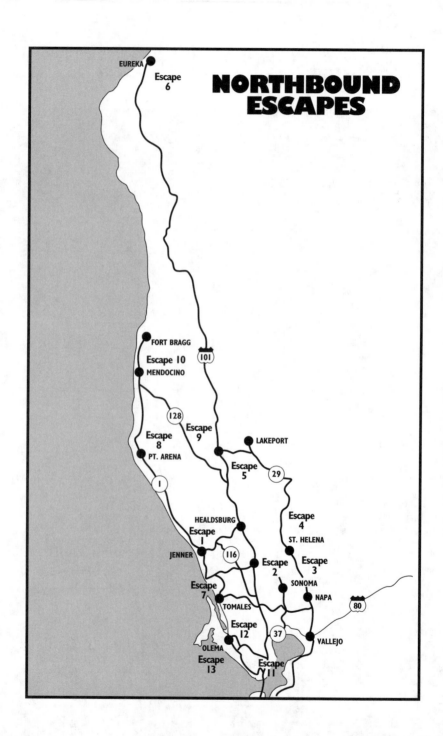

Wine Road to the Sea

A bridge spans the beautiful Russian River.

The Russian River Route, Healdsburg

——————————— 1 NIGHT ———————————

Wineries • Farm trails • Antiques shopping
Redwoods • River rambling • Victorian town

———————————————————————————————

In the mid-1800s tourists from San Francisco rode ferries across the bay and hopped onto a narrow-gauge railroad to reach summer resorts on the Russian River. The arrival of the motorcar and the decline of lumbering, followed by a disastrous fire that raged through the entire river valley in 1923, caused the towns along the river to fall into a deep sleep for a few decades. The town of Guerneville never missed a beat, however, thriving through the Big Band era when Benny Goodman and Harry James kept the weekenders coming. In the 1970s the tremendous growth of wineries began a new era of tourism. Now more than fifty wineries can be discovered on the backroads of the Russian River and Dry Creek valleys.

Russian River Valley grapes thrive in warm days and cool, fog-blanketed nights, maturing slowly and with a high degree of acidity. Early ripening varieties—Chardonnay, Pinot Noir, and Gewürztraminer—ripen and are harvested before the threat of fall rains and lower temperatures.

From high in the Mendocino National Forest, the **Russian River** winds through redwood canyons, past sandy beaches, orchards, and vineyards, sliding calmly all the way to the Pacific Ocean at Jenner. If you vacationed on the river before the winter of 1995, you may now find beaches and river bends changed in appearance or disappeared altogether. A devastating flood—more than a dozen feet above official flood level—rearranged the landscape, stranding canoes in treetops and fish in backyards. But now, aside from the vestiges of high-water marks here and there, the river and the resorts and towns along her banks are completely recovered and the surroundings are lush and green as before. Rustic inns, casual cafes, leafy walking trails, great fishing holes, and magnificent redwood groves are reason to spend several weekends following its path.

Canoeing, kayaking, and tubing on the Russian are very popular activities. The river is generally slow-moving and calm, with quiet coves and sandy beaches along the way. A good place to try out these activities is on the scenic 10-mile stretch from Forestville to Guerneville, where you will find many nice beaches and stopping points for fishing and picnicking. It will take a half-day, including rest stops. Osprey, blue herons, deer, and turtles are some of the wildlife that will accompany your trek. Canoe and kayak companies will shuttle you back to you starting point. Bring plenty of water, secure your car keys with a safety pin in your pocket, and beware of sunburn on the top of your legs.

The westernmost destination of your Russian River Wine Road escape is the tiny town of Jenner-by-the-Sea, on a high bluff overlooking a marshy bird sanctuary at the mouth of the river.

Day 1

Morning

Head north from the Golden Gate Bridge on Highway 101 to

Healdsburg, about one and a quarter hours, taking the central Healdsburg exit into the center of town, parking on the **Healdsburg Plaza,** a lovely, tree-shaded Spanish-style plaza built when the town was established in 1867. The plaza is surrounded by shops and restaurants. Band concerts and outdoor festivals are held here on many weekends. Between the Alexander Valley and the Dry Creek Valley, the small town of Healdsburg is prime Sonoma County wine country. Grown here are some of California's finest Zinfandels, a hearty red of Italian heritage. The Dry Creek Valley also produces excellent Sauvignon Blanc, a dry but fruity white wine. Several winetasting rooms are within a block or so of the plaza, including **Windsor Vineyards** (707–433–2822), **White Oak** (707–433–8429), **Clos du Bois** (707–433–5576), and **William Wheeler** (707–433–8786). Also nearby are the **Sonoma County Wine Library,** Piper and Center streets (707–433–3773), and the **Healdsburg Historical Museum,** 221 Matheson (707–431–3325). Get a walking-tour map at the **Chamber of Commerce,** 217 Healdsburg Avenue (707–433–6935).

Evans Designs ceramics, the world's largest producer of Raku pottery, has a factory outlet and gallery worth visiting at 355 Healdsburg Avenue (707–433–2502). Fifty antiques dealers hold court in the big blue building at **Vintage Plaza Antiques,** 44 Mill Street (707–433–8409).

The **Dry Creek Valley** west of town is top biking and winetasting territory. (Throughout the Sonoma and Napa wine regions, bike rental companies will pick you up at any point on your route and return you to your vehicle, by prior arrangement.) A nice 20-mile loop on gently rolling hills starts at the town plaza, heads south to Mill Street, crosses under the highway, and joins Dry Creek Road going north. Endless vineyards and rows of low, forested mountains remain in view throughout the ride. At Yoakim Bridge Road, make a stop at the Dry Creek Peach and Produce stand for juicy snacks. At the old Dry Creek General Store (3495 Dry Creek Road, 707–433–4171), you can buy sandwiches and picnic here or take provisions in your bike basket.

Ferrari-Carano, at 8761 Dry Creek Road (707–433–6700), comes as a surprise in the valley where most of the wineries are small, country places. A tasting room and an upscale shop are in the impressive Italianate Villa Fiore (House of Flowers), elegant with stone columns and arches and Roman tile roof and balconies, and surrounded by lush gardens. The prestigious magazine, *Wine Spectator*, rates Ferrari-Carano wines fifth in their list of the top 100, characterizing their Alexander Valley Chardonnay as "ripe, generous fruit flavors, layers of pear, pineapple, honey, vanilla and almond, amazingly long and complex finish."

If Zinfandel is your passion, be sure to stop at **Quivira Winery,** 4900 West Dry Creek Road (707–431–8333).

Five minutes south of town at 1147 Old Redwood Highway (707–433–8843), **Piper Sonoma's** sparkling wine cellars offers self-guided tours, followed by bubbly tasting on breezy terraces surrounded by vineyards.

On the south end of town on a bend of the Russian River, **Healdsburg Memorial Beach Park** is a popular place to sun and swim (13839 Old Redwood Highway; 707–433–1625).

Lunch: **Bistro Ralph,** 109 Plaza Street, (707) 433–1380. Locally raised produce, meats, and poultry are used to create miracles: roasted garlic and polenta with baby lamb, Hog Island oysters, peach shortcake, creme brulée. Ask for the Local Stash, a special wine list of older vintages from the Dry Creek and Alexander Valley wineries.

Afternoon

Proceed southwest out of town on Westside Road, stopping at the sharp left turn and driving through the arch to see **Madrona Manor,** 1001 Westside Road (707–433–4231), one of California's largest and finest Victorian masterpieces. Built in 1881, the huge manor is now an inn and restaurant surrounded by magnificent gardens. Walk in and ask for a tour of the museumlike rooms and outbuildings; depending on their bookings, it may or may not be possible but is definitely worth a try.

Mill Creek Vineyards, at 1401 Westside Road (707–433–5098), is a small, family-owned winery on a knoll overlooking the valley; it's fun to see their wooden mill wheel turning beside the creek. The redwood tasting room is modeled after the many mills that dotted Dry Creek at the turn of the century. Two picnic areas offer panoramic views of the valley and beyond. Mill Creek Vineyards makes several wines, from a good "Old Mill Red" table wine to a superb Cabernet Sauvignon.

You'll be following the Russian River now, all the way to the ocean. Valley foothills become mountains, oaks give way to dark redwood and fir forests, and the roadsides become ferny and damp. Along the riverbank in freshwater marshes grow silvery gray-green willows and cottonwoods.

Take a left onto Wohler Road, passing more than a half-dozen wineries on your way to River Road, then turn west. Stop at **Korbel Champagne Cellars,** 13250 River Road (707–887–2294), for a tour of the winery and the gardens. Founded in 1886 by Czech immigrants, the ivy-covered stone winery is a piece of Old Europe tucked into the rolling, vineyard-carpeted hills of the Russian River Valley. The guided winery tour, including museum, film, garden walk, and champagne tasting, is one of the most complete and enjoyable of all California wineries.

You'll follow the river and the redwoods a few minutes further down the road to the summer-vacation town of **Guerneville**, chockfull of souvenir shops, cafes, and art galleries.

In the middle of town, turn north onto Armstrong Woods Road a mile or so to **Armstrong Grove Redwoods State Reserve** (707–869–2015), 750 acres of glorious redwood groves along Fife Creek. Easy paths lead to sunny picnic areas and old-growth trees up to 300 feet tall. For a half-day horseback ride into the wilderness bordering Austin Creek State Recreation Area, call the **Armstrong Woods Pack Station** (707–887–2939). Even beginning riders will love the lunch ride, which meaders gently out of the redwood forest through a variety of wildlife habitats to ridgetops overlooking the Russian River Valley. On top of the world with a 360-degree view of five counties, you'll be served a gourmet lunch laid out on white tablecloths in a wildflower-strewn meadow. You can also ride your own horses on the guided pack trips and bring your own food.

Accessed from Armstrong Grove, the **Austin Creek Recreation Area** (707–869–2015) is 4,200 acres of hills, canyons, and river glens that campers, hikers, and horseback riders love to explore. Wildflowers in the spring, deep forests, good birding, bluegill and black bass fishing in Redwood Lake, and primitive camping sites are a few of the attractions. It is hot and dry in the summer, glorious in the spring with blooming wild azaleas, rushing creeks, and maples, ash, and alder in full leaf. Wildlife abounds on Austin Creek, from great blue herons, woodpeckers, and ravens to deer, foxes, and, occasionally, bobcats. Bullfrog Pond is a popular family campground here, with tent sites and RV sites for vehicles up to 20 feet.

Lodging: **Applewood**, 13555 Highway 116, Guerneville 95446. (707) 869–9093. An elegant 1920s California Mission Revival mansion in the redwoods, featuring a heated swimming pool, six acres of gardens and forest, hot tub, in-room Jacuzzis and double showers, and verandas. Ten romantically decorated rooms with down comforters, garden views. You could forget the sightseeing and just settle in here.

Dinner: Applewood. Candlelight gourmet dinners in the solarium by the fireplace.

Day 2

Morning

Breakfast: Applewood.

Ten minutes west of Guerneville, bear left across the bridge onto Moscow Road, through the tiny burg of **Monte Rio** to **Villa Grande,** a small riverbend village that's changed little since the 1920s, when it was built as a summer encampment for vacationers from San Francisco. There is a beach here, a delightful array of early Craftsman-style cottages, and not much else.

Back on the main road, it's not far to **Duncans Mills,** where a dozen or so shops nestle in a Victorian-era village, another 1880s railroad stop. Take a look at the only remaining North Pacific Coast Railroad station.

The **Duncans Mills General Store** (707–865–1240) stocks fishing gear, groceries, and antiques. At the **Gold Coast Oyster and Espresso Bar,** Steelhead Boulevard (707–865–1441), oysters are barbecued in a garden courtyard in the summertime, and you can smell fresh-roasted coffee beans year-round. Shops in Duncans Mills sell everything from fishing gear and fine jewelry to top-notch wildlife art.

As you head further west, the river widens and sheep graze on open, windswept hillsides. The Russian River meets the sea at **Bridgehaven,** the junction of Highways 116 and 1, where you'll turn north toward **Jenner-by-the-Sea.** In the winter ocean waves and the river clash here in a stormy drama. In the summer the mouth of the river is cut off from the ocean by temporary dunes. Salmon and steelhead runs attract crowds of seals hoping for delicious bites of their favorite food. In the spring seals hide in the river's mouth to give birth away from the sharp eyes of hungry sharks and whales. Ospreys in their treetop nests are some of the thousands of land and shore birds that feed and fly in this area.

Lunch: **River's End,** Highway 1 at the north end of Jenner. (707) 865–2484. On the cliffs overlooking Goat Rock, the Pacific, and the Russian River, this restaurant's European chef creates extraordinary cuisine, including Indonesian specialties, German veal dishes, fresh fish of all kinds, rack of lamb, wild game, and clam chowder. People come from the Bay Area just to have lunch and dinner here; reservations are absolutely necessary.

Afternoon

Drive back on Highway 116 to Guerneville, turning south on 116 past Forestville to **Kozlowski Farms,** 5566 Gravenstein/Highway 116 (707–887–1587), for luscious berries, jams, fresh fruits, and pies—the ultimate Sonoma County farm store. Pick up a **Sonoma County Farm Trails** map at Kozlowski's to locate the many produce outlets and nurseries in these verdant rolling hills. Nearby are the **Green Valley Blueberry Farm,** 9345 Ross Station Road (707–887–7496); **Campbell's Green Valley Orchard,** 9753 Green Valley Road (707–823–3580), selling herbs, flowers, and Rome Beauty apples; **Carriage Charter,** 3325 Gravenstein Highway (707–823–7083), offering horse-drawn carriage rides; and **Bennett Valley Farm,** 6797 Gio-

vanetti Road (707–887–9557), with dried flowers, garlic, and wreaths.
 Between Sebastopol and Highway 101 are dozens of antiques shops on Gravenstein Highway.
 Proceed south on Highway 101 and back to the Golden Gate Bridge.

There's More

Kiwi Kayaks, 10070 Old Redwood Highway, Windsor. (800) K–4–KAYAK. Rentals, shuttle service, learn-to-kayak classes, guided trips, retail store selling kayaks and accessories. The Kiwi Kayak is a revolutionary new design that is light years away from the old-style tippy, heavy kayaks. The inventor of the easy to paddle, super-stable Kiwi Kayak, Ann Dwyer, owns this business and she often leads the river tours. Ask for Granny Ann.
 Canoeing. Trowbridge Canoes, 20 Healdsburg Avenue, Healdsburg, 95448. (707) 433–7247.
 Burke's Canoe Trips, 8600 River Road, Forestville. (707) 887–1222. Paddle the Russian River, stopping at quiet coves and sandy beaches along the way; easy and safe for all ages. The canoe companies shuttle you back to your car.
 Johnson's Beach, wide stretch of sandy beach at Guerneville. (707) 869–2022. Site of the annual Russian River Jazz Festival.
 Northwood Golf Course, 19400 Highway 116, Guerneville. (707) 865–1116. Eighteen holes in a redwood grove.
 Fishing. Salmon runs on the Russian River occur late September through early November; steelheads follow, continuing through March. It's catfish in February and March, shad in April, several types of bass in the summer, plus crappie and bluegill. An excellent map to fishing access in the entire Russian River area is available from Russian River Region, P.O. Box 255, Guerneville 95446. (707) 869–9000.
 Lake Sonoma, a 2,700-acre lake for fishing, water sports, and camping. (707) 433–9493.
 Jimtown Store, 6706 Highway 28, a few miles northeast of Geyserville, just north of Healdsburg off Highway 101. (707) 433–1212. A destination in itself, this is an upscale general store/souvenir and antiques shop/gourmet deli/refreshment stand.

Special Events

February. Winter Wineland, Healdsburg. (707) 433–6782. A weekend of tasting, live entertainment, and celebrity events at the wineries.

March. Russian River Slug Fest, Monte Rio. (707) 869–9000. Banana slugs compete in races and contests—it's true.

March. Russian River Wine Road Barrel Tasting. (707) 433–6935.

April. Passport to Dry Creek, Healdsburg. (707) 433–3031. Wine tastings, winery and vineyards tours, food pairings, entertainment at several wineries.

May. Russian River Wine Festival, Healdsburg. (707) 433–6935. Fifty wineries, food, arts and crafts, music in the plaza.

Memorial Day Weekend Antiques Fair, Healdsburg. (707) 433–4315. An extravaganza of antiques displays and sales.

September. Russian River Jazz Festival. (707) 433–6935. Huge crowds at the beach in Guerneville; big-name performers.

October. Beer and Sausage Tasting, Villa Chanticleer, Healdsburg. (707) 433–8871. More than two dozen microbreweries, sausage tasting, live entertaiment, prizes.

Other Recommended
Restaurants and Lodgings

Guerneville

Sweet's Cafe and Bakery, 16251 Main. (707) 859–3383. The best place for Belgian waffles, omelettes, homemade croissants, espresso, and lunch.

Breeeze Inn Bar-B-Q, 15640 River Road. (707) 869–9208. Super burgers and ribs, take-out or delivery.

Ridenhour Ranch House Inn, 12850 River Road. (707) 887–1033. Next to Korbel Champagne Cellars, a turn-of-the-century redwood ranchhouse with comfortable rooms and a cottage; European chef and owner cooks incredible breakfasts.

The Estate, 13555 Highway 116. (707) 869–9093. A spacious, elegant country home, circa 1912: ten luxurious guestrooms, pool, spa; dinners some nights.

Duncans Mills

Casini Ranch Family Campground, 22855 Moscow Road. (707) 865–2255. Some 120 acres on the river, tent and RV camping, good fishing, small store, boat rentals.

Healdsburg

Charcuterie, 335 Healdsburg Avenue. (707) 431–7213. Deli sandwiches, pasta; casual cafe a few steps from the plaza.

The Haydon Street Inn, 321 Haydon Street. (707) 433–5228. A 1912 Queen Anne Victorian on a quiet, tree-shaded street. French and American antiques, down comforters, designer touches. Clawfoot and Jacuzzi tubs, full breakfasts, air-conditioning.

Healdsburg Inn on the Plaza, 110 Matheson Street. (707) 433–6991. Victorian bed and breakfast with ten antiques-chocked rooms, private baths, fireplaces, afternoon wine and tea, full breakfast.

Madrona Manor, 1001 Westside Road. (707) 433–6831. California cuisine, French and Italian classic dishes, a much-heralded restaurant in one of the largest and most elegant Victorian mansions in California. Reservations absolutely necessary. Twenty elaborately decorated inn rooms in the mansion, plus stunning traditional decor, large rooms and suites in a carriage house and other cottages. Swimming pool, fireplaces, private baths.

Raford House, 10630 Wohler Road. (707) 887–9573. On five acres of vineyards, an 1880 Victorian with seven lovely rooms, two with fireplaces. Full breakfast.

Samba Java, 109A Plaza Street. (707) 433–5282. Wild and crazy Caribbean decor, breakfast, lunch, and dinner. Housemade lox, world-class scones and pastries, exotic salads, roasted and rotisseried local poultry, meats, and fish. Daily menus change according to the season.

Jenner-by-the-Sea

Jenner Inn and Cottages, 10400 Coast Highway 1. (707) 865–2377. Comfortable bed-and-breakfast rooms with antiques and wicker, fireplaces, hot tubs, private baths, sea views.

Forestville

Topolos at Russian River Vineyards, 5700 Gravenstein/Highway 116, Forestville. (707) 887–1562. Greek and California cuisine in a circa 1870 estate home, in the dining room by the woodburning stove or outside on the garden patio. Local seafood, duckling in black currant Madeira sauce, souvlaki, spinakopita, pork in raspberry Riesling sauce, seasonal specialties. Adjacent to Russian River Vineyards, built in an interesting hop kiln style reminiscent of a century ago. The winery owners are the restaurant owners, and the bottle of wine at your dinner table may be opened by one of the winemakers, Jerry or Michael Topolos.

Santa Rosa

Lisa Hemenway's Restaurant, 714 Village Court in the Montgomery Village Shopping Center. (707) 526–5111. A nice lunch or dinner stop on the way to or from the Sonoma Valley or the Russian River. Long-established and one of the best restaurants in Northern California, bright, light, elegant decor, wine bar where you can order appetizers. Lunch is casual, dinner romantic. Asian and Pacific flavors come together in a unique California cuisine menu. Lisa expands her expertise and knowledge of ethnic cuisines by traveling and teaching internationally.

For More Information

Healdsburg Chamber of Commerce, 217 Healdsburg Avenue, Healdsburg, CA 95448. (707) 433–6935.

Russian River Region Information Center, 14034 Armstrong Woods Road, Guerneville, CA 95446. (707) 869–9212.

Jenner Visitors Center, Highway 1, Jenner, CA 95450. (707) 875–3483. Maps; boat launch.

Sebastopol Chamber of Commerce, 265 South Main, Sebastopol, CA 95472. (707) 823–3032.

Southern Sonoma Valley

The circa-1841 Mission San Francisco Solano de Sonoma.

On Country Roads

_____ 2 NIGHTS _____

Early California history • Wineries • Shopping • Hiking, biking, golf
Cheese, wine, produce • Mountain and valley parks

Between the rugged Mayacamas Mountains and the Sonoma Mountains, the 17-mile-long Sonoma Valley is a patchwork of vineyards and rich farmlands. Two-lane roads meander along rivers and creeks, through oak-studded meadows and foothills to country villages and to towns with entire neighborhoods that are National Historic Monuments. The Victorian and early California Mission eras come alive in museums and in hundreds of restored homes, inns, and commercial buildings all over the valley.

More than thirty premium wineries are located here, the birthplace of the California wine industry. Their production facilities and tasting rooms, in many cases, are of significant architectural and historical interest. Thousands of acres of vineyards create a tapestry of seasonal color and texture that cascades across the hills and streams out onto the valley floor.

Moderate climate and rich soil produce world-famous gourmet foods—cheeses, sausages, foie gras, orchard fruits and berries, nuts, and sourdough French bread. California Wine Country cuisine, a gastronomic genre all its own, attracts diners and chefs from afar.

Exploring the Sonoma Valley on quiet backroads by car, foot, or perhaps bike, you'll enjoy the landscape and discover some of Old California. After a day of winetasting, browsing in the shops, gourmet dining, and maybe a round of golf, a cozy bed-and-breakfast inn will be a welcome refuge.

Day 1

Morning

From the Golden Gate Bridge, drive north forty-five minutes on Highway 101 to the waterfront town of **Petaluma.** Take the Central Petaluma exit west into town, turning left onto Petaluma Boulevard, then right onto Western and right onto Kentucky to **New Marvin's,** 145 Kentucky (707–765–2371). Sit at an oilcloth-covered table and tuck into a hearty breakfast of nutty banana waffles. You're in the heart of a unique historical district that includes the finest block of iron-front buildings in the western United States. One of California's largest cities in the 1860s and the Egg Basket of the World early in this century, Petaluma harbors a precious collection of restored Victorians. Before heading back to 101, drive through the neighborhoods west of downtown to see gingerbread-clad, turret-topped homes.

Drive 1 mile south on Highway 101 to the Sonoma/Napa Highway 116 exit, then turn east. Passing a marina where fishing boats and rowing shells ply the Petaluma River, you'll go 5 miles to the 116 East left turn. ROAD NARROWS and SLOW road signs mean you're officially in the Sonoma Valley wine country. Lush rolling pasturelands are dotted with black-and-white cows, dairy farms, and giant valley oaks. Undulating along on the curvy two-lane road, you'll turn right at a stop sign, still on 116, then emerge into a wide valley. Passing **Los Arroyos Golf Club** (707–938–8835)—an inexpensive, three-par, nine-hole course—turn left onto Arnold Drive, heading north 8 miles, past vineyards, pony farms, country homes, and the **Valley of the Moon Winery** (707–996–6941), to the foresty village of **Glen Ellen.** On the way you'll see the tile roofs of the **Sonoma Golf Club** (707–996–4852); one of the most challenging courses in the state, it's a veritable botanical garden of trees, flowers, and waterways.

This is the **Valley of Moon,** named by its most famous (sometimes infamous) resident, Jack London, author of the classic adventure tales *Call of the Wild* and *The Sea Wolf.* You'll pass the **Jack London Bookstore and Research Center,** 14300 Arnold Drive (707–996–2888), across the road from a wonderful old gristmill, still creaking slowly over a rushing creek next to **Amedeo of Glen Ellen Ristorante,** 14301 Arnold Drive (707–996–3077), an indoor/outdoor Italian cafe.

When you see the large **London Lodge** banner, you've arrived in Glen Ellen, just a few blocks long. Turn left at the lodge, driving 1 mile up into dense oak forests to **Jack London State Historic Park** (707–938–1519). Once London's home ranch, the park is 800 magnificent acres of walking trails through groves of oaks, madrones, Douglas fir, redwoods, ferns, and explosions of wildflowers. There are shady picnic sites, mountain and valley views, a romantically spooky ruin, and a museum. Remnants of **Wolf House,** London's gigantic stone mansion, lie deep in a forest glade, at the end of a delightful short path through the trees (handicapped accessible by golf cart). Only walls and chimneys remain of the elaborately decorated and furnished home, which burned to the ground before London and his wife, Charmian, could enjoy it. Filled with London memorabilia and most of the original furnishings, his smaller home, the **House of Happy Walls,** is open to visitors.

On the way back to Glen Ellen, make a winetasting and -touring stop at **Benziger Family Winery,** 1883 London Ranch Road (707–935–3000). Beautiful valley oaks and gardens, an art gallery and picnic grounds are here, in addition to the tasting room. This is the only winery in the valley to offer a motorized tram tour of the vineyards. Call ahead for reservations.

In Glen Ellen, cross the stone bridge, bear left, and turn left onto Warm Springs Road for a 6-mile drive. First you'll see **Glenelly Inn,** 5131 Warm Springs Road (707–996–6720), a peach-and-white confection built in 1916 as a railroad inn for train passengers from San Francisco who gamboled their summers away at nearby mineral springs resorts. If you're up for a strenuous bike ride and some breathtaking scenery, take the 15-mile Sonoma Mountain Road loop, starting and ending on Warm Springs Road. Feeling lazy and warm? Stop at **Morton's Warm Springs** (707–833–5511) for a picnic on sweeping lawns or a swim in one of three heated pools. You'll come into Kenwood, a tiny, overgrown hamlet of cabins and rustic homes, then meet up with Highway 12; still a two-lane country road, it's a main route through the county. **Smothers Winery,** 9575 Sonoma Highway (707–833–1010) is on the corner—yes, *the* Smothers Brothers—and **Kenwood Vineyards,** 9592 Sonoma Highway (707–833–5891), is across the road. Even if you're not a winetaster, you'll want to visit Sonoma Valley tasting rooms. Wineries sell souvenirs and gifts, and some have extensive displays of historical memorabilia and art; most have picnic areas.

Lunch: Turn left onto Highway 12 and stop for a late lunch at **Cafe Citti,** 9049 Sonoma Highway. (707) 833–2690. A deli cafe with tables outdoors under the trees.

Afternoon

You'll see signs nearby for wineries: **Chateau St. Jean** (707–833–4134), **Landmark** (707–833–1144), and **Kunde Vineyards** (707–833–5501).

Go north on Highway 12 for half a mile, then turn right on Adobe Canyon Road and drive 3 miles to **Sugarloaf Ridge State Park** (707–833–5712), a 3,000-acre green and golden jewel of mountains, redwood groves, creeks, wildflower-strewn meadows, and *views*. You may take a short walk or a strenuous hike, picnic in the pines, park your RV overnight, or camp out in your tent. In the late afternoon cool off with strawberry margaritas, alcoholic or non-, under a grape arbor at **Vineyards Inn,** 8445 Sonoma Highway (707–833–4500), a Mexican cantina and restaurant at the corner of Highway 12 and Adobe Canyon Road.

Dinner: **Buckley Lodge,** 1717 Adobe Canyon Road, Kenwood. (707) 833–5562. Perched above a rushing creek in a forest, the restaurant offers casually elegant dining rooms and a beautiful outdoor stone terrace, lyrical on a summer night. Menu highlights include risotto, duck with Port sauce, lamb with pomegranate, salmon with lemon caper sauce, and seasonal offerings. Brunch, lunch, and dinner.

Lodging: **Beltane Ranch,** 11775 Sonoma Highway, Glen Ellen 95442. (707) 996–6501. A big yellow ranch house at the foot of Hood Mountain. Rooms open to verandas overlooking vineyards and orchardlands. Owned decades ago by a San Francisco madam from Louisiana, the ranch has a southern look, with hospitality generously dispensed by innkeeper Rosemary Wood, who grew up here.

Day 2

Morning

Breakfast: At Beltane Ranch.

Proceed back through Kenwood on Highway 12 toward Sonoma, a 12-mile drive. You'll go through **Boyes Hot Springs,** where you may wish to stop for a look at the buildings and grounds of the **Sonoma Mission Inn,** 18130 Highway 12 (707–938–9000), a pink, 1920s-style Mediterranean extravaganza of a luxury hotel and spa. It's five minutes farther to **Sonoma Plaza,** a typical Spanish town square, the largest and one of the oldest in California, laid out by General Mariano Guadalupe Vallejo in 1834. The site of many fiestas, parades, and historical events, it's a National Historic Landmark, and a beautiful one— huge bay and eucalyptus trees, a meandering stream with chattering ducks, a playground, picnic tables, the monolithic stone **City Hall,** and the **Visitor's Bureau,** 453 First Street East (707–996–1090).

Surrounding the plaza, and for several blocks around, are many historic buildings, including the **Mission San Francisco Solano de Sonoma,** circa 1841, the last of the California missions built, with a beautiful small chapel and museum. The commandant who held sway in the Sonoma area when Mexico owned California, General Mariano Vallejo built a barracks compound for his soliders, which is now a state park and a museum on the plaza (707–938–1519). Thick-walled adobes, Victorians, and Classic Revival and Mission Revival structures line the plaza and adjacent streets. Park your car, get out your camera, and explore the plaza and the streets and alleyways for a block or so in each direction. The visitor's bureau has good walking-tour maps.

Not to be missed on the plaza: **The Wine Exchange,** at 452 First Street (707–938–1794), to taste and buy the wines of almost every winery in the Sonoma and Napa valleys; the **Sonoma French Bakery,** 468 First Street (707–996–2691), famous for sourdough bread; the **Arts Guild** gallery, 460 First Street (707–996–3115); and **Kaboodle,** 447 First Street (707–996–9500), a feminine fairyland of country French gifts and accessories.

The **Zimbabwe Sculpture Gallery** at 452 First Street displays dramatic African Shona stone sculpture and there are interesting large photographs of Africa and a video to watch (707–935–6254). Next door at **Artifax International,** 450 First Street, take a look at African and Asian carvings, masks, jewelry, and doodads of great color and variety in an exotic incensed environment (707–996–9494). **Zambezi Trading Company** at 107 West Napa Street is an emporium of farm furniture, palm baskets, clay pots, rugs, and home accessories, all from the Zambezi River Valley and southeastern Africa. Some of the furniture is handmade from hundred-year-old teak and jarrah railroad ties. **Good Day Sunshine,** 29 East Napa Street, has been voted the best gift shop in Sonoma and for good reason—wearable art, a glowing collection of art glass, lots of exotic jewelry, Native American crafts, and more (707–938–4001).

Lunch: Buy locally made cheese, meats, bread, and wine at the **Sonoma Cheese Factory and Deli,** 2 West Spain Street (707–996–1931), for a picnic in the plaza, or have Mandarin Chicken Salad or a burger in the **Feed Store Cafe and Bakery**'s patio just off the square, at 529 First Street West (707–938–2122).

Afternoon

Even if you're not interested in winetasting, you'll want to walk, bike, or drive 1.5 miles (take East Napa Street to Lovall Valley Road, then go left onto Old Winery Road) from the plaza to the **Buena Vista Winery** (707–938–1266) and the **Hacienda Winery** (707–938–3220), both enchanting wine-country estates with old, vine-covered stone buildings, ancient trees, and rampant flower gardens. Tasting rooms are stocked with guidebooks, artwork, and museum-quality antiques. Buena Vista's Hungarian founder, Count Agoston Haraszthy, engaged in friendly winemaking competition with General Vallejo in the mid-1800s. The interconnected small roads on this western outskirt of town are pretty and quiet for walks, drives, and bike rides to several other wineries.

A paved path for walking, biking, and roller-blading winds 1.5 miles from one end of Sonoma to the other, passing through parks and playing fields, and ending on the west side at a big park with a playground. A block from the plaza on the walking path, **Depot Park** has a playground, barbecue grills, and picnic tables under the trees, a good choice when the plaza is crowded.

Accessible by the walking path and by car, the **General M. G. Vallejo Home** is a classic, Yankee-style two-story Gothic Revival shipped around the Horn and erected in 1851 (707–938–1519). You can tour the home, which is called *Lachryma Montis,* meaning "Tears of the Mountain." Original and period furnishings in every room recreate the days when Vallejo and his several daughters lived here. There is a glorious garden with huge magnolia, fig, and oak trees, and a fish pond with turtles and koi. The home is part of the state park property, so one admission ticket is good at the mission, the barracks compound, and the Vallejo home.

Dinner: **Eastside Oyster Bar and Grill,** 133 East Napa Street. (707) 939–1266. The fireplace creates a cozy atmosphere for fancifully prepared fresh seafood from both coasts; intimate in the winter, popular and fun on the patio in the summer.

Lodging: **Kenwood Inn,** 10400 Sonoma Highway, Kenwood, 95452. (707) 833–1293. Two-story European-style villas on a courtyard with swimming pool, all within a walled compound. All suites, with featherbeds, antiques, and fireplaces. Second-floor rooms look across at rolling vineyardlands and hillsides. Full-service spa with a variety of massages, beauty treatments, aromatherapy; day use also available.

Day 3

Breakfast: Kenwood Inn.

Leaving Sonoma, head south from the plaza on Broadway/Highway 12 for less than 1 mile, then turn left onto Napa Road, another view-filled country byway. If you're extending your trip to the lower Napa Valley (see Northbound Escape Three), turn left at the Highway 121 junction; otherwise turn right at the junction and proceed a couple of miles to the **Cherry Tree,** 1901 Fremont Drive (707–938–3480), just past the cow manure farm on your left (you'll sense it before you see it). At the Cherry Tree, pick up fresh black cherry juice and jalapeño-stuffed olives to take home. Go straight on through the Schellville–Highway 121 intersection and down the road to **Schug Carneros Estate** (707–939–9363), a winery tucked up against a low range of hills, a lost little corner of the valley. German-owned Schug makes a traditional California Chardonnay, a sparkling red wine, and a German-style Gewürztraminer, unusual for this area.

Continue on Highway 121 south at a slow pace along a 10-mile stretch of rolling hills. You'll soon see glimpses of wetlands at the top of San Pablo Bay. You can take a scenic ride in an antique biplane at **Aero-Schellville** (707–938–2444). Turn right at the **Gloria Ferrer Champagne Caves** sign and drive up toward the hills to the tile-roofed Spanish hacienda built by the largest sparkling wine company in the world—Freixenet, based in Spain—at 23555 Highway 121 (707–996–7256). Gloria Ferrer has a luxurious tasting salon with a fantastic view. Many annual events are scheduled here, such as Catalan cooking classes and fireside concerts.

Back on Highway 121 heading south, you'll have a last chance to buy fresh fruits and veggies at a large produce stand. Just south of the fruit stand on your left, a vine-draped arbor leads to **Viansa Winery and Marketplace,** a red-tiled, terra-cotta–colored Italian winery on a hill above the highway. There is much to enjoy at Viansa besides their unusual Italian wine varieties (707–935–4700). Sangiovese, Vernaccia, Nebbiolo, Aleatico, Trebbiano, and Chardonnay are the grapes blended into their traditional wines. At the huge gourmet delicatessen and Italian marketplace you can buy a sandwich, a salad, prepared party foods, packaged gourmet foods, cookbooks, ceramics, and wa-terfowl-related gifts. Barbecues and special events open to the public are held here in the summertime.

Viansa has restored the ninety-acre wetlands below the winery, one of the largest private waterfowl preserves in the state. More than 10,000 birds have been spotted in a single day. The wetlands is on the Pacific flyway, the route that ducks and geese use when migrating from Canada and Alaska to Mexico each winter.

On weekends there are stock car and motorcycle races at **Sears Point Raceway** (800–870–7223) at the junction of Highways 121 and 37, where you turn right, head west toward Marin County, and take Highway 101 south to the Golden Gate.

There's More

Walking tour. To see architectural styles circa 1860 to 1925, stroll an 8-block historic area in Petaluma. Detailed maps with historical notes are available from the Chamber of Commerce (707–762–2785).
Horseback riding. Sonoma Cattle Company. (707) 996–8566. Sugarloaf Ridge State Park. (707) 833–5712.
Bike rental. Sonoma Cyclery in Sonoma. (707) 935–3377. Good Time Bicycles in Boyes Hot Springs. (707) 938–0453.
Balloon rides. Once in a Lifetime. (707) 578–0580. Air Flambuoyant. (800) 456–4711.
Train Town, 1 mile south of Sonoma Plaza on Broadway/Highway 12. (707) 938–3912. A twenty-minute steamtrain trip through ten acres of landscaped park.
Sonoma County Wine Center and Winery, Rohnert Park, just north of Petaluma. (707) 527–7701. Educational tours, winetasting and sales, food demonstrations, wine industry displays.
More wineries. A visitor's guide to the Sonoma Valley, with all winery information listed, is available from the Sonoma Visitor's Bureau. (707) 996–1090.
Spas and mineral springs. Agua Caliente Mineral Springs. (707) 996–6822.
Spa at Sonoma Mission Inn. (707) 938–9000. Sonoma Spa. (707) 939–8770.
Golf. Oakmont Golf Club, Santa Rosa. (707) 538–2454 or 539–0415.
Sonoma Valley Regional Park, Highway 12 between Arnold Drive and Madrone Road near Glen Ellen. Some 135 acres; picnicking; bike and walking trails.

Special Events

March. Heart of the Valley Barrel Tasting, Sonoma. (707) 996–1090.
April. Butter and Eggs Days, Petaluma. (707) 762–2785.
June. Annual Ox Roast, Sonoma. (707) 996–1090.
June. Plaza Art and Artisan Show in Sonoma Plaza. Wine, food, music, art. (707) 996–2115.
June through August. Ravenswood Winery, 18701 Gehricke Road,

on the outskirts of Sonoma. (707) 938–1960. Overlooking a spectacular part of the Wine Country, afternoon barbecues on Saturdays, Sundays, and holidays.

July. Old-fashioned Fourth of July Celebration, Sonoma. (707) 996–1090.

July. Sonoma Valley Wine Festival, Sonoma. (707) 996–1090.

August. Sonoma County Wine Auction, Boyes Hot Springs. (707) 996–1090.

August. Sonoma Valley Shakespeare Festival, outdoors at Gundlach Bundschu Winery, Sonoma. Colorful, lively performances for all ages. Bring a picnic. (707) 575–3854.

August. Petaluma River Festival. (707) 762–2785.

September. Valley of the Moon Vintage Festival, Glen Ellen. (707) 996–1090.

October. Artrails of Sonoma County, throughout the county. (707) 996–1090.

October. World Wristwrestling Championships, Petaluma. (707) 762–2785.

November. Kenwood Wineries Open House. (707) 996–1090.

December. Christmas at the Sonoma Mission. (707) 996–1090.

Other Recommended Restaurants and Lodgings

Sonoma

Piatti, 405 First Street West. (707) 996–2351. Lively dining room and gracious tree-shaded patio, wood-fired pizza ovens, rotisserie roasting, contemporary Northern Italian food.

Thistle Dew Inn, 171 West Spain Street. (800) 382–7895. Five antiques-filled rooms and a suite, garden hot tub, fireplaces, private decks and private entrances, free use of bicycles, lovely gardens, gourmet breakfast, afternoon refreshments. Book well in advance.

Food to Go, 603 Broadway. (707) 938–0301. Sumptuous box lunches, gourmet picnics.

Victorian Garden Inn, 316 East Napa Street. (707) 996–5339. A dream of a turn-of-the century home a block from the plaza; pool, fireplaces, and full breakfast.

Sonoma Hotel, on the plaza, at 110 West Spain Street. (707) 996–2996. European-style country inn with Victorian charm, restaurant and bar, continental breakfast, pretty outdoor patio.

Pasta Nostra, 139 East Napa Street. (707) 938–4166. Lively, casual atmosphere; Italian food; indoors or garden patio with music; lunch and dinner.

Depot 1870 Restaurant, 241 First Street. (707) 938–2980. Looks like an inn in the south of France; mesquite-grilled meats, pasta, and seafood are served poolside or in small dining rooms; lunch and dinner.

Boyes Hot Springs

Sonoma Mission Inn and Spa, Highway 12. (800) 862–4945. Like a triple-layer cake with pink icing and white trim, the inn is a 1920s-style extravaganza of a building guarded by tall palms and surrounded by gardens. Rooms in the original building are beautiful but small, rooms and suites in the annex buildings are spacious, some with fireplaces. Two swimming pools, tennis courts. Spa and fitness center where some guests participate in a complete daily weight-reduction and health program, including meals.

Sonoma Mission Inn Cafe, 18140 Sonoma Highway. (707) 938–9000. Hearty Northern Italian cuisine, upscale cafe; three meals.

Glen Ellen

RV park in Sugarloaf Ridge State Park takes RVs to 24 feet. (800) 444–7275.

Gaige House Inn, 13540 Arnold Drive. (707) 935–0237. An Italianate Victorian on the outside, an eye-popping mix of styles and periods on the inside. Eight spectacular inn rooms with Ralph Lauren linens, eclectic art, some canopy beds and giant whirlpool tubs, garden rooms within steps of a 40-foot swimming pool, fireplaces. Big country breakfast. Unique among wine country inns.

Glen Ellen Inn, 13670 Arnold Drive. (707) 996–6409. A small Cape Cod cottage. Lunch and dinner in the tiny dining room or on the tree-shaded patio. Pasta with wild mushrooms, breast of duck with Asian dressing, rosemary-burgundy pork loin, grilled quesadilla with sun-dried tomatoes and roasted chiles, a lively daily menu.

For More Information

Petaluma Area Chamber of Commerce, 215 Howard Street, Petaluma, CA 94952-2983. (707) 762–2785.

Sonoma Valley Visitor's Bureau, in the plaza, 453 First Street East, Sonoma, CA 95476. (707) 996–1090.

Sonoma County Farm Trails, P.O. Box 6032, Santa Rosa, CA 95406. (707) 586–3276.

Schedule of events in Sonoma Valley. (707) 935–1111.

Bed and Breakfast Association of Sonoma Valley. (800) 969–4667.

Sonoma Reservations. (800) 576–6662. Motels, inns, spas, condos, homes.

Lower Napa Valley

A ride in a hot-air balloon is a great way to see the Wine Country.

The Carneros, Napa, Yountville, Rutherford

_____ 1 NIGHT _____

Art and architecture • Wineries • Shopping • California cuisine
Vineyard walks • Gourmet picnics • Country lanes

Even those who decline to taste the grape will enjoy the museumlike exhibits and the architectural richness of wineries in the Napa Valley. Thirty miles long, just one-sixth the size of Bordeaux, this valley is home to the densest concentration of wineries in North America and to some of the state's most highly regarded California cuisine restaurants, several championship golf courses, dozens of charming bed-and-breakfast inns, and scenery that attracts visitors from all over the world.

Your escape begins in the Carneros wine-growing district at the top of San Pablo Bay, cooled by ocean breezes and summer fogs. Grapes ripen more slowly here than in the hot, dry, upper valley, creating notable Chardonnays and Pinot Noirs. Vineyards and wineries here are relatively new in Napa's 150-year history of winemaking, and many tourists are unaware of the quiet lanes of the Carneros. (Carneros is one of the "appellations" into which the valley is divided. Just as in France, each area has a designated geographic appellation, producing grapes that differ in character according to topography, climate, and soil.)

There is time for some lesser-known sights near the town of Napa, a day in Yountville, and a meander down the Silverado Trail. Stretching from Napa 35 miles north to Calistoga, the trail winds along at the foot of high mountain ridges past venerable oaks, their trunks hoary with moss and tickled by buttercups. Sprinkled along the way are wineries and champagne cellars, gargantuan mansions, small stone cottages, luxurious hotels, and quaint inns, each in its own idyllic corner of the wine country.

Many Napa Valley wineries and restaurants are world-famous. It's wise to make reservations at the restaurants of your choice, and call wineries in advance, to determine if it is necessary to make an appointment for a tour and tasting.

Day 1

Morning

From the Oakland Bay Bridge, drive forty-five minutes north on Highway 80, *past* the Napa/Highway 37 exit, to the American Canyon exit a few miles north of Vallejo, turning west and connecting with Highway 221 north to Napa; staying to the left, you'll be on Soscol Avenue. From Soscol, take a left onto Third Street, crossing the Napa River, and park a few blocks down, across from a bright blue Victorian, at 1517 Third.

Breakfast: **Alexis Baking Company,** 1517 Third Street, Napa. (707) 258–1827. Inventive breakfasts, the best pastries and desserts in the county, cappuccino, local color.

Need maps and brochures? The **Napa County Visitor's Center** (707–226–7459) is in the Napa Town Center, accessed from First Street, within a few blocks of the bakery.

Head west on First Street to Highway 29, then south two minutes to Highway 12, turning west. Within a minute, turn left onto Cuttings Wharf Road and get lost for a while in the rolling vineyards and country roads of Carneros; biking is great on these empty lanes. Although a brandy distillery, not a winery, **Carneros Alambic Distillery** makes an interesting stop at 1250 Cuttings Wharf Road, (707) 253–9055. You can take a guided tour in a lovely garden setting to see the huge copper pots, a labyrinth of equipment, and the cellars, and learn about how brandy is made. Rather than tasting, as you do at the wineries, you participate in an aroma sampling. The shop here is one of the best places to buy Wine Country gifts.

Going west on Las Amigas, take a left onto Buchli Station Road to **Bouchaine** (707–252–9065), a winery specializing in Chardonnay and Pinot Noir; an appointment will be necessary. Farther west on Las Amigas, **Acacia Winery** (707–226–9991) produces superb Chardonnays. Going right onto Duhig Road, you'll wind up back on Highway 12.

The supercolossal French château on the hill is **Domaine Carneros,** 1240 Duhig Road (707–257–0101), a French-American winery producing sparkling wines. Scamper up the quadruple staircase to the tasting room for a tour.

Cross Highway 12 onto Old Sonoma Road; go left onto Dealy Lane a couple of miles to a Spanish champagne maker, **Codorniu Napa Valley,** 1345 Henry Road (707–224–1668). The architecture here is New Age, to say the least, something like a spaceship partly hidden in a vineyard-draped hillside. Enjoy the small museum, the wide views of the Carneros district, and the bubbly!

Carneros Creek Winery, 1285 Dealy Lane (707–253–9463), is a small, friendly place with picnic tables under a vine-covered arbor. If you are up for a walk on a quiet country lane, past vineyards, cow pastures, and rolling hills, park across the road from Carneros Creek Winery and walk west (past the entrance to Cordorniu) for a couple of miles until you reach a private property sign, then return. Along the way, you will hear the alarming call of peacocks, and, as you approach the peacock farm, a gaggle of guardian geese may appear.

Connect again with Highway 29 and head north five minutes to a left onto Redwood Road, then 6.5 miles through redwood and oak forests to **Hess Collection,** 4411 Redwood Road, Napa (707–255–1144). A large and important European and American contemporary art collection resides here in a historic winery building. Take the self-guided tour and enjoy the gardens and the views.

Return to Napa, crossing over Highway 29 onto Trancas, and turn right on Jefferson; drive 2 blocks to Pasta Prego, in a shopping center on the left.

Lunch: **Pasta Prego,** 3206 Jefferson Street, Napa. (707) 224–9011.

The best-kept secret and one of the best restaurants in the wine country; 1990s-style Italian cuisine, polenta with mushroom sauce, smoky grilled veggies, risotto, grilled local fish, poultry, meats, and many pastas. Noisy and fun; patronized by the "in crowd" of local winery families; dining is indoors in the cafe or on the outdoor patio.

Afternoon

On Highway 29 five minutes north of Napa is a monument-size white rooster, heralding **Red Hen Antiques,** 5091 St. Helena Highway (707–257–0822)—18,000 square feet housing the wares of more than forty dealers.

Proceed another five minutes to Yountville; across the highway near the old soldiers' home is **Domaine Chandon,** 1 California Drive (707–944–2892), a French-owned sparkling wine cellar where you can enjoy the beautiful oak-studded grounds and learn about the *méthode champenoise* style of winemaking. A flute of champagne and complimentary hors d'oeuvres await in the tasting room; try the Blanc de Noirs, a blossomy pink champagne.

The streets of the tiny town of Yountville are lined with vintage cottages in overgrown country gardens. On Washington Street, the main drag, a blizzard of shops, restaurants, and inns make this a popular destination.

The landmark building in Yountville is **Vintage 1870,** a massive pile of brick on twenty-two landscaped acres; once a winery, it's now many shops and cafes. You might come out of here with antiques, haute couture, or a book on winemaking. Try the apricot Danish at the **Pastry Shop** (707–944–2138), a European-style bakery. In **Groezinger Wine Merchants** (800–356–3970), more than one hundred locally produced wines are available to taste; shipping is available nationwide. **Wineoceros** (707–944–0827) sells every wine country T-shirt imaginable. Other shops sell toys, Victorian gewgaws, gourmet cooking accessories, fashions, art—more than enough to wear the numbers off your credit cards.

Near Vintage 1870, the **Overland Sheepskin Company** (707–944–0778) has sheepskin coats, leather jackets, and Western hats. **Depot Gallery,** 6526 Washington (707–944–2044), has for over three decades displayed the best of local artists' works. **Raspberry's,** at Beard Plaza, 6540 Washington (707–944–9211), is a gallery of art glass created by the country's most celebrated artists.

At the north end of town, Yountville Park is an oak-shaded grassy commons with a fantastic children's playground and picnic tables. For a 3-mile round-trip walk or bike ride, walk east from the park through the fascinating old cemetery to Yount Mill Road and follow it north to

Highway 29 and back. Running along a tributary of the Napa River, the road is shady and bedecked with lovely views of the mountains and vineyards. Watch for a plaque about George Calvert Yount, the first white settler in the valley. Yount wangled from Mexico the huge land grant of Rancho Caymus in the 1850s—comprising much of the heart of the valley, including Yountville—and built grist and saw mills on the river. You will see the remains of one of his large wooden barns.

From the intersection of Yount Mill and Yountville Cross roads, you can head east a couple of miles to connect with the Silverado Trail. On Yountville Cross Road at the bridge, the Napa River Ecological Reserve is a place to walk beside the river under oaks and sycamores. You can wade and fish here, too.

Raku Ceramics Collection in Beard Plaza, at 6540 Washington (707–944–9424), exhibits and sells ceramic creations by some of the country's most celebrated artists. And don't miss **Canard,** showing fine wildlife art, at the same address (707–944–0131).

Arrive at your lodgings in time to enjoy the gardens and perhaps a dip in the pool.

Dinner: For a snazzy, upscale atmosphere and renowned California cuisine, **Mustard's** (707–944–2424), two minutes north of Yountville on the highway. Go for the smoky baby-back ribs, mountains of feathery onion rings, inventive pastas, grilled and spit-roasted poultry and meats, and the super-colossal wine list. This is a very popular, fun place and you may need to make reservations several days ahead.

Lodging: **Vintage Inn Napa Valley,** 6541 Washington Street, Yountville 94599. (707) 944–1112. An eighty-room luxury garden hotel; elegant, spacious rooms with fireplaces, spa baths; 60-foot lap pool, tennis, buffet breakfast. Available on the grounds are a hot-air balloon and bikes.

Day 2

Morning

Breakfast: **The Diner,** 6476 Washington Street, Yountville. (707) 944–2626. Big, beautiful breakfasts, cornmeal pancakes, *huevos rancheros,* fresh local produce, local eggs and bacon in a 1940s-style cafe. At lunch and dinnertime, you may see a small, hungry crowd waiting for booths and stools at the counter for the American and Mexican food, huge desserts, soups, and sandwiches.

Just past Oakville Cross Road, stop at the **Oakville Grocery Company** (707–944–8802) for the makings of a French country picnic: pâtés, baguettes, Perrier, Yoplait, quiches, *fromages,* charcuterie, baby vegetables, salads.

Up the road, **St. Supery Vineyards and Winery,** 8440 St. Helena Highway, Rutherford (707–963–4507), is multifaceted. Here you can walk through a demonstration vineyard, see an art show, tour a lovely Queen Anne Victorian farmhouse, and enjoy elaborate exhibits about grape growing and winemaking. And taste wine, too.

Take a right onto Rutherford Cross Road to **Rancho Caymus Inn,** a unique Spanish-style hacienda, a showplace for Mexican, Central American, and South American arts and crafts. Ask to see a room or two. They're decorated with specially commissioned wall hangings, rugs, hand-carved furnishings, and stained glass. The courtyard blooms with wisteria and bougainvillea. A walk from Rancho Caymus over the stone bridge to the Silverado Trail and back takes about an hour; you'll pass historic mansions, blooming orchards, and mossy oaks.

Drive to the Silverado Trail and turn left, then turn right up the hill to **Auberge du Soleil Resort,** 180 Rutherford Hill Road, Rutherford 94573 (707–963–1211), where you'll feel as though you've dropped suddenly into an olive grove in the south of France. Wisteria-draped arbors and riots of flowers beckon you past fat stucco walls into a tile-floored entry, flooded with light from the terraces where beautiful people dine al fresco on California cuisine. Enjoy the heartstopping view and ask to see a villa, for future getaways.

Lunch: Picnic under the oaks at **Rutherford Hill Winery.** (707) 963–7194. Just up the hill from Auberge du Soleil, with the same panoramic view. This winery has 40,000 square feet of cool underground caves, seen on thirty-five-minute tours. Enjoy the picnic you packed from the Oakville Grocery Company at tables under the oaks or in the olive grove with wide valley views, or you can buy juices and picnic goodies here (although this is the not the best place to purchase provisions). Try **Katz's** in Yountville at 6770 Washington, (707) 944–1393. Katz's specializes in gourmet salads and sandwiches, and it's a good place to taste local olive oils and vinegars, which they will ship home for you.

A little south of Rutherford Hill, **Mumm Napa Valley,** at 8445 Silverado Trail (707–963–1133), is a French-American sparkling wine cellar with a pleasant tasting-terrace, big vineyard views, and a great gift shop. A permanent collection of Ansel Adams photographs is on display here.

A little south of Mumm, **Pine Ridge Winery,** at 5901 Silverado Trail (707–253–7500), is a small but top-notch winery where you can tour the caves, taste medal-winning Chardonnay, and picnic in a grassy grove under tall pines. There are swings for the kids and a nice walking trail through the vineyards and along the ridge overlooking the winery.

Afternoon

Watch for the left turn to the **Silverado Country Club Resort,** 1600 Atlas Peak Road, Napa (707–257–0200), a 1,200-acre resort famous for its two eighteen-hole Robert Trent Jones golf courses. Towering eucalyptus, palm, magnolia, and oak trees line the drive leading to a huge, circa-1870 mansion. A curving staircase and period chandeliers grace the lobby; a terrace bar overlooks sweeping lawns, waterways, and gardens. Silverado has several restaurants, one of the largest tennis complexes in Northern California, and condominium accommodations.

Head south to Napa and back to the Bay Area.

There's More

Marine World Africa U.S.A., 495 Mare Island Way, Vallejo 94590. (707) 643–6722. Highway 80 on the north end of Vallejo at Marine World Parkway/Highway 37; 160-acre oceanarium and wildlife park; live shows with killer whales, sharks, dolphins, tigers, tropical birds; water-ski show on a fifty-five-acre lake. Plan a whole day to talk to the animals and their trainers, pet the kangaroos, feed the elephants, and play with the chimpanzees. The most carefree way to visit Marine World is by way of ferry from San Francisco. Ask about ferry packages and special event days.

Old Town Napa. On the west side of the Napa River, charming Victorian neighborhoods are bounded by Franklin, Division, Elm, and Riverside drives; behind Alexis Bakery, drive up Franklin and down Randolph.

Golf. Chardonnay Club, 2555 Jameson Canyon, Napa. (707) 257–8950. On the south end of Napa, on the Highway 80 connector; two links-style, eighteen-hole courses in a challenging landscape of ravines, hills, and vineyards; predictably windy.

Chimney Rock Golf Course, 5320 Silverado Trail near Napa. (707) 255–3363. Nine holes in the vineyards; playing conditions are variable.

J. F. Kennedy Municipal Golf Course, just north of Napa. (707) 255–4333. Eighteen challenging holes, water on fourteen; reasonable rates.

Ballooning. Floating silently in a hot-air balloon is an unforgettable way to see the Wine Country. Always scheduled for the early morning, balloon trips are usually accompanied by champagne, breakfast, and much revelry. Rates average $100 per person.

Napa Valley Balloons, P.O. Box 2860, Yountville 94599. (707) 253–2224. Launches at sunrise from Domaine Chandon Winery.

Adventures Aloft, P.O. Box 2500, Yountville 94599. (707) 255–8688. Napa Valley Balloon Aviation, Yountville 94599. (707) 252–7067. Balloons Above the Valley, P.O. Box 3838, Napa 94558. (707) 253–2222. Departures from Monticello Cellars in Napa.

Napa Valley Wine Train. (707) 253–2111. Elegant restored dining and observation cars, a relaxing way to see the valley; lunch and dinner; no stops on the slow, three-hour chug from Napa to St. Helena and back.

Skyline Park, East Imola Avenue, Napa. (707) 252–0481. Hundreds of acres of hilly woodlands and meadows for hiking, horseback riding, picnicking, and RV and tent camping. Great for winter mushroom expeditions and springtime wildflower walks; find the waterfalls for a summer splash.

Hakusan Sake Gardens, junction of Highways 29 and 12 East. (707) 258–6160. Taste and tour at a sake factory.

Biking. The Napa Valley can be divided into three moderately strenuous bike trips: a circle tour around the spa town of Calistoga, a mid-valley tour in and around St. Helena and Yountville, and a third tour in the Carneros region. Dotted with wineries and adorned with views of the vineyards and the mountains, the mostly flat Silverado Trail, running along the east side of the valley, is a main biker's route. Criss-crossing the valley between Highway 29 and the Silverado Trail are myriad leafy country roads. Twelve- to twenty-one-speed hybrid, mountain, and tandem bike rentals and maps are available at several bike shops. You can arrange to have the bike rental company deliver bikes to your hotel and, at the end of your expedition, pick up you and your bikes at a winery or other destination.

Bicycle Trax, 796 Soscol Avenue, Napa. (707) 258–8929.

Napa Valley Cyclery, 4080 Byway East, Napa. (800) 707–BIKE. Pick-up service, scheduled and private tours, rentals.

Bicycle Events Information: (707) 226–7066.

Kayaking. Aqua Ventures, 1008 Main, Napa. (707) 257–7058. Kayak and canoe rentals on the Napa River and for use elsewhere in the county. Lifejackets provided.

Shopping. Napa Factory Stores, First Street exit off Highway 29 at Napa. More than twenty upscale outlet stores.

Vintage Cars. Napa Valley Model A Rentals, Washington Square, Yountville. (707) 944–1106. Take a spin around the valley in a yellow replica 1929 Model A Ford with a rumble seat.

Wine Education. Robert Mondavi Winery's 3.5-hour tour and wine essence tasting is one of the most comprehensive of the free educational tours offered by wineries. For reservations, call (707) 226–1395, ext. 4312. Located at 7801 St. Helena Highway (Highway 29) in Oakville.

Merryvale Vineyards holds a beginner's winetasting seminar in the cask room on Saturday mornings. For reservations, call (800) 326–6069. Located at 1000 Main Street in St. Helena.

One of the most renowned family-operated wineries in the valley, Cakebread Cellars offers a lively schedule of dinners and classes with celebrity chefs, as well as special outings throughout the year—even a fly-casting school. Call for the current calendar: (707) 963–5221. Located at 8300 St. Helena Highway in Rutherford.

Special Events

June. Concour de Elegance, Silverado Country Club, Napa. 707–257–0200.

June. Napa Valley Wine Auction. (707) 963–5246. Wine aficionados from all over the world come for three days of parties, barrel tastings, and events at wineries; auction benefits local hospital.

September. Harvest Fest, Charles Krug Winery, St. Helena. (707) 253–2353.

September. River Festival, Third Street Bridge, Napa. (707) 226–7459. Napa Valley Symphony performs at the riverside.

October. Yountville Days Festival. (707) 944–0904. Parade, music, entertainment, food.

November. Napa Valley Wine Fest. (707) 253–3563.

December. Napa Valley Jazz Festival, Yountville. (707) 944–0310.

Other Recommended Restaurants and Lodgings

Yountville

Ristorante Piatti, 6480 Washington Street. (707) 944–2070. One in an extraordinary, upscale chain of Northern Italian places in Northern California. It's fun to watch the chefs in the open kitchen prepare pastas, roasted and rotisseried poultry and meats, and vegetable specialties galore. Outdoors under the arbor is the place to be.

Frankie, Johnnie and Luigi, Too, 6772 Washington Street. (707) 944–0177. Pizza and pasta, lunch and dinner, food to go, box lunches. Pleasant patio and deck.

California Cafe Bar and Grill, Highway 29 and Madison at Washington Square. (707) 944–2330. California cuisine and a great wine list, indoors or on the patio.

Compadres, next to Vintage 1870. (707) 944–2406. Delightful outdoor patio under giant palms and oaks, zowie margaritas, good Mexican food.

Red Rock Cafe, under vine-draped arbors in front of Vintage 1870. (707) 944–2614. The best burgers and onion rings in the county, maybe the world; also in downtown Napa.

Napa Valley Lodge, Route 29 at Madison Street, on the north end of town. (707) 944–2468. A pretty, gardeny motel with spacious rooms, vineyard views, fireplaces, pool, spa, sauna.

Napa

Bistro Don Giovanni, 4110 St. Helena Highway (Highway 29), five minutes north of Napa. (707) 224–3300. Rub elbows with the beautiful Wine Country people in a lively cafe atmosphere. Country Italian cuisine, risotto, wood-fire roasted chicken, eclectic pasta, one of the valley's best wine lists. A little noisy but never boring.

P.J.'s, 1001 Second Street. (707) 224–0607. Fantastic salads, soups, pizza and pasta, vegetarian and Mexican specialties. Only the lucky locals know about P.J.'s. Everything can be delivered.

Oak Knoll Inn, 2200 East Oak Knoll Avenue. (707) 255–2200. In the middle of 600 acres of Chardonnay vines, four huge, elegant guest rooms with private entrances, fireplaces, king-size brass beds, hot tub, swimming pool. Full gourmet breakfast, wine and cheese in the evening.

Foothill Cafe, 2766 Old Sonoma Road. (707) 252–6178. In a tiny cafe tucked away in an unlikely strip center, a French-trained chef turns out mouthwatering pit-barbecued ribs and chicken, house-smoked salmon, crispy fried calamari, pasta, and daily specials. You may well be the only tourists in the place.

Inn at Napa Valley, 1075 California Boulevard. (707) 253–9540. All-suite, upscale hotel, very conveniently located at Highway 29 and First Street; full breakfast and cocktail hour included; golf packages.

The Fairways at Silverado, 100 Fairway Drive. (707) 255–6644. Two-bedroom condos on the golf course, long- or short-term rentals.

La Residence, 4066 St. Helena Highway, on the north end of Napa. (707) 253–0337. One of the most spectacular and romantic inns in the valley, a French barn and a circa-1870 mansion surrounded by gardens on two oak- and pine-studded acres. Rooms are elaborately decorated with antiques and designer fabrics and linens, four-poster beds, fireplaces, patios, and verandas. Full breakfast, wine and hors d'oeuvres, swimming pool.

Downtown Joe's Restaurant and Brewery, 902 Main. (707) 258–2337. Breakfast, lunch, or dinner on the patio overlooking the Napa River, adjacent to the downtown park. Salads, sandwiches, pastas, microbrewery. Live music on weekend nights is popular with the young set.

Napa Valley Reservations Unlimited, 1819 Tanen. (707) 252–1985.

Bed and Breakfast Exchange. (707) 942–2924.

Napa Valley

Tall Timber Chalets, between Napa and Yountville at 1012 Darms Lane. (707) 252–7810. Circa-1940 cottages in a grove of trees; fresh, bright decor; sitting rooms, kitchens, continental breakfast.

Rutherford

Rutherford Grill, 1880 Rutherford Road. (707) 962–1782. Grilled and spit-roasted ribs, chicken, burgers, old-fashioned mashed potatoes. Big booths indoors, umbrella tables, and a wine bar outside.

Oakville

Stars Oakville Cafe, 7848 Highway 29. (707) 944–8905. One of the inventors of California cuisine, Jeremiah Tower has opened a Wine Country version of his world-famous Stars in San Francisco. A casual cafe with an arbored patio where a seasonal menu of fresh local produce, fish, and poultry is memorably served.

For More Information

Yountville Chamber of Commerce, 6795 Washington Street, Yountville, CA 94599. (707) 944–0904. In Washington Square Center, north end of town.

Napa Valley Visitor's Bureau, 1310 Napa Town Center, Napa, CA 94559. (707) 226–7459.

Napa Valley Vintners Association, P.O. Box 141, St. Helena, CA 94574. (800) 982–1371. Ask for the excellent, free winery touring map.

Upper Napa Valley

The Culinary Institute of America is housed in a historic winery building.

Heart of the Wine Country

_____ 2 NIGHTS _____

Hot springs · Art galleries · Winery architecture tour
Shopping · Mud baths · Vineyard picnic

"Up valley," as the northern half of the Napa Valley is called, is anchored by Calistoga, a hot springs resort town founded in the 1840s. Steam rises from 200-degree mineral springs at a dozen or so health resorts; some are scatterings of historic clapboard cottages with simple facilities, while others are Roman-style spas with luxurious lodgings.

This is the place for rest and rejuvenation, for massages, mud baths, beauty treatments, and slow swims in warm pools. The mud-bath experience must be tried, at least once; be warned that après mud bath you won't feel like moving for quite a spell.

As you drive to Calistoga, through the valley bordered by the Mayacamas Range on the west and the Howell Mountain Range on the east, the tremendous variety of Napa Valley soils and microclimates becomes evident. It's fun to try the diverse wines produced from grapes grown on the dry hillsides, those from the valley floor, and especially the wines from grapes grown on the "benches," the alluvial fans of soil and rocks eroded down from the mountainsides into triangles of rich bedding for vineyards whose grapes have produced wines besting the best in France.

Besides winetasting and hot-bath soaking "up valley," there's tons of shopping to do in St. Helena, plus biking, hiking, golfing, and ballooning; perhaps you'll be forced to return for another weekend or two.

Day 1

Morning

From the Golden Gate Bridge, drive north on Highway 101 to the Napa/Highway 37 exit, connecting with Highway 121 east to Highway 29 at Napa, then driving thirty minutes north to **St. Helena**—about ninety minutes altogether.

Breakfast: **Gillwoods,** 1313 Main Street. (707) 963–1788. Unique breakfast specialties and all-American favorites.

Of the plethora of specialty shops on Main, a few are of particular note. **Stillwaters,** 1228 Main (707–963–1782), is about traveling to exotic places and about fishing: bamboo rods, fish cookbooks, decoys, safari clothes, unique picnic accessories. **Main Street Books,** 1371 Main (707–963–1338), is stocked with regional guidebooks. English country garden goodies can be found at **Mosswood,** 1239 Main (707–963–5883).

The Gallery on Main Street, 1359 Main (707–963–3350), shows the best of local artwork. Just off Main at 1124 Pine, **Henry Evans Printmaker** studio (707–963–2126) produces sophisticated botanical linocuts created by a world-famous artist.

If you're a Robert Louis Stevenson aficionado, you'll find 8,000 pieces of his memorabilia at the **Silverado Museum,** 1490 Library Lane (707–963–3757). Next door, the **Napa Valley Wine Library** (707–963–5145) houses 6,000 books, tapes, and reference materials on the art of winemaking and the history of the valley.

Driving north from St. Helena, you'll see redwood forests grow darker and deeper, maples and oaks crowd closer to the roadside, creating canopies of leaves and branches overhead, brilliant canyons of color in the fall. Watch for **Beringer Winery's Rhine House** on the left, built in 1883 as a reminder to the winery founder of his family home in Germany. This is a good place to take a full winery tour, which includes the huge cellar caves carved into the hillside by Chinese laborers more than a hundred years ago. The grounds and gardens are lovely. The original Beringer home now houses a Culinary Arts Center, headed by Madeleine Kamman, a world-renowned French chef and TV personality, who gives seminars and classes that are open to the public. Call (707) 963–7115 for information.

Lunch: **Culinary Institute of America (CIA),** just north of Beringer on Highway 29. From 1889 until about a century later, the Christian Brothers Winery inhabited Greystone, a massive multistory European-style chateau with 22-inch-thick, hand-cut volcanic stone walls guarded by towering palm trees. After a three-year, $13 million renovation, Greystone was transformed into the western outpost of the most prestigious culinary college in the United States, the CIA in Hyde Park, New York. Lucky for visitors and valley residents, the architectural extravaganza of Greystone today houses not only a state-of-the-art training facility for professional chefs, but a restaurant and dining terrace overlooking an ancient oak forest and rolling vineyards. Here you can watch graduate chefs in action while enjoying California cuisine and Mediterranean classics, such as Spanish tapas, created from the fresh herbs and organic produce gathered daily in the school's gardens and orchards.

While at the CIA, take a look at the food and wine museum and browse the school store, where CIA-logo jackets, shirts, and chef's attire and CIA cookbooks are available. Prized souvenirs of a Wine Country vacation, CIA-logo items make great gifts for gourmands back home.

In addition to comprehensive classes for professional chefs, one-week workshops on subjects such as Napa and Sonoma wines, Chinese cuisine, or seafood cookery are open to experienced chefs and serious foodies. Request a catalog by calling (707) 967–0600. For restaurant reservations and information, call (707) 967–1010.

Afternoon

Two minutes north of the CIA on Highway 29 at the Freemark Abbey sign, turn right into the parking lot and go into the **Hurd Beeswax Candle Factory and Store** (707–963–7211) to see wild and weird candles of every description being created for shipment worldwide.

Just up the road, **Bale Grist Mill State Park** (707–963–2236) is a wooded glade with a 36-foot waterwheel beside a rushing creek. Walk from here into **Bothé–Napa Valley State Park** (707–942–4575) to find a lovely campground in Ritchie Creek canyon, a swimming pool, and shady picnic sites under redwoods and firs along the creek. Both of these parks are home to the endangered spotted owl. You can take a one- or two-hour guided horseback ride along Ritchie Creek and up along the ridges overlooking the valley. Call **Napa Valley Trail Rides** at (707) 996–8566.

Proceed on another ten minutes to Calistoga.

Have a glass of wine with the local winery workers and well-heeled weekenders from San Francisco at the **Silverado Tavern,** 1374 Lincoln Avenue. (707) 942–6825. The wine cellar here is legendary, regularly winning *Wine Spectator* awards. You can get a hefty chunk of prime rib here, with garlic mashed potatoes, but the All Season's Cafe across the street is a much better restaurant. Curiously, the same people own both places.

Dinner: **All Season's Cafe,** 1400 Lincoln. (707) 942–9111. A classically trained chef holds forth in the kitchen, inventing American versions of Mediterranean food with all locally grown and produced ingredients. Home-smoked salmon and chicken, grilled Petaluma duck breast, pizzettas, pasta, fresh fish, killer pies. Salads are tops here, such as warm spinach with smoked chicken and lemon dressing. The greens come from fields just a few blocks away.

Lodging: **Scott Courtyard,** 1443 Second Street. (707) 942–0948. Private, roomy suites (some with full kitchens) in circa-1940 bungalows surrounded by lush gardens. Swimming pool, hot tub, library with fireplace, fully-equipped art studio, separate video/TV room. Full breakfasts served in a bistro setting, evening wine and cheese. Two blocks from downtown.

Day 2

Morning

Breakfast: Scott Courtyard.

Set off on a walking tour of town, a compact grid of tree-shaded streets. The architecture is an eclectic conglomeration of Victorian, art deco, 1950s funky, Craftsman, and Greek and Mission Revival. Get a map and some orientation at the **Sharpsteen Museum,** 1311 Washington (707–942–5911), where an elaborate diorama re-creates the 1800s resort town. Exhibits are lifelike and colorful, and a huge collection of old photos recalls the people who came here over a hundred years ago to "take the waters." Kids love the stagecoach and the unstuffy atmosphere of this museum, built and donated by a thirty-year veteran producer at the Walt Disney Studios; his Disney memorabilia is on display, too. Part of the museum is a charming Victorian cottage and gardens.

Just off the main street on Cedar, the green oasis of **Pioneer Park** on the Napa River has lawns, a gazebo, and a great kids' playground. Next door to the park, **The Elms,** 1300 Cedar (707–942–9476), is a bed-and-breakfast inn in a fanciful French Victorian mansion.

For a midmorning cappuccino, step into **Cafe San Marco,** 1336 Lincoln Avenue (707–942–4671); every variety of coffee and steamed milk specialty you can think of, as well as pastries, is served here. There are a dozen espresso bars in Calistoga, no doubt catering to the throngs of tourists who do the slow stroll of Lincoln Avenue every weekend in the summer and fall.

Galerie Chevrier, at 1219 Washington Street (707–942–6634), and **Donlee Gallery,** at 1319 Lincoln (707–942–0585), display large collections of well-known California artists' works.

The **Evans Designs** outlet at 1421 Lincoln (707–942–0453) sells one-of-a-kind, fine ceramic art. **Calistoga Pottery** (1001 Foothill Boulevard at Pine, 707–942–0216) sells oven-proof dinnerware and table accessories that are like no other.

The work of some of the best artisans in Northern and Southern California is shown and sold at **The Artful Eye:** jewelry, wine glasses, ceramics, glass, clothing, and more (1333-A Lincoln, 707–942–4743). If you are a wine aficionado and want to add to your wine book collection, or pick up guidebooks to the wine country, stop in at the **Calistoga Bookstore,** 1343 Lincoln, (707) 942–4123.

Lunch: **Wappo Bar Bistro,** 1226B Washington Street. (707) 942–4712. A small cafe with patio tables beside a fountain, serving ethnic-inspired inventions such as Middle Eastern pomegranate-glazed pork, Ecuadorean hornada, Central American duck carnitas, Asian noodle salads, and homemade ice cream. Try to arrive either before or after the traditional mealtimes, or you may wait for a table.

Afternoon

A restored 1868 Southern Pacific train station on Lincoln houses the visitor's bureau and the **Calistoga Wine Stop,** 1458 Lincoln Avenue (707–942–5556), where you can choose from more than 1,000 Napa and Sonoma Valley wines and arrange for them to be shipped.

Spend the rest of the day at one of Calistoga's health resorts being herbal-wrapped, enzyme-bathed, massaged, and soaked in mineral-rich mud; expect to feel like warm Jell-O when it's over.

Calistoga Hot Springs at 1006 Washington Street (707–942–6269), is one of the largest. You come for the day or stay overnight in spacious motel units equipped for light housekeeping. Float blissfully in three large, naturally heated mineral pools and take advantage of full spa services.

One of the oldest resorts in town, founded in 1865, **Indian Springs Hot Springs Spa and Resort,** at 1712 Lincoln Avenue (707–942–4913), has an old-fashioned air about it, but they offer all the spa treatments that the newer resorts do. Built in 1913 and still restoring the spirits of bathers is the Olympic-size pool filled with mineral water from three natural geyers, heated to 92 degrees in the summer and 101 in the winter. From a studio cottage to a large house, accommodations are simple and comfortable, including gas fireplaces, soft terry robes, and air-conditioning.

White Sulphur Springs, five minutes east of St. Helena at 3100 White Sulphur Springs Road (707–963–8588), is the oldest hot springs resort in the state. Open to day-trippers are an outdoor hot sulfur pool, an Olympic pool, Jacuzzi, a museum, horseshoe pits, and hiking trails in 330 acres of redwood and madrone.

The **Lavender Hill Spa** (1015 Foothill Boulevard at Hazel, 707–942–4495) is the newest and most elegant. They specialize in treatment for couples, offering everything from massage to acupressure, aromatherapy, and "Vibra Sound" in addition to the traditional mud baths.

Not in the mood for mud and massage? Take a hike in **Robert Louis Stevenson State Park** (see page 41) or on the **Oat Hill Mine Trail,** a historic landmark that starts at the junction of Lincoln Avenue and the Silverado Trail. Mountain bikers, horseback riders, and hikers like this rocky, rigorous 5-mile climb to China Camp.

Dinner: **Catahoula Restaurant and Saloon,** in the **Mount View Hotel** at 1457 Lincoln Avenue. (707) 942–2275. One of a precious covey of nationally celebrated chefs who have escaped to the gourmet mecca of the California Wine Country, Louisiana-born Jan Birnbaum adds Cajun spice to his cooking. Try the rooster gumbo, pecan-crusted catfish, zippy sausages, poultry and meats smoked in a wood-fired oven. Gooey desserts to die for. Reservations absolutely necessary.

Lodging: Scott Courtyard.

Day 3

Morning

Breakfast: Choose from one of the coffeehouses.

Proceed a few minutes north on the Silverado Trail, north of Calistoga to **Chateau Montelena** (707–942–5105), at the foot of Mount St. Helena. Secluded in a piney wood, the winery is a spectacular castle built of French limestone brought around the Horn in 1880, enchantingly poised above a small lake surrounded by gardens and weeping willows, with a vineyard view. A Chinese junk floats serenely, and red lacquered gazebos provide private places for conversation and sipping of the renowned estate-grown Cabernets and Reislings, available only here. In 1972 a Chateau Montelena Chardonnay exploded the myth that French wines are best by winning a blind tasting against France's finest.

Head south on the Silverado Trail and turn right onto Dunaweal Lane to **Clos Pegase** (707–942–4982), a russet-colored, postmodern extravaganza of a winery, the result of an international architectural competition. Besides winetasting here, you'll enjoy the vineyard views, sculpture garden, frescoed murals, and a slide show about the history of winemaking.

A minute farther on Dunaweal, the sparkling white Mediterranean aerie of **Sterling Vineyards** (707–942–3300) floats like an apparition high on a hilltop. For a small fee a tram will take you on a four-minute gondola ride to a sky-high terrace with valley views.

Back on the Silverado Trail, continue south through the valley to a left onto Meadowood Lane for a stroll on the grounds of the **Meadowood Resort Hotel** (707–963–3646), a posh country lodge reminiscent of the 1920s, residing regally on a rise overlooking 250 densely wooded acres, a golf course, and tennis and croquet courts. Meadowood is the home of the annual Napa Valley Wine Auction, a spectacular four-day event attended by deep-pocket bidders and wine lovers from all over the world. The complete health and beauty spa is open to day use: fitness and relaxation classes, aromatherapy, reflexology, Swedish massage, salt glow, facials. Try the day-long spa sampler.

Lunch: **Fairway Grill,** on the terrace at Meadowood. Or, for a picnic lunch, take a right onto Zinfandel Lane, crossing over to Highway 29, and head south a few minutes to Oakville, stopping for gourmet goodies at **Pometta's Deli** (707–944–2365), at the Oakville Cross Road. Drive two minutes up this road to **Vichon Winery,** 1595 Oakville Grade (707–944–2811), to shady picnic tables on a hill overlooking the world. Or try **V. Sattui Winery,** at 111 White Lane south of St. Helena (707–963–7774), which has the largest and one of the prettiest winery picnic groves in the entire valley. Two acres of lawns under spreading oaks are sprinkled with picnic tables around the stone-walled 1885 winery buildings. A gourmet deli sells literally hundreds of varieties of cheeses and meats, fresh breads, juices, and drinks, along with myriad picnic accessories. The only disadvantage here is the sight of busy Highway 29.

Afternoon

Head south to the Bay Area (or turn to Northbound Escape Three and make this a *long* weekend).

There's More

Gliders. Calistoga Soaring Center, 1546 Lincoln Avenue, Calistoga. (707) 942–5592.

Spas. Golden Haven Hot Springs, 1713 Lake Street, Calistoga 94515. (707) 942–6793. Complete spa facilities, mineral pool.

Lincoln Avenue Spa, 1339 Lincoln Avenue, Calistoga 94515. (707) 942–5296. Mud baths, body and beauty treatments, pools.

Roman Spa, 1300 Washington Street, Calistoga 94515. (707) 942–4441. Mineral pools, beauty treatments, mud baths, enzyme baths, saunas, rooms around a tropical garden.

Calistoga Village Inn and Spa, 1880 Lincoln Avenue, Calistoga 94515. (707) 942–0991. Complete spa facilities in a country setting with vineyard views.

Old Faithful Geyser, 1299 Tubbs Lane, Calistoga. (707) 942–6463. Blows its top every forty minutes.

Petrified Forest, 4100 Petrified Forest Road, Calistoga. (707) 942–6667. Six million years ago a volcanic explosion turned redwoods to stone.

Robert Louis Stevenson State Park, 7 miles north of Calistoga on Highway 29. (707) 942–4575. Some 3,670 acres, 2,200 to 4,343 feet elevation, day use only; 5-mile trek to the top of Mount St. Helena for wide views of Northern California. Watch for the rare peregrine falcon; the fastest animal in the world, the falcon dives at speeds of up to 200 miles an hour. Spyglass Hill in Stevenson's *Treasure Island* is based on the landscape of Mount St. Helena. RLS afficionados make pilgrimages to the **Silverado Museum** at 473 Main in St. Helena (707–963–7411), where hundreds of his artifacts, photos, and memorabilia are displayed.

Biking. Palisades Mountain Sports, 1330B Gerrard Street, behind the fire department. (707) 942–9687. Rentals. Mountain bike specialists, rock climbing equipment.

Getaway Bicycle Tours, Calistoga. (800) 499–BIKE. Guided daytrips. Try the thrilling Downhill Cruise guided bike descent from the top of Mount St. Helena, with stops on the way down for photo ops and catching your breath. It's perfectly safe, even for kids nine years old and older and for toddlers in bike trailers.

Backroads, 1516 Fifth Street, Berkeley 94710-1740. (800) 462–2848. Longer guided bike expeditions and inn tours.

Golf. Mount St. Helena Golf Course. (707) 942–9966. Nine holes, reasonable rates.

Safari West, 3115 Porter Creek Road, Santa Rosa 95404. (707) 579–2551. Giraffes in Napa? Yes, at the far northern end of the valley on open grasslands and rolling hills in a wildlife preserve with over

400 exotic animals and birds, African plains animals, including zebras, elands, endangered antelope, giraffe, impala, and Watusi cattle. Private half-day tours in safari vehicles. A once-in-a-lifetime expedition. Advance reservations required.

Lake Berryessa, east of Napa off Highway 128. Lake Berryessa is one of the state's most popular recreation lakes, with 165 miles of hilly oak-covered shoreline. Year-round fishing for trout and bass, warm water for waterskiing and swimming, complete resort, camping, and water-sports facilities and rentals.

Ballooning: Once in a Lifetime Balloon Company, Inc, P.O. Box 795, Calistoga 94515. (800) 722–6665.

Special Events

February. Napa Valley Mustard Celebration, Calistoga. (707) 942–9762. At the county fairgrounds, dozens of food, wine, and brew booths, live entertainment, games.

April. Cajun Gumbo Ya Ya Festival, Napa Valley Fairgrounds, Calistoga. (707) 361–1309. Exotic food, wine and beer, wild and crazy entertainment.

July. Napa County Fair, Calistoga. (707) 942–5111.

September. Flivvers and Flyers Auto and Air Fair, Calistoga Gliderport. (707) 942–6333. Food, sky divers, live music, hangar dance.

September. Hometown Harvest Festival, Oak Street, St. Helena. (707) 963–4456. Dancing, parade, arts and crafts, music, food, wine.

October. Old Mill Days, Bale Grist Mill State Park. (707) 963–2236. Costumed docents grind grain and corn on the millstones and make bread; demonstrations of traditional trades and crafts, games, entertainment.

October. Calistoga Beer and Sausage Fest. (707) 942–6333. Local microbreweries.

December. Pioneer Christmas Celebration, Bale Grist Mill State Park. (707) 963–2236. Costumed docents help kids make traditional Christmas decorations; grain grinding, refreshments, entertainment.

Other Recommended Restaurants and Lodgings

St. Helena

Tra Vigne, 1050 Charter Oak Avenue at Highway 29. (707) 963–4444. At stone-topped tables under the trees and umbrellas, keep your eyes peeled for movie stars and winery owners. It's easy to imagine you are at a villa in the Italian countryside. The terra-cotta–toned stone walls are rampant with vines and a glimpse through iron-framed windows discloses a vibrantly painted high-ceilinged bar and restaurant. A rich balsamic vinegar game sauce blankets roasted polenta, house-cured prosciutto melts in your mouth. Exciting varieties of homemade ravioli, roasted poultry rubbed with exotic spices, and more.

Cantinetta Tra Vigne, at same address. (707) 963–8888. Cozily residing in a nineteenth-century sherry distillery, an Italian deli and market like no other, probably the best in the valley. Fresh pizzettas, salads, sandwiches, sweets, house-brand oils and vinegars. Eat here or take away.

Model Bakery, 1357 Main Street. (707) 963–8192. A circa-1920 brick oven turns out sourdough and rustic breads, pizzettas, fruit tarts, amazing desserts. Buy breakfast rolls and picnic sandwiches.

Spring Street Restaurant, Spring at Oak. (707) 963–5578. Indoors in the historic bungalow or outdoors in a garden patio, American favorites loved by the locals.

Terra, 1345 Railroad Avenue. (707) 963–8931. In a historic stone building, warm and romantic; exotic California cuisine with French and Japanese accents, miraculous wine list. Chef Hiro Sone made a name for himself at Spago in Los Angeles.

Trilogy, 1234 Main. (707) 963–5507. Intimate, casual cafe; bistro cuisine for lunch and dinner; wine and appetizers on the patio.

Showley's Restaurant, 1327 Railroad Avenue. (707) 963–1200. On the patio under a big old fig tree or in the cozy dining room of the 135-year-old building, homemade pasta, big salads, famous garlic mashed potatoes, roasted meats and poultry.

Brava Terrace, at the Freemark Abbey complex, just north of St. Helena, 3010 St. Helena Highway. (707) 963–9300. French bistro menu, delightful garden terrace with waterfalls and carp pond, cozy dining room with fireplace. Risotto, pasta, cassoulet, homemade ice cream, a mixture of ethnic specialties such as spicy Vietnamese chicken, Caribbean jerked pork, excellent burgers.

Harvest Inn, 1 Main Street, 94574, just south of town. (707) 963–9463. Antiques, four-posters, an eclectic collection of elaborate furnishings in luxury rooms and suites surrounded by acres of lush English gardens, a labyrinth of shady pathways, lawns, and bowers. Private balconies, fireplaces, two pools. Expanded continental breakfast. Try to book the King Arthur suite, a romantic venue with a private patio looking onto vineyards and mountains.

El Bonita, 195 Main Street. (707) 963–3216. Hidden behind the original 1930s art deco motel are new two-story motel units with private balconies looking into the trees and over the gardens. Large, two-room suites have micro kitchens. Small pool, sauna.

Calistoga

Calistoga Inn, 1250 Lincoln Avenue. (707) 942–4101. Breakfast, lunch, and dinner; hearty country fare; chili, burgers, *huevos rancheros,* crabcakes, fresh fish, and homebrewed beers and ales. Also eighteen comfortable inn rooms.

Comfort Inn, 1865 Lincoln Avenue. (707) 942–9400. East end of town. Reasonably priced, simple, modern; pool, sauna, spa.

Cafe Pacifico, 1237 Lincoln Avenue. (707) 942–4400. A Mexican motif is the backdrop for incredible breakfasts, lunches, and dinners. Try the blue-corn buttermilk pancakes, fresh enchiladas, and chili rellenos. During happy hour in the late afternoon, a special menu of Mexican appetizers is offered. The bar is a lively, fun place to talk about wine and drink Mexican beer.

Calistoga Ranch Club, 580 Lommel Road. (707) 942–6565. Popular, rustic camping resort off upper Silverado Trail in an oak forest with creek, meadows, Olympic-sized pool, indoor/outdoor games, short hiking trails, small fishing lake. Tent and RV sites, basic cabins. Fewer people and greener surroundings in winter and spring.

Palisades Market, 1506 Lincoln Avenue. (707) 942–9549. Looks like an old grocery store on the outside, gourmet surprises await within. Gourmet market and deli with miraculous sandwich and salad combinations.

For More Information

Calistoga Chamber of Commerce, Old Depot, 1458 Lincoln Avenue, Calistoga, CA 94515. (707) 942–6333.

St. Helena Chamber of Commerce, 1080 Main Street, St. Helena, CA 94574. (707) 963–4456.

You may find it difficult and time consuming to find a bed-and-breakfast accommodation or a hotel room in the Napa Valley on your desired dates. Representing a wide variety of accommodations, the following agencies will send brochures and make reservations for you. Most bed-and-breakfast inns require a two-night minimum stay.

Accommodations Referral. (800) 240–8466.
B & B Style. (800) 995–8884.
Napa Valley Reservations. (707) 252–1985.
Wine Country Reservations. (707) 257–7757.

Lake County Loop

The tasting room of the Fetzer Winery.

Clear Lake, Hopland, Ukiah

_____ 2 NIGHTS _____

Hot springs • Indian history • Fishing and water sports
Beer- and winetasting • Country roads • Wildlife preserves

The mountains, lakelands, and wine valleys of Lake County and western Mendocino County are some of the least visited and most rewarding weekend destinations in Northern California. Traffic and tourist crowds occur only at Clear Lake when summer vacationers arrive with boats and fishing gear. In winter you'll see bald eagles and waterfowl that have come from Alaska and Canada to spend the season at the lake and at Anderson Marsh and Boggs Lake Preserve.

The smooth green flanks of 4,200-foot Mount Konocti, a dormant volcano, loom dramatically above Clear Lake's placid blue waters. Holding more fish per acre than any other lake in the United States, it's the largest natural lake in the state. Resorts, marinas, and camp-grounds dot the 100-mile shoreline, and the lake is stocked regularly with warmwater fish, such as bass, crappie, trout, bluegill, and catfish. A lively competition for the big ones takes place at the Clear Lake Bass Tourney in February.

More discoveries: the surprising Wine Country village of Hopland, champagne baths at Vichy Hot Springs, and a world-famous Indian museum in Ukiah. The **Blue Lakes** are two small lakes in the densely wooded mountains along Highway 20 west of **Upper Lake.** Here you will have a quieter experience, with no water-ski boats or jet skis. A few miles from Clear Lake, **Lake Mendocino** and **Lake Pillsbury** are also tops for striped bass and catfish fishing, water sports, camping, and hiking.

Day 1

Morning

From the Golden Gate Bridge, drive north on Highway 101 to the Napa/Highway 37 exit, connecting with Highway 121 east to Highway 29 at Napa, then driving thirty minutes north to Calistoga—about ninety minutes altogether. Stop for picnic supplies along the way or in Calistoga. The **All Seasons Cafe,** 1400 Lincoln Avenue, Calistoga (707–942–9111), makes up gourmet box lunches including utensils and wine.

Follow Highway 29 through town and five minutes beyond to **Robert Louis Stevenson State Park** (707–942–4575). If you're up for a morning hike, set out into 3,000 wild acres of hillside forest trails; a steep scramble to 4,343 feet, the summit of Mount St. Helena, rewards with views of the entire Napa Valley.

From here to Middletown is a scenic drive like no other, on a roller-coaster road through stream canyons and woods scented with bay and pine. Bicyclers and walkers love the quiet side roads off Highway 29 where big-leaf maples turn red in the fall and oaks are green umbrellas on hot summer days. You'll emerge in a valley of walnut, pear, and kiwi orchards; tumbledown farmhouses; scrub oaks; and rocky meadows. Vast vineyards were planted here in the past decade, creating an increasingly more prominent wine region. Passing through Middletown, watch for the GUENOC WINERY sign and make the

5.5-mile drive on Butts Canyon Road to **Guenoc Estate Vineyards and Winery,** 2100 Butts Canyon Road (707–987–2385). Surrounded by gracious verandas and gardens, the former home of nineteenth-century British actress Lillie Langtry was lovingly restored by current owners, who've established the winery and vineyards on thousands of acres stretching to Napa County.

Lunch: Picnic here in the vineyards on Guenoc Lake or at Anderson Marsh State Historic Park.

Afternoon

Proceed on Highway 29 to Lower Lake, taking the Highway 53 exit to **Anderson Marsh State Historic Park** (707–994–0688). The 900 acres you see from here to the horizon are the wetlands habitat for herons, pelicans, ducks, grebes, coots, cormorants, bald eagles, and hundreds more species of waterfowl. The sight of a bald eagle fishing for its dinner is a moment to remember. Numerous ancient Native American sites are here, some dating from 8000 B.C., when the shores and swamps surrounding Clear Lake were almost exactly as they are today. At the historic **Anderson Ranch House** is a small museum and visitor's center; ask for directions to the re-created Pomo village and ceremonial roundhouse. To see the natural sights, hike through **Redbud Audubon Society's McVicar Preserve** or rent a boat at Garner's Resort (707–994–6267) or Shaw's Shady Acres (707–994–2236).

Back on Highway 29, it's another twenty minutes to the right turn onto Soda Bay Road, then a 5-mile descent to **Konocti Harbor.** In the shadow of Mount Konocti, Konocti Harbor Resort and Spa is a sprawling lakeside resort and marina, with two large swimming pools, tennis courts, minigolf, playgrounds, and a lot more. After enjoying some of the recreational opportunities, have a twilight cocktail on the deck overlooking the action of the marina. Get ready for plenty of live action indoors; *big* country-and-western stars perform here all year long.

Dinner: **Konocti Landing Restaurant.** (707) 279–4286. Seafood, steak, lobster, hearty American fare.

Lodging: **Konocti Harbor Resort and Spa,** 8727 Soda Bay Road, Kelseyville 95451. (800) 862–4930. Rooms, beach cottages, condo units, family packages; complete health spa (707–279–4261) with body and beauty treatments, exercise classes, lap pool.

Day 2

Morning

Breakfast: In the resort coffee shop.

On the way to Lakeport on Highway 29 is **Konocti Winery,** on Thomas Drive (707–299–8861), and **Kendall-Jackson Winery and Vineyards,** at 600 Mathews Road (707–263–5299), both open for tasting every day. Lakeport, a busy summer-vacation town, has a few historic buildings and an old-fashioned band shell and playground in a grassy lakefront park.

From here it's 18 miles on a zigzaggy mountain road, a 2,500-foot ascent up and over the craggy **Mayacamas Range** to Hopland, a route not recommended for large RVs or for stormy days—light snow is not uncommon on this road in midwinter. The road descends on the west side of the mountains into a peaceful vineyard valley, finally crossing an arm of the Russian River, entering Hopland on Highway 101.

Lunch: Purchase picnic goodies in the **Fetzer Tasting Room** gourmet deli, 13500 Highway 101, Hopland (707–744–1737), and settle into one of several woodsy picnic venues around the Fetzer complex. Or go up the street to **Hopland Brewery and Beer Garden,** 13351 South Highway 101 (707–744–1361). Red Tail Ale, Peregrine Pale Ale, Black Hawk Stout, and other exotic brews are fun to try; the lunch menu, served in the century-old pub or outside on a sunny deck, features hearty sausages, burgers, chili, and salads. Brewing operations are open to view, and if you're here on a Saturday night, hang around for the live music and dancing. The joint really jumps during Hopland's Octoberfest celebration.

Afternoon

Hardly 1 mile long, **Hopland** could be the cutest one-horse town you've ever seen, an enclave of art galleries, antiques shops, winery tasting rooms, and small cafes, wrapped snuggly around with vineyards and farmlands.

The ivy-covered Fetzer tasting room is also a large store specializing in food products from the Wine Country: mustards; jams, jellies, and pickles; cheeses; fresh garlic; olive oil and vinegars; and regional cookbooks and guidebooks. A wide variety of Fetzer's wines, from table wines to estate reserves, are available to taste, buy, and ship home, including a line of organically grown varieties.

Adjacent to Fetzer, **Made in Mendocino** (707–744–1300) sells art, weavings, jewelry, and fine crafts produced in the region.

If you dare, take your chances at the **Cheesecake Lady,** 13325 Highway 101 (707–744–1441), for espresso and guess-what.

Real Goods (13201 Highway 101, 707–744–2100) is an unusual retail showplace of renewable energy products: solar, recycled, biodegradable, nontoxic, energy-efficient items for sustainable living. Even the building itself demonstrates "green" concepts.

Like an elderly lady, perfectly preserved and in splendid Victorian dress, the **Thatcher Inn,** Highway 101, Hopland 95449 (800–266–1891), takes up ½ block of Hopland's main street. The hundred-year-old hotel, with peaked dormers and sweeping verandas, shelters an elegant restaurant, bar, dining terrace, swimming pool, and twenty elaborately furnished rooms with private baths. The bar is distinguished by one of the country's largest collections of single malt scotch whiskeys; the library, by 4,000 volumes, one of which will keep you reading in an armchair by the green marble fireplace.

Drive north to Ukiah on Highway 101 and take a right onto Vichy Springs Road, 2 miles through pear orchards to Vichy Hot Springs, arriving in time for a relaxing late-afternoon soak in the warm, bubbly mineral-water baths or the pool.

Dinner: **North State Cafe,** 801 North State Street, Ukiah. (707) 462–3726. Sophisticated specialties in a casual setting, exotic pizzas from the brick oven, pasta, fresh fish, local poultry, meats, and produce.

Lodging: **Vichy Hot Springs,** 2605 Vichy Springs Road, Ukiah, 95482. (707) 462–9515. Since 1854, a country resort famous for carbonated mineral-water springs. From 25,000 feet below the surface of the earth, the magical waters rush forth, sixty-five gallons a minute, filling a large swimming pool and several tubs. Simple, spacious rooms have verandas overlooking sweeping lawns, meadows, and gardens.

Day 3

Morning

Breakfast: A substantial continental breakfast in the sunny dining room at Vichy Springs. Stoke up for a morning hike in the surrounding 700 acres of woods, meadows, streams, and hillsides.

The main attraction in Ukiah, formerly a lively logging town, is the **Grace Hudson "Sun House,"** at 431 South Main Street (707–462–3370), an impressive museum complex housing American Indian baskets, artifacts, and paintings. The late Hudson painted the faces and the domestic life of native Pomo Indians, and her ethnologist husband assembled the extraordinary collection, one of the most important in the Northern Hemisphere. Open to inspection, their home is a wonderful redwood Craftsman-style bungalow. A tree-shaded park surrounds the museum buildings.

On the East Fork of the Russian River near Ukiah, **Lake Mendocino** has 15 miles of oak-studded shoreline and is excellent for striped bass and catfish (707–462–7581). There is a large U.S. Corps of Engineers campground and a great marina resort.

The **Lake Mendocino Marina** has 300 campsites and self-contained RV camp sites, each with a view of the lake (707–485–8644).

The attractive, meticulously maintained resort provides complete water sports, fishing, camping facilities, and boat rentals. Rent a "patio boat"—an easy-to-handle sort of barge, just the thing for families or people who like to party.

Head south to the Bay Area, about two hours away. The Russian River follows you down the highway; watch for access points if you're of a mind to play along the riverbanks. And if you can't bear to return to the city, refer to Northbound Escape One.

There's More

Clear Lake State Park, 3.5 miles northeast of Kelseyville on Soda Bay Road. (707) 279–4293. Some 565 acres; RV, camper, and tent sites. Behind the visitor's center look for great blue herons on the banks of Kelsey Creek; the large nests in the treetops are heron rookeries.

Boggs Lake Preserve, at Middletown. Take Highway 175 to Cobb, then a left onto Bottle Rock Road; proceed 6.5 miles, then take a right onto Harrington Flat Road and drive for 1 mile. A 141-acre tract of fir and pine forest with a unique vernal pool, a lakeland habitat for 141 species of birds, including wintering wildfowl and songbirds, plus a myriad of common and endangered wildlflowers. Early May to mid-June is best for flowers; wintertime, for osprey and bald eagles. Tours April through June. Information: Nature Conservancy, 785 Market Street, San Francisco 94103. (415) 777–0487.

Gliders. Crazy Creek Soaring, Middletown. (707) 987–9112. Scenic glider rides.

Golf. Hidden Valley Lake Golf Course, Highway 29, 5 miles north of Middletown. (707) 987–3035. Eighteen-hole championship course.

Clear Lake Riviera Golf Course, 10200 Fairway Drive, Kelseyville. (707) 277–7129. Eighteen holes and a restaurant.

Hoberg's Forest Lake Golf Club, Highway 175 and Golf Road. (707) 928–5276. Nine holes.

Indian crafts. Owl's Flight, 6292 Highway 20, Lucerne. (707) 274–7734. Native American crafts, jewelry, art, games, supplies.

Parasailing. On the waterfront, 60 Third Street, Lakeport. (707) 263–6789.

Fishing. The fishing season here is 365 days a year, with trout excellent in 160 miles of the Eel River drainage at Blue Lakes, Lake Pillsbury, and small streams throughout southeastern Lake County. A great guide to best trout spots, hot fishing spots for other species, and a map showing launch ramps is found in the Lake County Marketing Program annual magazine, available by mail: 875 Lakeport Boulevard, Lakeport, CA 95453.

Biking. On quiet country roads, special bike roads and lanes called the "Pathways" have been developed all over Lake County. Go to the Visitor's Center in Lakeport or call (707) 525–3743 to get a booklet with a map and detailed descriptions of bike routes for beginners and experienced bikers, from the relatively easy 15-mile Cobb Mountain loop to the 101-mile tri-county Century loop, which includes a demanding ascent of Mount St. Helena.

Lake County Museum, 255 North Main, Lakeport. (707) 263–4555. In a beautiful 1877 building that served as a school for more than fifty years, the extensive collection features stone tools, arrowheads, pioneer costumes and exhibits, antique firearms, and a shop selling jewelry made by local Indians. The jewels of the collection are the superb Pomo Indian baskets.

Casinos. New in the county, video card and slot machines, card tables, bingo. Four Native American tribes operate the gaming halls: Twin Pine, 22223 Rancheria Road, Highway 29, Middletown, 707–987–0197; Elem Casino, 1 Elem Drive, Clearlake Oaks, 707–998–4938; Robinson Rancheria Bingo and Casino, 1545 East Highway 20, between Nice and Upper Lake, 800–809–3636; Konocti Vista Casino, Mission Ranchera Road off Soda Bay Road, Lakeport, 707–262–1900.

On the Waterfront, 60 Third Street, Lakeport. (707) 263–6789. Parasailing, rentals for jet skis, pedal boats, ski boats, fishing and patio boats. Purchase beach wear and water-ski accessories.

Disney's Shirts and Sports, 160 Main, Lakeport. (707) 263–0969. Jet ski, fishing boat and paddle boat rentals, Parasail rides.

Lake Pillsbury, at Upper Lake. Sixty-five miles of shoreline in a mountain setting at 1,800 feet. This is the headwaters of the Eel River, great trout and salmon fishing, all-vehicle gravel roads, tent and RV camping, hiking, horse trails, and boat rentals (707–275–2361).

Special Events

April. Spring Wine Adventure, Lake County Wineries. (707) 525–3743.

April. Pear Blossom Festival, Lakeport. (707) 263–6182. Square dancing extravaganza and other events.

May. Native American Cultural Day, Anderson Marsh. (707) 994–0688. Dancing, displays, demonstrations of traditional arts and crafts.

May. Model Seaplane Fly-In, Lakeport. (707) 263–5092.

May. Lower Lake Daze, Lower Lake. (707) 994–6153. Parade and barbecue, entertainment.

June. Lakeport Revival Classic Car Show. (707) 525–3743. Parade, dance.

June. Lake County Wine and Food Renaissance, Lake County Fairgrounds, Lakeport. (707) 263–6658. Grand garden party, wine and food tasting, entertainment.

July. Lake County Rodeo, Lakeport. (707) 525–3743.

August. Blackberry Festival, Anderson Marsh. (707) 994–0688. Homemade pies, demonstrations of traditional trades, arts and crafts, entertainment, games, tours.

August. Native American Cultural Day, Anderson Marsh. (707) 994–0688. Dancing, displays, demonstrations of traditional arts and crafts.

September. Lake County Fair, Lakeport. (707) 263–6181.

October. Octoberfest, Lakeport and Hopland. (707) 263–7231.

Other Recommended Restaurants and Lodgings

Clearlake

El Grande Inn Best Western, P.O. Box 4598. (707) 994–2000. On the lake; forty-four very nice rooms and suites, pool, sauna, spa, garden courtyard, restaurant, bar.

Nice

Featherbed Railroad Company, 2870 Lakeshore Boulevard. (707) BR–GUEST. On Clear Lake. Eight narrow, cozy caboose sleeper cars, featherbeds, Jacuzzi tubs, swimming pool, in a forest setting across the street from Clear Lake. Extended continental breakfast.

B. J. Wall's Lakeside RV and Campground, 2570 Lakeshore Boulevard. (707) 274–3315. On Clear Lake, full hook-ups, camp sites, shade trees, private beach, boat dock, showers, laundry. Walk to restaurant and boat rentals.

Middletown

Harbin Hot Springs, 18424 Harbin Springs Road. (707) 987–2477. Hot, warm, and cold mineral pools; sundecks, sauna, gym; 1,160 acres of nature trails; camping, restaurant, store.

Lakeport

Forbestown Inn, 825 Forbes Street. (707) 263–7858. Built in 1863, a Victorian masterpiece chock-full of antiques and designer touches. Hearty breakfast, pool, spa; 1 block from the lake.

Park Place, 875 Lakefront Boulevard. (707) 263–0444. Lunch and dinner, fresh produce, seafood, pasta, burgers, steak; casual, with windows overlooking the city park and the lake.

Rainbow Restaurant, 2599 Lakeshore Boulevard. (707) 263–6237. Dinner house with boat dock and lake view.

Cobb Mountain

Beaver Creek RV Park and Campground, 14417 Bottle Rock Road. (707) 928–4322. In a forested mountain area, full hook-up RV spaces, horse rentals, and guided horseback rides.

Kelseyville

Bellhaven Resort, on Clear Lake's Soda Bay, 3415 White Oak Way. (707) 279–4329. Nice beach, fishing and swimming pier, knotty-pine cabins with kitchens, private dock.

For More Information

Lake County Visitor's Center, 875 Lakeport Boulevard, Lakeport, CA 95453. (707) 525–3743.

Greater Ukiah Chamber of Commerce, 495 East Perkins Street, Ukiah, CA 95482. (707) 462–4705.

Mendocino County Vintner's Association, P.O. Box 1409, Ukiah, CA 95482. (707) 463–1704.

MISTIX (state park campground reservations). (800) 444–7275.

The Redwood Route

The Gingerbread Mansion, one of the premier Victorian homes on the West Coast.

Seacoast Towns, Path of the Giants

—————————— 2 NIGHTS ——————————

Logging towns • Rivers and seacoast • Victorian village
Ancient redwoods • Seafood cafes • California history

The drive up Highway 101 to the seaside logging town of Eureka is a respite from summer's heat and a cozy adventure on foggy winter weekends. You'll stop along the way to see the redwoods and play on the Eel River. California's coastal redwoods are the world's tallest living things. Walking beneath a 300-foot forest canopy among these silent giants from the age of the dinosaurs is an unforgettable experience.

Eureka and smaller coastal towns look much as they did in their Victorian heyday—streets lined with gracious old homes and elaborate gingerbread-trimmed hotels. Settled during the California Gold Rush in the mid-1800s, the county's founding coincided with the birth of Victorian architecture, and in every town are glorious examples of the era, from Greek Revival to the later and more ornamental Second Empire, Italianate, Eastlake, and Queen Anne styles. A stand-out example is the William Carson Mansion in Eureka, a mixture of several styles that took one hundred men more than two years to build, from 1882 to 1884. Another stunner called the Elegant Victorian Mansion in Eureka, one of the most elaborate Eastlake structures ever constructed, is now a bed-and-breakfast inn.

From partaking of bed-and-breakfast inns, fresh seafood, logging and Indian history, wildlife sanctuaries, and sea air to fishing for the mighty salmon, biking on forest paths, and going river rafting or beachcombing, you'll find that there's more than a weekend's worth of enticements here. In addition, Humboldt County is home to nearly 8,000 artists—more artists per capita than any other county in California—whose works you will see and experience in shops, galleries, and performing arts venues.

Expect foggy mornings, even in the summer, and winter rains December through March. These tremendous northern woods are true rain forests, thriving on drizzle and damp. But don't let drippy weather keep you at home. Fishing is best from October through March, and Eureka is misty and romantic then, too.

Day 1

Morning

Begin the 280-mile trip at the Golden Gate Bridge, going north on Highway 101 for 80 miles to **Healdsburg.** Take the Central Healdsburg exit and go 2 blocks north to the plaza, the palm-shaded green heart of the wine regions of the Alexander and Dry Creek valleys (see Northbound Escape One).

Breakfast: **Healdsburg Coffee Company,** 312 Center Street, on the plaza. (707) 431–7941. Cappuccino, muffins, fresh pastries, and many breakfast goodies.

Back on 101, head north. Crisscrossed by the Russian River, the serene **Alexander Valley** opens up, its folded foothills carpeted with vineyards and scattered with giant oaks and poufs of yellow broom. At **Cloverdale** you'll begin to see redwood groves and logs piled up at sawmills on the roadside. Slowing up through Cloverdale (a notorious speed trap), notice old stone landmark buildings and Victorians.

Between Cloverdale and Leggett you'll share the road with logging trucks as the highway winds along the rugged, forested spine of the Coast Range. Mountains become jagged and canyons deep. Redwoods, pines, maples, and madrone crowd the hillsides, vivid in the fall. Above Leggett watch for the **Redwood Tree House,** a fun tourist trap with a good collection of guidebooks and maps. The vestibule is formed from the burned-out shell of a giant sequoia; the tree, however, is still alive and thriving.

Hartsook Inn, 900 Highway 101, Piercy, CA 95587 (707–247–3305), 8 miles south of Garberville, is another stretch-your-legs opportunity. In a grove of towering redwoods, the inn has been famous for fresh trout dinners since the 1920s. Take a peek at the old photos in the lobby and walk down to the river, the south fork of the Eel, past simple vacation cabins; families spend their summers here, fishing and swimming in the river.

Twenty-three miles north of Leggett, you'll see a sign for the **Benbow Road,** a pretty byway running close along the Eel, making a nice little drive, walk, or bike ride, ending up at the **Benbow Inn,** 445 Lake Benbow Drive, Garberville (707–923–2124). Built in 1925, the inn is a Tudor monolith overlooking a twenty-six-acre summer lake. Here you can fish and rent a canoe; for a refreshing sidetrip, go with the park rangers (707–946–2311) on a one-hour interpretive canoe tour to absorb some natural history and see osprey, turtles, herons, and belted kingfishers.

Now on to the **Avenue of the Giants,** a world-famous 33-mile scenic drive, the highlight of your visit to redwood country. The avenue bypasses the highway and its many attractions are well marked; turnouts and parking areas access short loop trails into the forest. Some 51,222 acres of spectacular redwood groves along the Eel and its south fork are contained here in **Humboldt Redwoods State Park** (707–946–2311). These are the biggest of the 2,000-year-old beauties remaining in a 30-mile-wide belt of coastal redwoods stretching from Monterey to Oregon.

Pick up picnic goodies at one of the small groceries along the first few miles of the avenue, then begin your tour at the **Visitor's Center** (707–946–2311), about 4 miles from the south end of the avenue. Here you'll get oriented by a movie, exhibits, and trail maps. Ask for advice on the lengths and types of walks and drives you'd like to take in the park. Docents will show you a special binder of trail maps, pointing out new trails and those that may be closed due to weather or maintenance.

Not to be missed is the **Rockefeller Forest** in the **Big Trees** area, a 5-mile drive in on Mattole/Honeydew Road. Since the former champion sequoia Dyerville Giant, 362 inches in diameter, fell in rain-saturated ground in the spring of 1991, the new champ is a 363-footer in the Rockefeller Forest. Tiptoeing along boardwalks and spongy pathways in the damp, cool stillness at the foot of these magical giants, you'll hear only the bustle of chipmunks. Under a fragrant green canopy hundreds of feet above your head, the shade on the forest floor is deep and dark, even on a hot summer's day. Wildflowers—trillium, wild iris, and redwood orchid—spring from a carpet of moss and fern, while brilliant blue Stellar's jays flash through the branches overhead. A spooky rush of air signals the flight of a black raven; the shiny and silent 2-foot-long ravens are aggressive guardians of their thousand-year-old forest. A short trail leads to a sandy riverbank, for sunbathing, wading, picnicking, and fishing.

Lunch: Have your picnic here or at Bull Creek Flats.

Afternoon

Returning toward the highway on the Mattole/Honeydew Road, watch for the sign to **Bull Creek Flats,** a sunny pebbled beach and picnic area at a lovely bend in the river; wild lilacs bloom here in great purple clouds in the spring. In the rainy season the river runs with salmon and steelhead. Summer fishing—carp and eels—is for fun, not for food.

One hundred miles of trails in Humboldt Park are maintained for walkers, backpackers, bikers, and horseback riders. Meanderings will turn up old homesteaders' cabins and a plethora of campgrounds, some for RVs and others consisting of simple sites in the backcountry. Apple blossoms bloom in orchards planted by early settlers. In fall big-leaf maples, alders, and buckeyes turn red and gold. In the farthest outback are bobcats, black-tailed deer, foxes, ring-tailed cats, and even black bears.

Reaching Eureka by day's end, you'll be warmly welcomed by Doug Vieyra, the mustachioed proprietor of the **Elegant Victorian Mansion,** 1406 C Street, Eureka 95501 (707–444–3144). Lily Vieyra will hand you a glass of wine and take you on a tour of the house, perhaps the finest of Eureka's great treasure trove of Victorian bed-and-breakfast inns. Built in 1888, it's an extravagantly antiques-filled Queen Anne surrounded by a garden of 150 antique roses; there are four large, comfortable rooms. The Vieyras offer saunas, massages, croquet, vintage movies, fireplace chats, and a library of guidebooks.

Dinner: **The Sea Grill,** 316 E Street. (707) 443–7187. In historic Old Town on Humboldt Bay; biggest seafood menu in town, legendary salad bar, steak; reservations necessary.

Stroll around under the gaslights in nineteenth-century **Old Town** for a last whiff of sea air before bedtime. It's 12 blocks to the mansion.

Day 2

Morning

Breakfast: Lily's hearty eggs benedict and Dutch pancakes, with fresh fruits and juices.

A font of local sightseeing and historical information, Doug will clue you in to secret spots to visit in the area. With an architectural/ scenic walking-tour map, start the day with an exploration of the surrounding Victorian neighborhood, ending up in Old Town. On the waterfront, home port to more than 500 fishing boats, are several blocks of 1850–1904 Queen Anne, Eastlake, and Classic Revival buildings. The Victoriana is enhanced by parks, fountains, playgrounds, and shaded benches for resting between shopping, photo snapping, and museum discoveries.

Not to be missed is the **Indian Art Gallery,** 241 F Street (707–445–8451), where Northwestern Indian artists exhibit and sell their works. The **Clarke Memorial Museum,** at Third and E streets (707–443–1947), a 1920s Italian Renaissance–style former bank with a glazed terra-cotta exterior, houses an extraordinary collection of Indian basketry, antique weapons, maritime artifacts and photos, furniture, and memorabilia of early Humboldt days. The **William Carson Mansion,** at Second and M streets, said to be the most photographed home in America, is a wedding cake of an Italianate/Queen Anne mansion built in the 1880s by a lumber baron; it's a private club, and the interior is off-limits to the public.

Lunch: **Bristol Rose Cafe** in the Eureka Inn off the elegant main lobby, Seventh and F streets. (707) 442–6441. Rub shoulders with loggers and tourists. Or, for a picnic lunch, go to **Sequoia Park,** Glatt and W streets, in fifty-two acres of virgin redwoods with a zoo, a kids' playground, formal gardens, walking paths, and a duck pond.

Afternoon

From June through September a seventy-five-minute cruise of the bay, departing from the foot of C Street, can be had on the *M.V. Madaket* (707–444–9440), a wooden steamer built in the 1920s. You'll get a narrated tour of historical and natural sights around the bay, passing oyster farms, flocks of aquatic birds, and the third largest colony of harbor seals in the West. If it's a clear, mild day, try the cocktail cruise, leaving at 4:00 P.M.

One of the magic places in Eureka that will catch and keep you longer than you planned to stay, the **Blue Ox** (800–248–4259) is an old mill at the foot of X Street, 3 blocks north of Fourth. This is a museumlike job shop and sawmill that makes custom trim for Victorian buildings, using the same machines that were used to create the originals. Owner Eric Hollenbeck collected machines from junked mills and from the briarpatches of Mendocino County, restoring dozens of them for turning columns, carving rosettes, and forming wooden gutters. In the huge main building, you can take a self-guided tour on catwalks above the workers; call ahead to see if Eric happens to be giving one of his special personal tours. A loggers' camp, a bird sanctuary, and other attractions make this a worthy stop.

Dinner: **Hotel Carter Restaurant,** 301 L Street, Eureka. (707) 444–8062. Opulent Victorian decor, California cuisine, and nouvelle Italian specialties; scallops in garlic, lemon, and herbs; oysters with basil and chèvre; filet mignon in Burgundy wine; grilled breast of duck in Zinfandel-blueberry sauce; extensive wine list.

Lodging: Fall into a big, comforter-covered bed here at the **Carter House Country Inn.** (707) 445–1390.

Day 3

Morning

Breakfast: **The Samoa Cookhouse,** on Woodley Island in the bay. (707) 442–1659. Reached by the Highway 255 bridge on the north edge of Old Town, this is the last surviving lumber camp cookhouse in the West. In the dining room, where giant breakfasts are served from 6:00 A.M., historical photos and logging artifacts add to the turn-of-the-century atmosphere. Woodley Island affords breezy seaside walks, bike rides, and views of the bay and Eureka; watch for the egret rookery in cypress trees on Indian Island.

From the Samoa Cookhouse take scenic Highway 255 north fifteen minutes around Humboldt Bay to **Arcata,** home of Humboldt State University. This is another old logging town with unique attractions, such as the **Historic Logging Trail** in Arcata's 600-acre **Community Forest** (707–822–7091). Enter Redwood Park at the corner of Fourteenth and Union, following Redwood Park Road to the parking lot. On foot, take Nature Trail #1 on the west side of the parking lot and follow signs and a map that's provided to see logging sites and equipment from a century ago. A few old-growth sequoias remain in these groves, but most are second-growth.

Arcata Marsh and Wildlife Sanctuary, at the foot of I Street in Arcata (707–822–7091), is a birdwatcher's mecca. For the best photography settle into one of the bird blinds. Guided nature walks are scheduled on Saturdays, rain or shine.

Twenty-two miles south of Eureka, take the Ferndale exit, driving 5 miles west across the Eel through flat, green dairylands to **Ferndale.**

Just two long streets of glorious Victorian buildings, the entire tiny town is a State Historic Landmark. To attract tourists and cheer themselves through long, damp winters, residents have painted more than 200 of their homes and businesses in a cacophony of bright colors. Art galleries, antiques shops, ice cream parlors, and cafes abound. The **Gingerbread Mansion,** at 400 Berding Street (707–786–4000), is one of the premier Victorian masterpieces on the West Coast. Dressed in bright yellow and peach with cascades of lacy white trim, and surrounded by whimsical formal gardens, the gigantic hundred-year-old beauty is ½ block long. Nine elaborately decorated rooms have clawfoot tubs (one room has two tubs, toe to toe) and the mansion has four parlors. This was the only Victorian in town to survive undamaged a monster earthquake in 1992; Ferndale has since been completely restored. It will take a couple of hours to stroll Main Street, take pictures of the old buildings, and browse in the shops. (On the way into town, watch for a large, light green building with striped awnings and a red door: the **Ferndale Antiques Mall,** a veritable bazaar of forty dealers selling everything from estate jewelry to Victorian furniture, 597 Fernbridge Drive, 707–725–8820.)

At **Golden Gait Mercantile** (421 Main, 707–786–4891), time is suspended in the 1850s with barrels of penny candy, big-wheeled coffee grinders, and glass cases lined with old-fashioned restoratives and hair pomades.

Dave's Saddlery (491 Main) has cowboy boots, beaded hatbands, and silver buckles. Dave will probably be in residence creating a hand-tooled saddle.

Many of Ferndale's beautiful gardens are visible from the sidewalk in town, but some of the most spectacular are open to the public in odd-numbered years, at a July event benefitting the Ferndale Museum (707–786–4477).

Ferndale sparkles all over and decorates to the max at Christmastime. The lighting of the tallest living Christmas tree in America, a parade, a Dickens's Festival, and concerts are among the blizzard of holiday activities.

Victorian Village Mysteries is a popular event in February, when residents, guests, and actors come to town in costume for a weekend of clue-hunting, a dinner and masquerade party, a theater performance, and a reception with the cast, all starting on Saturday morning and ending with Sunday lunch (707–786–4477).

Lunch: **Curley's Grill,** 460 Main. (707) 786-9696. Surprisingly sophisticated California cuisine, indoors or on the patio. Grilled prawns with Thai peanut sauce, homemade foccacia, local fresh fish, grilled sandwiches.

Afternoon

On the south end of Main, go left onto Ocean Street to **Russ Park** to stretch your legs in a 110-acre closed-canopy spruce and redwood forest with more than 3 miles of wildflower trails and good bird-watching.

Head back to the Bay Area, stopping along the way to walk again under the great redwoods.

There's More

Fishing. K Street and the F Street piers; the south jetty, 11 miles south of Eureka on 101; the north jetty, 6 miles from the west end of Samoa Bridge, for surf and rock fishing, lingcod, salmon. Trolling and shorecasting for salmon and steelhead in coastal lagoons between Trinidad and Orick, north of Eureka; clamming on several nearby beaches. The Eel, the Mad, the Van Duzen, the Little River, and Redwood Creek all are near Eureka; the Klamath, a little farther. River runs of king and silver salmon start after the rains have begun in October. Steelhead runs begin in late November. Twenty lakes in Humboldt County are stocked with trout. To check for fishing conditions, call North Coast Fishphone (707–444–8041) or Eel River Headquarters (707–946–2311).

Celtic Charter Service, 5105 Woodland Way, Eureka 95501. (707) 442–7580. From Woodley Island Marina, Phil Glenn takes you out on his sportfishing boat, daily from May to September, for salmon and rock cod fishing and for whale-watching.

Rivers West Fishing Expeditions, P.O. Box 53, Redcrest 95569. (707) 722–4159. A veteran jetboat operator customizes camping, fishing, and sightseeing jaunts on local rivers.

Golf. Eureka Municipal Golf Course, 4750 Fairway Drive, Eureka. (707) 443–4808. Eighteen holes.

Henry A. Merlo State Recreation Area, at Big Lagoon, 32 miles north of Eureka on Highway 101. (707) 488–2171. A beautiful lagoon inhabited by thousands of birds with 7 miles of beaches, windsurfing for the experienced.

King Range National Conservation Area, in an area known as the Lost Coast, preserves 24 miles of shoreline, mountain streams, trails, and forests for camping, hiking, fishing, hunting, and sightseeing. Five campgrounds are available. (707) 822–7648. Horse Mountain is a popular spot for birdwatching and nature photography, 23 miles northwest of Redway. The Mattole Campground, 5 miles west of Petrolia, is known for seabirds, sea lions, harbor seals, and sea otters.

The part of the Lost Coast between Mattole Point and Shelter Cove is rugged and largely inaccessible except for a few wilderness trails off the Mattole Road. One of your options is to head south from Ferndale to the tiny town of Petrolia, then take Lighthouse Road west to the beach and spend a wonderful day hiking the 6-mile route from the mouth of the Mattole River south to the Punta Gorda Lighthouse and back. It's mostly on and along the beach, with tidepools, wildflowers, high cliffs, and the sea in view. For maps and information, call the BLM headquarters at 1695 Heindon Road, off Janes Road in Arcata. The BLM also administers the King Range area.

Prairie Creek Redwoods, 50 miles north of Eureka on Highway 101, 6 miles north of Orick, a World Heritage Site. Twelve thousand acres of magnificent coastal redwoods, 70 miles of mountain biking and hiking trails, Roosevelt elk, museum, beaches, campgrounds, Fern Canyon. (707) 488–2171.

Mad River Salmon and Steelhead Hatchery, 2 miles south of Blue Lake on Hatchery Road. (707) 822–0592.

Winter fun. Horse Mountain cross-country skiing, sledding. Take Highway 299 to Titlow Hill Road.

Scenic drive along wild Humboldt County rivers. Take Highway 36 along Van Duzen and Mad rivers to Ruth Lake in Trinity County (three to four hours) or beyond to Red Bluff (five to six hours).

Tours. Trees to Sea Interpretative Tours, 2006 Street Maru, McKinleyville 95521. (707) 839–8066. Five- and seven-hour guided tours of Eureka and Humboldt County.

Eureka Image Tours, 1401 East Avenue, Eureka 95501. (707) 445–2117. Guided tour of Victorian districts, Fort Humboldt, Humboldt Bay, lumberjack lunch.

Tall Trees Outfitters, P.O. Box 12, Orick 95555. (707) 488–5785. Guided horseback rides in the national and state parks, daytrips and pack trips.

Aurora River Adventures, P.O. Box 938, Willow Creek 95573. (916) 629–3843. Daytrips on the wild and scenic Klamath River.

Skunk Train, 1 West Laurel, Fort Bragg. (707) 964–6371. Having hauled logs to sawmills in the 1880s, the Skunk Train—actually several historic diesel and steam trains—now delivers provisions to people living in isolated places along the tracks and takes tourists on half- or full-day trips to Willits and back. The route runs along Pudding Creek through redwood forests, crossing many bridges and trestles. In the Fort Bragg train depot are two dozen retail shops and places to eat, scattered among huge railroad and logging artifacts.

Special Events

February. Annual Trinidad Clam Beach Run, Patrick's Point State Park, Trinidad. (707) 677–3448. One thousand runners and walkers; 8.5-mile route ending at the beach.

March. Annual Oyster Shooter Eating Contest and April Fools' Day Eve Ball, 102 F Street. (707) 445–3970.

March. Redwood Coast Dixieland Jazz Festival, Eureka. (707) 445-3378.

April. Rhododendron Festival, Eureka. (707) 442–3738.

April. Dolbeer Steam Donkey Days, Fort Humboldt State Historic Park. (707) 445–6567. Logging competition; operation of steam donkeys, locomotives, and equipment; rides.

May. Avenue of the Giants Marathon. (707) 442–1226.

May. World Championship Great Arcata to Ferndale Cross-County Kinetic Sculpture Race, Arcata. (707) 725–3851.

June. Scandinavian Festival and Barbecue, Main Street, Ferndale. (707) 786–9853. Dancing, food, a parade, and festivities for descendants of Scandinavian lineage and for visitors; food, music, and fun.

June. Rodeo and Western Celebration, Garberville. (800) 338–7352.

August. Humboldt County Fair and Horse Races. (707) 786–9511.

November. Humboldt County's Coastal Christmas celebrations begin, two months of festivites. (800) 338–3482.

December. Truckers' Parade, downtown Eureka. (707) 443–9747. Some 150 big rigs decorated in Christmas lights; logger-style floats. You've never seen anything like this parade.

Other Recommended Restaurants and Lodgings

Eureka

Bay City Grill, 508 Henderson Street. (707) 444–9069. Bistro-style menu, fresh seafood, great salads, upbeat, lively.

Cafe Waterfront Oyster Bar and Grill, 102 F Street at First. (707) 443–9190. Bay view, Victorian decor, casual; seafood, pasta, chicken, beef.

Ramone's Bakery, 209 E Street. (707) 445–2923. Where the locals go for cappuccino, killer bagels, and scones.

Lazio's, 327 Second Street. (707) 443–9717. Great seafood since 1944.

Camellia Cottage, 1314 I Street. (707) 445–1089. French country–style.

Eureka Inn, Seventh and F streets. (707) 442–6441. Hundred-room hotel with a pool, spa, and three restaurants. A National Historic Landmark, reminiscent of an English Tudor estate. Grand lobby has cushy leather sofas, backgammon tables, and a huge fireplace. Rooms are spacious, with traditional decor.

Red Lion Inn, 1929 Fourth Street. (800) 547–8010. 175 nice motel rooms in town, pool, restaurant, and bar.

Eureka KOA Kampground, Highway 101, 4 miles north of Eureka. (800) 462–KAMP.

E-Z Boat Landing and Trailer Park, 4 miles south of Eureka at King Salmon turnoff. (707) 442–1118. All services; good clamming and sportfishing.

Garberville

Knight's Restaurant, Myers Flat on the Avenue of the Giants. (707) 943–3411. Casual cafe serving all day and evening, basic good food, impeccable, comfortable.

Ferndale

Diane's Cafe and Espresso, 553 Main. (707) 786–4950. Cafe au lait in a vat, homemade sandwiches, salads, soups.

For More Information

California State Park Campsite Reservations. (800) 444–2775.

Redwood Empire Association, 785 Market Street, Fifteenth Floor, San Francisco 94103. (415) 543–8334.

Eureka/Humboldt County Convention and Visitor's Bureau, 1034 Second Street, Eureka 95501. (800) 338–7352.

Eureka Chamber of Commerce, 2112 Broadway, Eureka 95501. (707) 442–3738.

Ferndale Chamber of Commerce, 248 Francis Street, Ferndale 95536. (707) 786–4477.

Bodega Bay

One of the many farms featured on the Sonoma County Farm Trail map.

A Weekend at the Coast

_____ 1 NIGHT _____

Beachcombing · Waterfront cafes · Harbor life
Whale-watching · Kite flying · Fishing · Birdwatching

From the Gravenstein Apple Capital of Sebastopol, through Sonoma County's rolling pastures, to the major fishing port of Bodega Bay, there is much to fill a weekend. Some of the warmest and most beautiful of the Northern California beaches are found near **Bodega Bay,** a small fishing village where seals and sea lions, boats, windsurfers, and thousands of birds share a harbor. Some of the best weather days are in October, November, and December, when other places in the Bay Area are chilly. Dense fog occurs only about twenty days annually. On the way to the wild beaches of the central coast and the lively harbor town, relaxing meanders on country roads are enlivened with frequent stops for antiques and art-gallery browsing, sightseeing, and coastal contemplation in cafes.

Day 1

Morning

Drive north from the Golden Gate on Highway 101 for forty-five minutes to Cotati, turning west onto Highway 116 to Sebastopol. You'll pass more than a dozen antiques shops on the way into town; stop if you dare at the **Antique Society,** 2661 Gravenstein Highway South (707–829–1733), the county's largest antiques collective. **Julien's Sebastopol Antiques,** at 1190 Gravenstein Highway South (707–836–0595), has nine rooms of goodies.

Breakfast: **East West Cafe,** 128 North Main, Sebastopol. (707) 829–2822. Simply the best local produce in inventive breakfasts; vegetarian specialties.

Set off through the orchardlands of western Sonoma County on the **Bodega Highway,** after 6 miles taking a right turn onto the Bohemian Highway to **Freestone. The Wishing Well Nursery,** 306 Bohemian Highway (707–823–3710), is like no other nursery. Surrounding a 200-year-old hotel are acres of fabulous plants and flowers, outdoors and in greenhouses. Exotic birds, fancy chickens, ducks, swans, peacocks, pheasants—you name it—twitter in cages, glide on ponds, and strut around as if they owned the place. Decorating the grounds are statuary remnants of Bernard Maybeck's turn-of-the-century Palace of Fine Arts in San Francisco. **Trude's Antiques** (707–823–3710) is in the same building; a player piano accompanies your antiques discoveries in the large shop.

Continue on the Bodega Highway a few miles to the wide-spot-in-the-road town of **Bodega,** 2 miles west of Bodega Bay; take a left onto Bodega Lane. The old school on the hill that looks vaguely familiar is the **School House Inn,** 17110 Bodega Lane (707–876–3257), a comfortable bed-and-breakfast establishment. When Alfred Hitchcock filmed *The Birds* in 1962, this was the school where the black beauties lined up menacingly on the schoolyard jungle gym and chased the children down the road. Near the inn is St. Teresa's Church, circa 1860, and a few antiques and gift shops. On the highway watch for **Bodega Landmark Studio Collection,** 17255 Bodega Highway (707–876–3477), a regional center for art and fine crafts of all kinds.

Lunch: **The Tides Wharf and Restaurant,** 825 Highway 1, midtown Bodega Bay. (707) 875–3652. Dine at a sunny window table overlooking the action of the wharf and the harbor. Fresh local seafood: clam chowder, Dungeness crab, salmon, mussels, sand dabs—the list goes on.

Afternoon

Whale-watching cruises and deep-sea fishing party boats leave from the wharf, headquarters for Bodega Bay's harbor and the home port for many northern coast fishing vessels. Fishermen unload their catch and shoppers choose from local and imported fresh seafood at **The Tides Wharf Fresh Fish Market** (707–875–3554). It's crab in the fall, herring in the spring, salmon in the summer—and rock and ling cod all year. Mingled with weathered clapboard houses are a handful of seafood restaurants along with a few shops and motels scattered around the edges of a large, protected harbor where pleasure boats from all over the world come to anchor away from the open sea. Although the town was founded in the 1870s, most of the buildings of architectural interest are circa-1910 California Craftsman–style bungalows.

On the north end of town, turn left onto Eastshore Road, then right onto Westshore Road, circling the bay. Notice a swampy area on your right, near an old boat skeleton, where blue herons often stalk about in the reeds. Fishing boats and sailboats are lined up at **Spud Point Marina** (707–875–3535), and there's a long fishing pier where you can try your luck. At **Westside Park** (707–875–2640), you can picnic, dig for clams and bait, and launch a boat. Most days sailboarders flit like butterflies in the harbor breezes. Every April, thousands come to the park for the **Bodega Bay Fishermans' Festival** to see the blessing of the fleet and a decorated boat parade, and to enjoy a big outdoor fair with food and entertainment, arts and crafts (707–875–3422).

There's a sign for the **University of California Bodega Marine Laboratory** (707–875–2211), open to tours on Friday afternoons. About .5 mile of coastline and surrounding marine habitat is protected and studied; the exhibits and working research projects—such as aquafarming of lobsters—are fascinating.

At the end of the road, park and get out onto the bluffs of **Bodega Head** (707–875–3540), a prime whale-watching site. Hundreds of whales migrate north along the coast from December through April. Footpaths from here connect to 5 miles of hiking and horseback-riding trails in grassy dunes.

Back on Eastshore Road near the highway, stop in at the **Branscomb Gallery,** 1588 Eastshore Road (707–875–2905). There are three floors of galleries with sea views, featuring local and internationally known artists, wildlife etchings, seascapes, and vineyard scenes, one of the best galleries in gallery-rich Sonoma County. Next door is **Bodega Bay Baking Company,** 1580 Eastshore Road (707–875–2280). Fresh batches of muffins, cinnamon rolls, breads, pastries, and cookies baked all day, espresso and cold drinks. At **Candy and Kites,** 1425 Highway 1 (707–875–3777), get you-know-what for your beach walks. The **Ren Brown Collection,** 1781 Highway 1 (707–875–2922), features works from California and Japan—wood blocks, etchings, silkscreens.

From Bodega Bay north to Bridgehaven, the **Sonoma Coast State Beach** (707–875–3483) is 13 miles of sandy beaches and coves accessible in a dozen or so places; dramatic rocky promontories and seastacks, tidepools, and cliffsides make this a thrilling drive. You can camp at **Wright's Beach** or **Bodega Dunes** (800–444–7275). On the north end of the Bodega Bay area, the Bodega Dunes comprise more than 900 acres of huge sand dunes, some as high as 150 feet. There is a 5-mile riding and hiking loop through the dunes and a hiking-only trail to Bodega Head. In a spectacular show of color, thousands of monarch butterflies flock to a grove of cypress and eucalyptus trees adjacent to Bodega Dunes every October through February. Overwintering in Bodega Bay, the monarchs disburse throughout the state seeking the milkweed plant to lay their eggs.

For rock fishing and surf fishing, **Portuguese Beach** is a good choice; for beachcombing and tidepooling, try **Shell Beach.** Across Highway 1 from Shell Beach, a trail runs up and over the hills to a small redwood forest. It takes about an hour and passes through beautiful meadows, under big shade trees, and over creeks, with coastal views all the way. The path goes on from the forest to the **Russian River** and the Pomo/Miwok campground, described below.

Surf fishing is good at **Salmon Creek Beach** (campsite reservations, 800–444–7275), a beautiful dune area planted with European grasses. The creek is dammed up with sand, forming a lagoon inhabited by throngs of seabirds. At the north end of the beaches, **Goat Rock,** a notoriously dangerous place to swim, is popular for seashore and freshwater fishing at the mouth of the Russian River; seals like it, too. This coastline is home to more than 200 species of sea- and shorebirds. You don't need to be an official birdwatcher; they're easy to see in saltmarshes, mudflats, tidepools, and bays—great blue herons, white and brown pelicans, gulls, ospreys, even peregrine falcons.

At **Bridgehaven,** where the Russian River meets the sea, are a simple restaurant and lodgings (see Northbound Escape Eight).

Dinner: **Duck Club** at Bodega Bay Lodge, Highway 1 on the south end of Bodega Bay, near Bodega Harbour Golf Links. (707) 875–3525. Fresh Sonoma County seafood, poultry, cheeses, and produce on a California cuisine menu. One of the top dining experiences on the Northern California coast.

Lodging: **Bodega Bay Lodge.** (707) 875–3525. Among pines and grassy, landscaped dunes overlooking the Pacific, Doran Beach, bird-filled marshes, and the bluffs of Bodega Head. Seventy-eight spacious, deluxe rooms with views, terraces, or decks; comforters; Jacuzzi tubs; robes; fireplaces. The lobby has a giant stone fireplace and two 500-gallon aquariums filled with tropical fish. Sheltered swimming pool with sea view, spa, sauna, fitness center, bikes, golf packages. Afternoon wine hour.

Day 2

Morning

Breakfast: Complimentary continental breakfast in the Duck Club restaurant. Later in the morning the **Sandpiper Dockside Cafe,** on the water at 1410 Bay Flat Road (707–875–2278), is the place to tuck into eggs with home fries, *huevos rancheros*, or crab omelettes.

From the lodge take a morning walk in **Doran Beach Regional Park** (707–875–3540), a 2-mile curve of beautiful beach separating Bodega Bay and Bodega Harbor. Clamming in the tidal mudflats and wind surfing in the harbor waters are two popular activities. The combination of freshwater wetlands, salt marshes, and the open sea attracts a great variety of shorebirds and waterfowl, such as sanderlings, plovers and herons, cormorants, marsh wrens, and red-winged blackbirds; you may even see pond turtles, harbor seals, or sea lions. RV and tent camping sites are breezy (707–875–3540).

Head out of town, south on Highway 1 through Bodega Bay to the Valley Ford cutoff/Highway 1 road just west of Bodega, to Valley Ford. You'll drive past lush green hills, dairy farms, and ranches to the town of **Tomales,** a 2-block-long headquarters for crabbing, clamming, and surf fishing at **Dillon Beach** and in the skinny finger of **Tomales Bay,** between the mainland and the peninsula of Point Reyes National Seashore. A number of nineteenth-century buildings remain near the intersection of Main Street and Dillon Beach Road; the Church of the Assumption, just south of town, was built in 1860.

The town of Dillon Beach, 4 miles west of Tomales, consists of a collection of Craftsman-style beach cottages from the 1930s; on the beach are some of the richest tidepools on the entire coastline. You can walk on the dunes or drive 1 mile south to Lawson's Landing, where hang-gliders often ride the winds. Camping, boating, and fishing equipment and advice are available at **Lawson's Landing Resort** (707–878–2204). At low tide in the winter, catch a clammer's barge out to the flatlands around Hog Island in Tomales Bay. Hog Island and nearby Duck Island are private wildlife sanctuaries frequented by harbor seals.

Lunch: **Old Town Cafe,** 26950 Highway 1, Tomales. (707) 878–2526. A false-front, hundred-year-old building, antiques bedecked. Sandwiches, homemade soup, fresh fish. Across the street is the **U.S. Hotel,** 26885 Highway 1 (707–878–2742), a circa-1860 bed-and-breakfast inn. If inn guests have checked out, ask for a tour of the museumlike hotel.

Afternoon

To connect with Highway 101 south to the Golden Gate, drive east on Tomales Road, a eucalyptus-lined lane winding through coastal farmlands; it's 15 miles to **Petaluma.** If you have some of the afternoon remaining, pick up a walking-tour map at the Chamber of Commerce, 215 Howard (707–762–2785), and sightsee in the riverport town.

There's More

Golf. Bodega Harbour Golf Links, P.O. Box 368, Bodega Bay 94923. (707) 875-3538. One of the most beautiful courses in the state, with all the characteristics of a traditional links layout, including sand, sea, and breezes. Islands of gorselike scrub and a huge freshwater marsh—inhabited by loons, grebes, marsh wrens, pond turtles, herons, egrets, and ducks—add challenge and beauty. It is located at 21301 Heron, off Highway 1 on the south end of Bodega Bay.

Sportfishing. The Challenger, 1785 Highway 1, Bodega Bay. (707) 875-2474.

New Sea Angler and Jaws, at the Boathouse, 1145 Highway 1, Bodega Bay. (707) 875–3495.

Horseback riding. Sea Horse Stables, 2660 Highway 1, Bodega Bay. (707) 875–2721. Two-hour guided dune ride.

Chanslor Guest Ranch, 2660 Highway 1 on the north end of town, Bodega Bay 94923. (707) 875–2721. Guided horseback rides on the beaches, along the bluffs, and through wetlands, plus haywagon rides, barbecue rides. Special rides for kids ages four and up on gentle horses, ponies, or donkeys around the ranch, and a petting zoo.

Special Events

April. Bodega Bay Fisherman's Festival, Bodega Bay. (707) 875–3422. Thousands come for the blessing of the fleet and boat parade, outdoor fair, food, entertainment, and arts and crafts.
June. Sonoma-Marin Fair, Petaluma Fairgrounds. (707) 763–0931.
August. Sonoma County Wineries Association Auction. (707) 579–0577.
August. Old Adobe Fiesta, Petaluma. (707) 762–2785.
August. Petaluma River Festival. (707) 762–5331. A hundred craft and food booths, steamboat and sternwheeler rides, entertainment.
August. Sebastopol Apple Fair. (707) 586–FARM.
September. Bodega Bay Allied Arts Show, Bodega Harbour Yacht Club. (707) 875–2585. Large, annual exhibition of the work of the regional arts community.
September. Bodega Bay Sandcastle Building Festival, Doran Beach. (707) 875–3422.
October. Sonoma County Harvest Fair, Santa Rosa. (707) 545–4203.
November. Festive Bay Days, Bodega Bay. (707) 875–3777. Seasonal festival; Santa arrives.

Other Recommended Restaurants and Lodgings

Bodega Bay

Inn at the Tides, 800 Highway 1. (800) 368–2468. Spread out on a hillside overlooking the town and the harbor, a large complex of two-story inn buildings on landscaped grounds. Rooms have quite comfortable amenities, like fireplaces, sitting areas, sea views. Completely protected indoor/outdoor pool, spa, sauna. The restaurant here is casual in feel, top-notch in quality, and a place to linger when the sun is on the terrace.
Breakers Cafe, 1400 Highway 1, in the little shopping center across from the kite shop on the north end of town. (707) 875–2513. Great view from a sunny deck and killer breakfasts, fresh seafood, pasta, homemade pies, soups.
Vacation Homes. (707) 875–4000. From cabins to spacious homes, a variety of rentals are available in the Bodega Bay area.
The Bay Hill Mansion, 3919 Bay Hill Road. (707) 875–3577. Modern rendition of a Queen Anne, six view-filled rooms, full breakfast.
Bodega Coast Inn, 421 Highway 1. (707) 875–2217. Forty-four sim-

ple, contemporary rooms, each with ocean view and balcony, some with fireplaces and spas.

Chanslor Guest Ranch, 2660 Highway 1. (707) 875–2721. A historic 700-acre working ranch with a ranch house where guests relax and watch the sea, the wetlands, and the horses in the pasture; sunsets are memorable. Three rooms in the ranch house, a guest house with living room and three bedrooms, and a two-room loft suite with private balcony, fireplace, and whirlpool tub. The entire ranch can be rented for special occasions. Horseback riding tours can be arranged.

Sonoma Coast Villa, 16702 Highway 1. (707) 876–9818. A few miles east of town, six guest rooms in a Mediterranean-style villa, fireplaces, Jacuzzi spa, pool, secluded, unique.

Pomo/Miwok Campground, where the Russian River meets the sea at Bridgehaven, ten minutes off Highway 1. (800) 444–7275. Forty walk-in tent sites in a dense redwood forest at the end of the paved road (great for biking). A few sites are near the parking lot; it's a five- to fifteen-minute walk to the others. Pomo/Miwok is best in summer, a little chilly in winter. If you arrive without a campsite reservation, look at the bulletin board to see if some sites are still available; they usually are.

Willow Creek Campground, on the same road as Pomo/Miwok, but closer to the highway, although you can't see or hear the traffic. (800) 444–7275. A dozen sheltered walk-in tent sites on the Russian River. A few sites are near the parking lot, the others are a five- to ten-minute walk away. Sites 2, 8, and 9 are the prettiest and most private. At both Pomo/Miwok and Willow Creek are fire rings, tables, and portable potties. Willow Creek is a sunny choice when the coastal campgrounds are foggy and windy.

Freestone

Osmosis Enzyme Bath and Massage, 209 Bohemian Highway, Freestone 95472. (707) 823–8231. Japanese-style heat treatment and blanket wrap, massages, Japanese gardens.

Occidental

Union Hotel (707–874–3555) and Negri's (707–823–5301), two Italian restaurants in an old mountain village, famous for decades for their supercolossal, multicourse, family-style dinners, on the main street of a one-street town. Very popular places on Sunday afternoons and evenings and on holidays. Take the Bohemian Highway through Freestone, about twenty minutes on the winding, scenic mountain road, to Occidental. The restaurants, along with a few galleries and shops, are on the highway, which runs through town.

Valley Ford

Dinucci's, downtown on Highway 1. (707) 876–3260. For decades a destination in itself. Huge home-style Italian dinners; seafood and steaks; a friendly long bar.

For More Information

Vacation Homes. (707) 875–4000. Vacation home rentals.

Petaluma Chamber of Commerce, 215 Howard Street, Petaluma, CA 94952. (707) 762–2785.

Bodega Bay Chamber of Commerce, 855 Highway 1, Bodega Bay, CA 94923. (707) 875–3422.

Russian River Region Visitor's Center, 850 Highway 1, Bodega Bay, CA 94923. (707) 869–9212.

Jenner to Point Arena

The beaches of Sonoma County make for great horseback riding.

North Central Coastline on Highway 1

——————————— 1 NIGHT ———————————

Rugged coastline • Rocky beaches • Russian history
Whale-watching • Fishing harbors • Seacoast villages

The north Sonoma/south Mendocino coast is a stretch of wild, rocky shoreline with jewel-like beaches, a few resorts, a harbor or two, and a handful of seagoing towns where fishermen and loggers have lived since before the turn of the century. When San Francisco exploded with growth during the California Gold Rush of the mid-1800s, the demand for lumber from the great coastal redwood forests resulted in the establishment of the communities of Anchor Bay, Point Arena, Manchester, Elk, and Albion.

Following the rebuilding of San Francisco after the great earthquake of 1906, the logging boom finally subsided, due to a lessening of demand and a scarcity of big trees. Subsequently, modern logging practices and overfishing affected the supply of ocean fish, and although commercial fishing is still a major activity on the coast, the fishing industry also diminished. Tourism, some agriculture, and the products of resident artists and craftspeople are what fuel the economy today in this idyllic region, a magical kingdom between the misty seas and the dark forests.

Spring, with its breezes and clear days, brings wildflowers and baby lambs in the roadside meadows and the migration of the great gray whale, easily seen from the entire coastline. Summer, a time of warm weather with some foggy days, is busy with visitors, fairs, and festivals. The spectacular, warm fall is the perfect time to come, when most tourists have gone home and the weather is perfect, each beach looking like a postcard view. Winter is for lovers, when magnificent storms turn every beach into a treasure chest of driftwood, shells, and discoveries washed up by the crashing surf, while cozy fireplaces beckon from bed-and-breakfast inns.

Day 1

Morning

From the Golden Gate Bridge, drive north on Highway 101 to the Guerneville Road exit on the north end of Santa Rosa, an hour's drive. Go west on Guerneville Road to Highway 116, proceeding west to Guerneville along the lush riparian corridor of the **Russian River.**

Breakfast: **Sweet's Cafe and Bakery,** 16251 Main, Guerneville. (707) 869–3383. Belgian waffles, omelettes, homemade croissants, espresso.

Proceed to the Highway 1 junction, turning north toward **Jenner.** Here the mild, meadowy headlands of the southern Sonoma coastline abruptly turn steep. The 11-mile stretch of road between Jenner and Fort Ross winds cruelly along a narrow marine terrace with precipitous bluffs on one side—some 900 feet above the shore—and high cliffs on the other side. This is a challenging, spectacular drive; take your time, and take advantage of pullovers and vista points.

From the west end of the parking lot at **Fort Ross State Park,** 19005 Highway 1 (707–847–3286), walk down to the small, protected beach below the fort. As you breathe in fresh sea air before starting your explorations of the fort, think about the Russians who arrived in

1812, accompanied by Aleut fur hunters. They came to harvest otter and seal pelts and to grow produce for their northern outposts. Their small settlement of hand-hewn log barracks, blockhouses, and homes, together with a jewel of a Russian Orthodox church, was protected with high bastions and a bristling line of cannons, just in case the Spanish decided to pay a call. At the visitor's center are exhibits, films, and guidebooks. Inside the restored buildings are perfectly preserved rifles, pistols, tools, furniture, and old photos. The "crib-style" architecture uses hand-adzed logs notched together and fastened with oakum, a jute-rope-and-tar combination. Several times a day costumed docents put on a demonstration of domestic activities.

Back on the highway, if you're ready for a snack, stop at the **Fort Ross Store and Deli** (707–847–3333) for an ice cream cone. Then go on to **Salt Point State Park** (707–847–3221), 6,000 acres of sandy beaches, tidepools, high cliffs, sunny meadows, and hiking and biking trails: a good place to beachcomb, scuba dive, or get a little exercise. Campground sites on both sides of the road are private and protected. The dense forestlands of Salt Point are inhabited by gnarly pygmy pines and cypress, their ghostly gray, mossy trunks tickled by maidenhair ferns. Seven miles of coastline are characterized by long, sandy beaches: rocky coves with tidepools rich in wildlife; and many breeding and nesting locations for birds, such as at **Stump Beach,** where a large number of cormorants reside. On both sides of the highway, a wide variety of weather-protected camp sites are available: developed and primitive tent sites and biker/hiker sites, RV sites for up to 31-foot vehicles, and walk-in sites (800–444–7275).

Near the park, **Salt Point Lodge Bar and Grill** is a wonderful spot for casual dining, indoors or outdoors, with an ocean view (707–847–3234). They specialize in mesquite-grilled fresh fish and a big salad bar. **Salt Point Lodge** here has comfortable rooms, a hot tub, and voluptuous gardens.

Kruse Rhododendren State Park (707–847–3221) should not be missed in the months of April, May, and June, when wild rhododendron glades up to 15 feet high are brilliant with bloom under redwood, oak, and madrone branches. It's a 1-mile dirt road into the park; a trail sign shows easy and challenging trails.

Lunch: **Sea Ranch Lodge,** 60 Sea Walk Drive, off Highway 1. (707) 785–2371. All along the bluffs in this area and from the Sea Ranch restaurant, you can see whales in the wintertime and a wide variety of other wildlife all year. Sandwiches, salads, homemade soups, fresh fish, lunch, and dinner.

Rooms at the rustic lodge are simple, each with a wide ocean view, within steps of sea-spray meadows and walking trails on the bluffs. The lounge bar has a big fireplace.

Afternoon

The Sea Ranch Lodge is headquarters for a unique residential development that pioneered the use of extensive open space and architectural restraint. Widely scattered, naturally weathered wood houses on the headlands and hillsides are barely visible; some have sod roofs. Cars are hidden, fences absent; grasses and trees are indigenous. Many of the homes are available to rent (Rams Head Realty, 800–785–3455).

There are great walking paths above the beaches and quiet, paved country roads on the highway side of the Sea Ranch in the redwood, madrone, fir, and pine forest. Wild azaleas, rhododendrons and irises bloom in the spring; wild mushrooms are colorful most of the winter and spring. A smashingly beautiful eighteen-hole, links-style golf course, laid out on the coastal bluffs and in the meadows and forestlands above the highway, makes this a weekend getaway destination. Designed by world-famous architect Robert Muir Graves more than two decades ago, the **Sea Ranch Golf Links,** in his words, "is the closest I've ever come to a true links course and it reminds me of Scotland every time I look at it. Wild vegetation or a natural landscape hazard is allowed to cross or encroach upon the fairways. The rough is natural and is left unmowed, right up to the edge of the fairways. Depending on the growth each year, this does not always make me a popular person." Call for tee times: (707) 785–2468.

A string of quiet, sandy coves and rocky beaches are accessible for several miles along the Sea Ranch coast; **Shell Beach, Pebble Beach,** and **Black Point Beach** are the best.

When you see the lace curtains and wooden porches of the ninety-year-old Gualala Hotel, you've made it to the town of Gualala, your final destination for the day. Once a logging center, Gualala is now an art colony and headquarters for steelhead and salmon fishing.

Several shops in the **Seacliff Center,** on the south end of town, are worth browsing. **Once upon a Time** (707–884–4910) specializes in imported dolls, art glass, and "chainsaw sculpture," an art form unique to the redwood forest areas. A yarn and sweater store, **Marlene Designs** (707–884–4809), has contemporary hand-knit sweaters glowing with vivid colors, not the styles your grandmother used to knit. Prowl around town a bit to find art galleries and antiques shops.

Dinner: **Gualala Hotel,** 39301 Highway 1, Gualala. (707) 884–3441. Family-style Italian dinners, homemade cioppino on Friday nights, country fried chicken with biscuits and gravy, thirty-ounce steaks, fresh crab, and seafood galore, all in a lively, friendly atmosphere. Come in early for a tall one at the long bar, where local fishermen and tourists rub elbows beneath a museumlike array of photos of early days and fishing on the Gualala. Breakfast and lunch, too, and simple hotel rooms.

Lodging: **Seacliff,** P.O. Box 697, Gualala 95445. (707) 884–1213. Contemporary suites with fireplaces, spas, and private decks overlooking **Gualala Beach;** a prime whale-watching and fishing spot. The Top of the Cliff is the restaurant here, specializing in gourmet seafood, with a cocktail lounge warmed up nightly by the sunset over the Pacific.

Day 2

Morning

Breakfast: Eggs and bacon with a sea view at the **Sandpiper,** at the south end of town. (707) 884–3398.

Drive north to **Point Arena.** At the south end of the main street, turn west onto Port Road, following it to the **Point Arena Public Fishing Pier,** which thrusts 330 feet out into the water from the edge of a cove seemingly protected by high cliffs on either side. The original wooden pier was dramatically smashed to pieces in 1983, along with all of the buildings in the cove. In the **Galley at Point Arena** restaurant, Port Road, Point Arena (707–882–2189), are photos of the storm as it ripped and roared. The Galley serves chowder, snapper sandwiches, homemade pies, salads, fresh crab in season. This is a good place to watch whales and crusty old salts. Fishing, crabbing, and whale-watching are good from the pier; tidepooling and abalone hunting, from the rocks.

Walk up to the **Wharf Master's Inn,** on the hill behind the pier. Built in the 1870s for wharf masters who watched over the port until the 1920s, this is the town's most elaborate building, a fantasy of turned posts, scroll brackets, and fancy window moldings. Prefabricated in San Francisco, the house was shipped here as a kit. Just below, the **Coast Guard House,** P.O. Box 117, Point Arena (707–882–2442), now a bed-and-breakfast inn, is a classic California Arts and Crafts–style house built in 1901 as a lifesaving station.

Rollerville Junction, 3 miles north of Point Arena, is the western-most point in the continental United States, the site of many a shipwreck; ten vessels went down on the night of November 20, 1865. The 115-foot **Point Arena Lighthouse** (707–882–2777) was erected here in 1870, then reerected after the 1906 San Francisco earthquake. The lighthouse is the all-time best location for California gray whale-watching; December through April are the prime months. Scramble around in the lighthouse and visit the museum of maritime artifacts below.

Few people know that the three small homes at the **Point Arena Coast Guard** facility are available to rent; neat and clean, with kitchens, they're perfect for a family or several couples (707–882–2777).

Proceed north on the highway to **Elk,** a tiny community perched on cliffs above a spectacular bay. You'll recognize the **Greenwood Pier Inn** complex, 5928 Highway 1 in Elk, by the multitude of blooming flowers and trees. Take your time poking around in the gardens and in the **Country Store** and **Garden Shop at Greenwood Pier Inn** (707–877–9997). Owners Kendrick and Isabel Petty are artists, cooks, gardeners, and innkeepers, their works found throughout the rooms, the store, and the cafe.

Lunch: **Greenwood Pier Cafe.** (707) 877–9997. Fresh local seafood, greens and vegetables from the inn gardens, sandwiches, salads, breakfast.

Afternoon

Drive back to the Bay Area by way of Highway 253 through Boonville and the beautiful Anderson Valley (see Northbound Escape Nine), or retrace your Highway 1 route.

Special Events

February to May. Gualala Arts Music Series. (707) 884–1138.
February. Annual Chocolate Festival, Gualala. (707) 884–1138.
March. Gualala Whale Festival. (707) 884–3377.
July. California Winetasting Championships, Anderson Valley. (707) 877–3262.
July. Fort Ross Living History Day, Fort Ross State Park. (707) 847–3286.
August. Art-in-the-Redwoods Festival, Gualala. (707) 884–1138. Art, music, vintage car show.

Other Recommended Restaurants and Lodgings

Point Arena

Wharf Master's Inn, 785 Port Road, P.O. Box 674. (800) 932–4031. New inn surrounding a landmark house from the mid-1800s; courtyards, private decks, firpelaces, spas, ocean views, upscale decor.

Pangaea, 250 Main Street. (707) 882–3001. In a warm, terracotta–colored Mediterranean environment, baby beet salad with goat cheese, cassoulet of duck confit, quail with pine nut dressing, a changing daily menu including pizza from the brick oven, local fresh seafood. Surprising sophistication in a laid-back village.

Coast Guard House Inn, 695 Arena Cove. (707) 882–2442. In a ro-

mantic, ocean view setting, rooms in a historic house, hot tub, fireplace, private cottage, full breakfast.

Elk

Greenwood Pier Inn, 5928 Highway 1. (707) 877–9997. Redwood
castles on a cliff with wonderful coastline views; fireplaces, decks,
amazing gardens, privacy. In a complex with a shop, plant nursery,
and cafe.

Sandpiper House Inn, 5520 Highway 1. (707) 877–3587. A sweet
old mansion in an English garden on a coastal bluff, white picket
fences, path to private beach. Three rooms with ocean view, one with
a fireplace and meadow view. Steps away from a good dinner house.

Jenner

Fort Ross Lodge, 20705 Coast Highway 1. (707) 847–3333. Comfortable ocean-view rooms and suites, some with fireplaces, spas; reasonable. Barbecues on your private patio, store across the road.

Sea Coast Hideaways, 21350 Highway 1. (707) 847–3278. Vacation
home rentals.

Timber Cove Inn, 21780 Highway 1. (707) 847–3231. Eclectic rooms
have fireplaces, decks, and hot tubs or Jacuzzis. On a whale-watching,
ocean-viewing point; good restaurant; three-story stone fireplace in the
lounge; romantic—a place for runaways.

Gualala

Gualala Country Inn, P.O. Box 697, Gualala 95445. (800) 564–4466.
Overlooking the Pacific and Gualala Beach, four rooms with traditional oak furnishings, comforters, with panoramic sea or river views,
fireplaces, window seats, whirlpool spas.

Whale Watch Inn by the Sea, 35100 Highway 1 (actually in Anchor
Bay, 5 miles north of Gualala). (707) 884–3667. Five contemporary-
design buildings on a cliff above the ocean, stained glass windows,
beautiful gardens. Eighteen luxurious guest rooms, whirlpool tubs,
fireplaces, private decks with ocean views. Common lounge is comfy
and lovely, with a coastal view, big fireplaces, leather couches, telescope. Full breakfast in your room. Private access to a half mile of
sandy beach with tide pools. No phones, bliss.

Old Milano Hotel, 38300 Highway 1. (707) 884–3256. Romantic
Victorian-inspired rooms in an inn established in 1905, on the National
Registry of Historic Places. On three acres of gardens and cliff-top
bluffs, a few rooms, a suite, and a cottage, with common outdoor spa
with sea view. One cottage includes a sleeping alcove with reading
loft and wood stove. An old train car comprises another unit, also with
a wood stove and two brakemen's seats upstairs for sunset viewing.

Big breakfast in your room, on the garden patio, or by the fire in the wine parlor. Massages available in your room.

Old Milano Restaurant. In a Victorian dining room with lace curtains and etched glass lamps, guests dine by candlelight by the fire; renowned continental menu and top wine list.

For More Information

Sonoma County Convention and Visitor's Bureau, 10 Fourth Street, Santa Rosa, CA 95401. (707) 575–1191.
California State Park Reservations, (800) 444–7275.

Advice: Driving can be hazardous on the twists and turns of Highway 1, and it's not recommended that you attempt it after dark or during storms. Farm animals and deer in the road can be a scary, and maybe deadly, surprise as you're coming around a blind curve.

The Anderson Valley

Mist on the vineyards in the Anderson Valley.

Boonville and the "Other" Wine Country

_____ 1 NIGHT _____

Redwood giants · Swimmin' in the river · Apple cider
Village life · Country wineries

"The other wine country" is what some people call the Anderson Valley, lesser-known than the the well-traveled Napa and Sonoma wine valleys. A flat plain carpeted with fruit orchards and vineyards, with dark redwood forests on one side, rolling hills on the other, and a river running through it, the Anderson Valley has quiet charm; it's a perfect place to get lost for the weekend.

Bisecting the valley, two-lane Highway 128 is sprinkled on either side with small winery tasting rooms and fruit stands, and anchored by a handful of small villages. The road follows the Navarro River from Cloverdale, at the southeast junction with Highway 101, to coastal Mendocino on the northwest.

A two-day jaunt from the San Francisco Bay Area offers plenty of time to drive slowly through the countryside, stop at a few wineries, discover a few top-notch restaurants and microbreweries, take a walk in a redwood grove, and swim or fish in the river. The half-dozen or so excellent bed-and-breakfast inns are in high demand on weekends and in the summertime.

Day 1

Morning

Head north from the Golden Gate Bridge on Highway 101 to Santa Rosa, an hour's drive.

Breakfast: Take the downtown exit and go under the freeway west to **Omelette Express,** 112 Fourth Street in Old Railroad Square, Santa Rosa. (707) 525–1690. Every omelette imaginable, wooden tables, hanging ferns, historical photos.

Gateway to the **Sonoma County** wine country, the **Russian River** region, and the Sonoma coastline, **Santa Rosa** is surrounded by apple orchards, magnificent redwood groves, wineries, campgrounds, and recreation along the Russian River. In town are a large regional park with a lake for fishing, sailing, and hiking, and a grid of tree-lined streets just east of downtown that is a treasure trove of turn-of-the-century mansions.

Continue on Highway 101 about forty minutes north to **Cloverdale,** then go northwest on Highway 128, 27 miles to **Boonville.** The landscape goes wild almost immediately when you leave Cloverdale. Cows teeter precariously on rocky mountainsides, eagles soar over redwood and pine forests, and an occasional old farmhouse comes into view. Rolling across the valley as it flattens out are vineyards, apple and pear orchards, and meadows dotted with sheep.

Not much more than a wide spot in the road, the tiny town of Boonville is famous for a language called "boontling," which was invented here and is spoken only in this town. Around the turn of the century, when the valley was still isolated from most of civilization, local farmers and shepherds made up their own lingo as a way of avoiding strangers and having a few laughs. It's fun to poke around town and take pictures of the boontling signs such as BUCKEY WALTER (phone booth), HORN OF ZEESE (cup of coffee) COFFEE SHOP, BAHL GOKRMS

(Good Food), and ROOKIE-TO GALLERY (Quail Gallery). The **Buckhorn Saloon,** at 14081 Highway 128 (707–895–2337) is a good place to sit a spell and listen to the strange speech. You can also get fish and chips here, burgers, and sausages steamed in beer. If you're a beer aficionado, check out the **Anderson Valley Brewing Company** in the basement of the saloon. They make almost a dozen kinds of beer and ale, and sometimes give tours of the brewery.

Across the road from the Boonville Hotel in midtown, at the **Boont Berry Farm Store** (13981 Highway 128, 707–895–3576), you can pick up fresh juices, fruits, deli items, and local wines, but as today you'll be stopping at fruit stands and wineries, perhaps this is a good stop on the trip home.

At the south end of town at 14300 Highway 128 (707–895–2204), the **Rookie-To Gallery** has an extraordinary collection of contemporary ceramics, paintings, prints, fine jewelry, and wearable art. The gallery features the work of over 150 artists and craftspeople, with emphasis on work from the North Coast. Shopping is limited in the valley, other than gourmet foodstuffs, wine, and produce, so Rookie-To Gallery is a place to remember.

Of the several roadside stands, the **Tinman,** just north of Boonville, has long been known for a wide variety of fresh apple juices and ciders, and they are all available to taste. They will ship their luscious juices, jams, vinegars, and organic herbs anywhere in the United States (707–895–2759).

At **Gowan's Oak Tree,** 6350 Highway 128 (707–895–3225), kids stay busy in the playground while their parents taste apple cider and choose berries, local apples, giant garlic, and veggies to take home.

At the **Apple Farm,** above Philo at 18501 Greenwood Road (707–895–2333), antique apple varieties are grown, and they smell wonderful at harvest time in the late summer and fall. All year-round, you can buy cider vinegar, apple butter, chutney, juices, and gift items made with dried apples. Formerly of the French Laundry and Tante Marie's, Sally Schmidt gives one-day, weekend, and midweek cooking classes on the farm that turn into house parties as students pick produce and learn how to cook like pros. Everything is grown organically and the complex of farm buildings is aglow with rampant roses, fruit trees heavy with fruit, and the cacophony of farm animals and four children.

Of the more than thirty wineries in the valley, most are open for tasting and most are within an 8-mile stretch of the highway between Boonville and Philo. The charm of the Anderson Valley wineries comes from the old-time atmosphere and the fact that, more often than not, your hosts are the owners themselves.

At **Obester Winery,** 9200 Highway 128 (707–895–3814), taste award-winning Chardonnay, Reisling, and the full-bodied Italian-style red table wine under the Gemello label, named for grandfather John Gemello who came from Italy in 1934 to found the winery. You can picnic here, pick your own produce, and buy homemade garlic mustard, herbal and flower blossom vinegars, and home-grown and pressed olive oils.

The octagonal wooden building at 5501 Highway 128 (707–895–2002) is **Greenwood Ridge Vineyards,** where you can try and buy Pinot Noirs and Cabernets. The mountain backdrop, pond, and gardens make this a good place to picnic. Every July they put on a winetasting championship event with food, entertainment, and . . . wine!

Across the road, **Navarro Vineyards** (5601 Highway 128, 707–895–3686) is a family-owned winery that produces renowned dry Gewürztraminers and Rieslings, and an interesting Pinot Noir, plus nonalcoholic "wines." You can buy Navarro wines only here or in restaurants. Umbrella-topped picnic tables have views of the vineyards and the hills.

A culinary and craft celebration that includes barrel tastings, live ethnic music, art and craft exhibitions, and lots of food, the annual Expressions of the Anderson Valley is held at **Handley Cellars,** 3151 Highway 128 (707–895–3876). Winemaker Milla Handley, the great-great-granddaughter of Henry Weinhard of brewing fame, is a young mother whose first Chardonnay for the winery won a gold medal, and her subsequent wines have won many more. The Handley tasting room exhibits folk art that the family has collected from around the world. If you are lucky enough to show up here on the first weekend of the month, you are in for a treat, when visitors are offered international foods paired with Handley wines. Perhaps you will try avocado-corn-shrimp salsa with gingered crab cakes, or Jamaican jerked pork, Thai chicken, or West African pepper and carrot salad.

Lunch: **Floodgate Cafe Store and Grille,** 1810 Highway 128 between Navarro and Philo. (707) 895–3000. Country cute in a clapboard building with an EATS sign over the door, serving buffalo burgers, famous smoked duck breast salad, homemade soups, fresh fish, grilled lamb and pork, vegetarian specialties, fudge pie, Anderson Valley pear or apple pie, and more, definitely worth the trip.

Afternoon

Just north of Philo is **Hendy Woods State Park** (707–937–5804), where a walk beneath a shady canopy of virgin redwoods might be the highlight of your trip. Here in eighty-acre Big Hendy and twenty-acre Little Hendy groves are some of the largest and oldest trees remaining in the state. Trails lead to the wide, calm **Navarro River,** which is enjoyed by anglers, canoeists, kayakers, picnickers, and sunbathers. There are almost a hundred developed campsites here, and sites for trailers and RVs up to 35 feet.

It's best to get settled at your lodgings in time to spend the cocktail hour at the Boonville Hotel, where you may meet movie stars or cowboys, tourists from Manhattan or local winemakers, and definitely hear some boontling.

Dinner: **Boonville Hotel,** 14050 Highway 128. (707) 895–2210. Southwestern, California, and Italian cuisine is prepared by a French-trained chef who picks his herbs and vegetables from the hotel garden. Pizza with goat cheese, fresh fish with avocado-lime salsa, *huevos con chorizo,* grilled ahi with mango chili, homemade ice cream, rhubarb shortcake, super wine list.

Lodging: Boonville Hotel. Eight simply decorated rooms and suites, with down comforters, wicker furnishings, some with valley or garden views, private balconies, sitting rooms.

Day 2

Morning

Breakfast: Boonville Hotel.

If you are going on to the Mendocino Coast from here on your way north on Highway 128, take the time to discover the glories of the Save-the-Redwoods League's 673-acre parcel of property along the Navarro River, found along a 12-mile stretch of the highway between Navarro and the coast. The road tunnels through groves of second-growth redwoods and ferny glens. Fishing, swimming, and exploring are available to the public throughout the tract of woods.

If you are retracing your Highway 128 route back to the San Francisco Bay Area, save time to tickle your nose with bubbly at these two champagne cellars (if you are a passenger).

Foggy mornings and winter frosts produce superb sparkling wines for **Scharffenberger Cellars** (7000 Highway 128, 707–895–2065), which is owned by the prestigious French megacorporation Moet Hennessy Louis Vuitton. At a tiny table in the garden, sip some Blanc de Blanc, made from Chardonnay grapes, and the lovely, pinky Brut Rosé.

Another French champagne house is represented in the valley at **Roederer Estate,** at 4501 Highway 128 (707–895–2288). If you are interested in learning more about the *méthode champenoise* process of creating sparkling wines, this is the place to take a tour. The contemporary redwood winery building is of architectural interest for its subtle integration into the landscape. Notice the two-century-old tiles on the floor, from a French château.

There's More

Paul Dimmick Wayside Campground. (707) 937–5804. Six miles east of Highway 1 on Highway 128, very pretty, wooded small campground with thirty sites for tents or RVs.
Indian Creek County Park, just south of Philo on Highway 128. (707) 463–4267. A nice little picnic spot along a creek with short pathways in the redwoods.

Special Events

April. Spring Wildflower Show, Boonville Fairgrounds. (707) 964–3153.
May. Spring Fair, Boonville Faigrounds. (707) 964–3153. Logging events, barbecue, entertainment.
July. Woolgrower's Barbeque and Sheep Dog Trials, Boonville Fairgrounds. (707) 964–3153. Barbecue, all-day events.
July. Greenwood Ridge Wine Tasting Championships, Greenwood Ridge Vineyards. (707) 895–2002. Food, wine, live music.
September. Mendocino County Fair and Apple Show, Boonville Fairgrounds. (707) 964–3153. Rodeo, sheep dog trials, animal judging, midway, hoedown, parade.

Other Recommended Restaurants and Lodgings

Boonville

Toll House Restaurant and Inn, 15301 Highway 253, Boonville.(707) 895–3630. On a 360-acre ranch, a circa-1910 ranch house and luxurious rooms with laid-back atmosphere.

Philo

Philo Pottery Inn, 8550 Highway 128. (707) 895–3069. A redwood farmhouse from the late 1800s, once a stagecoach stop. Four lovely rooms with private porches and a cottage with a wood stove in an English garden, owned by expatriates from the Silicon Valley. Patchwork quilts, antiques, down comforters, memorable breakfasts. Courtesy airport pick-up and local transportation.

Cottages at Shenoa, P.O. Box 43, Philo 95466. (707) 895–3156. On 160 acres, a retreat center that makes nice, new cottages available to travelers; a good deal for families or groups. Hot tubs and Jacuzzis, wood heat, kitchens, lovely views, tennis. Walk to Hendy Woods and the Navarro River. Vegetarian meals are available in the dining room.

For More Information

Anderson Valley Chamber of Commerce, P.O. Box 275, Boonville, CA 95415. (707) 893–3638.

Mendocino Coast Accommodations. (707) 937–1913.

Mendocino and Fort Bragg

A century-old water tower in the village of Mendocino.

A Romantic Victorian Village by the Sea

_____ 3 NIGHTS _____

Hidden coves • Redwood groves • Art galleries • Harbor views
Fishing, beachcombing, kayaking • Whale-watching • Bed and breakfasts

Floating like a mirage on high bluffs above a rocky bay, Mendocino seems lost in another century. The entire town is a California Historical Preservation District of early Cape Cod and Victorian homes and steepled clapboard churches. Though thronged with tourists in summer, the town somehow retains the look and feel of a salty fisherman's and lumberman's village.

Old-fashioned gardens soften weather-worn mansions and cottages; picket fences need a coat of paint; dark cypress trees lean into the sea breezes. Boutique and art-gallery shopping is legendary, charming bed-and-breakfast inns abound; in fact, there are more B&Bs per capita in and around Mendocino than anywhere else in California. Most of the mansions here were built by wealthy Maine logger barrons in the mid– to late–nineteenth century. So closely does Mendocino and this stretch of coastline resemble New England that much of the television show *Murder She Wrote,* is filmed in the historic buildings and on the streets of the town, and at nearby Noyo Harbor. Cabot Cove is, in fact, Mendocino.

Virtually abandoned in the 1930s when logging activities declined, Mendocino held its breath for years, as if lost in another era. In the 1950s, artists began to discover the rugged beauty of the area and the quaint charm of the little town. Gradually they began to gravitate to the isolated region, opening galleries and workshops. Today, Mendocino is a major cultural center with dozens of top galleries, a large art center, and a busy schedule of festivals and exhibitions all year long.

A few miles north, Fort Bragg lacks Mendocino's concentration of historic buildings, the cultural attractions, and the spectacular coastal setting, but this former logging town has its own subtle charms, and is located near great beaches, state parks, and a picturesque harbor with seafood restaurants.

Day 1

Morning

Head north from the Golden Gate Bridge on Highway 101 to Santa Rosa, an hour's drive (it's about three and a half hours from the bridge to Mendocino).

Proceed ten minutes north on 101 to the River Road exit, heading west toward the coast, then north at the Highway 1 junction at **Jenner.** On the roller-coaster road from here to Mendocino, make frequent stops to enjoy cliffhanging views of rocky coves, salt-spray meadows, redwood and pine forests, and a necklace of tiny fishing villages and loggers' towns along the way (see Northbound Escape Eight).

Lunch: **Salt Point Bar and Grill,** 23255 Highway 1, just north of Timber Cove. (707) 847–3238. Solarium windows overlooking gardens and Ocean Cove; mesquite-grilled specialties, fresh fish, salad bar, barbecue.

Afternoon

After you arrive in Mendocino, revive with a bracing walk along the bluffs, the grassy headlands that surround the town. The trail traces the very edge of the cliffs, above swaying kelp beds where otters tap-tap-tap their abalone shells and harbor seals play. The sea churns and boils through rocky arches and dark grottoes. Sandy, driftwoody beaches and tidepools are accessible and safe, unless it's stormy. December through April you may see whales offshore. From the bluffs are views of a deep river valley as it meets the sea at **Big River Beach,** and looking back at the town's skyline, you can imagine when horse-drawn carriages were parked in front of the Mendocino Hotel and ladies with parasols swept along the boardwalk in their long gowns.

Good old days in mind, now is the time to visit the **Kelley House Museum** on Main Street (707–937–5791). A sunny yellow house built in 1852, it's set back from the street next to a huge water tower and a pond surrounded by an old garden. Among the historical photos in the Kelley House are those of burly loggers hand-sawing ancient red-woods. Both the loggers and the redwoods are now endangered, imparting a bittersweet aspect to the contemplation of life as it was in Mendocino's heyday. Lumber for shipbuilding and for construction of the Gold Rush city of San Francisco brought Easterners here in the mid-1800s; it took them six months by ship from the East Coast to reach this wilderness of mighty river valleys and seacoast, inhabited only by Indians and fur trappers.

On Main Street's headlands is **Ford House** museum (707–937–5397), built in 1854. A scale model of Mendocino in the 1890s shows the dozens of tall water towers that existed at that time; more than thirty towers, some double- and triple-deckers, are distinctive features of the skyline today.

Have a sunset cocktail at the **Mendocino Hotel,** a gloriously overdecorated gathering place since 1878. A rough-and-tumble logging town until the 1930s, Mendocino languished quietly for several decades after the lumbermen left, only to be reborn as an art colony and, eventually, a tourist destination. The Mendocino Hotel underwent a $1 million restoration in the 1980s.

Dinner: **MacCallum House Restaurant and Grey Whale Bar,** 45020 Albion Street, Mendocino. (707) 937–5763. Haute cuisine in a rambling Victorian mansion. Oysters, *gnocchi,* lobster, fresh salmon, duck in blackberry sauce; sophisticated menu and wine list.

Lodging: **Joshua Grindle Inn,** 44800 Little Lake Road, Mendocino 95460. (707) 937–4143. One of the oldest homes in town, a circa-1880 beauty on two cypress-bordered acres overlooking the town. Spacious New England–style rooms in the main house; plus very private accommodations in the water tower and the "chicken coop." Escapees from corporate life, Jim and Arlene Moorehead are gleeful in their incarnation as innkeepers. Their lively spirit and the friendly ghost of Joshua Grindle pervade; guests return again and again.

Day 2

Morning

Breakfast: Baked pears, quiche, frittata, and fresh apple and orange juices, as well as merry conversation, at the old harvest table at Joshua Grindle Inn.

Set out from the inn to explore on foot. Browsing the boutiques and galleries in Mendocino village can take an hour or a week, depending on your love of discovery. At 400 Kasten is the **Mayhew Wildlife Gallery** (707–937–0453), where paintings and prints of whales, dolphins, seabirds, and seascapes are featured. Next door is wild and crazy **Eclectic** (707–937–5951), a gallery of Mexican art; walk through the shop to the sculpture garden in back. On to **Gallery Fair,** at Kasten and Ukiah streets (707–937–5121), a bright yellow building from the 1870s housing fine jewelry, art deco furniture, and paintings produced by local artists.

Many Mendocino artists are renowned not only throughout the state but internationally, and you will find galleries on every street of the town. The **Mendocino Art Center Showcase** at 560 Main (707–937–2829) shows a wide variety of fine art and crafts, including wearable art and home accessories. At **Creative Hands of Mendocino,** 45170 Main (707–937–2914), look for hand-crafted gifts for children and adults. The **Artists Co-op,** upstairs at 45270 Main (707–937–2217), is operated by artists who show and sell primarily landscape works in a variety of media.

Tiptoe into the **Gallery Bookshop,** at the corner of Kasten and Albion (707–937–2665), a crowded rabbit's warren of bookshelves, frequented by seriously browsing resident artists and writers.

When you see clouds of swirling birds, you're near **Papa Birds,** 45040 Albion Street (707–937–2730), a shop selling hundreds of birdfeeders, birdhouses, and bird paraphernalia. Their outdoor feeders attract feathered types. Free bird walks are conducted on Saturday mornings, starting at the shop. Just up the street is the **Nicky Boehme Gallery,** 45055 Albion (707–937–2048), showing the work of a famous local artist who paints the boats, harbors, and seagoing scenes of California and Oregon; you can get affordable print reproductions of the original paintings.

Main Street shops of note are the **Highlight Gallery** (707–937–3132), for burlwood sculpture; the **Irish Shop** (707–937–3133), for winter coats and sweaters; and **Mendocino Mercantile** (707–882–3017), a barnlike structure housing several shops selling art glass, ceramics, and gifts. Farther down the street is a feminine fantasy, the **Golden Goose** (707–937–4655), two floors of European antiques, country-luxe bed and table linens, and a children's boutique for heirs and heiresses.

Overgrown country gardens will draw you up and down the sidestreets and alleys; look for the two old cemeteries, not in the least spooky, whose headstones are fascinating relics of the days when European sailors, Russian soliders, and Chinese workers lived here. *Lunch:* Have **Good Taste,** at Lansing and Little Lake streets (707–937–0104), put a luscious picnic together for you with a bottle of Mendocino County wine and head for the headlands or the beach, or, go to **Chocolate Moosse Cafe,** corner of Kasten and Ukiah streets (707–937–4323). A cottage in a garden. Smoked salmon, blackout cake, wine-poached chicken, bread pudding, extensive Mendocino County wine list; popular all afternoon for cappuccino and dessert.

Afternoon

Three miles south of Mendocino on Highway 1, the beach, the campground, and the hiking trails of **Van Damme State Park** are popular weekend destinations (707–937–4016). This is the home of the uniquely beautiful **Pygmy Forest,** a Registered National Landmark. A .3-mile easy trail takes you through a lush fern canyon and spooky woods of dwarf cypress, rhododendrons, and other bonsai-like plants and trees. A fifty-year-old cypress, for instance, may be only 8 inches tall and have a trunk less than 1 inch in diameter. To reach the Discovery Trail and other trails, stop at the ranger station or take Little River Airport Road off Highway 1 and go 2.7 miles to the Pygmy Forest parking lot.

There are seventy-four developed campsites at Van Damme and sites for RVs up to 21 feet long. A few hike-in campsites are accessed by a 2-mile scenic trail.

If you crave a little more strenuous outdoor adventure for the afternoon, call **Catch a Canoe and Bicycles, Too!** (800) 937–0273, to ask about paddling the **Big River,** which runs into the sea below the high bluffs on the south side of Mendocino. Along banks lush with fir and redwood groves, wildflowers, and wild rhododendrons, you can paddle a canoe or a kayak from the mouth of the river 7 or 8 miles upstream on an estuary—the longest unchanged and undeveloped estuary in Northern California—stopping at a tiny beach or a meadow for a picnic. You will undoubtedly see ospreys, wood ducks, and blue herons, probably harbor seals and deer, and maybe even a small black bear.

Time your canoeing expedition to paddle up the river when the tide is coming in, and to be on the return trip as the tide goes out. The rental company can advise you on this; they also rent mountain bikes, outriggers and other types of boats, and auto racks for use on other coastal rivers.

Catch A Canoe and Bicycles, Too! is located at the wondrous **Stanford Inn by the Sea** complex on a hillside above the river across from Mendocino. The luxurious twenty-six-room country inn is surrounded by spectacular natural and introduced gardens and landscaping. Herds of llamas and horses graze in the meadows. The llamas are bred for sale; in the late spring, baby llamas are much in evidence. Guests enjoy a spa, a sauna, and an Olympic-size swimming pool enclosed in a greenhouse crowded with tropical plants. When it's foggy or rainy outside, swimming laps in the pool can be a voluptuous experience

Big River Nurseries is also located on the grounds of the inn and it's fun to browse the rows of organic plants, veggies, and herbs. The nursery also sells herbal wreaths, sprays, and braids, as well as herbs and spices, which they will ship home for you. Mendocino's most famous restaurant, Cafe Beaujolais, and other local restaurants buy produce here.

If you stay at the Stanford Inn (Highway 1 and Comptche-Ukiah Road, P.O. Box 487, Mendocino 95460, 800–331–8884), you will enjoy a fireplace or woodburning stove in your sitting area, a down comforter on your four-poster or sleigh bed, a private deck from which to watch the sun set over the sea, complimentary wine, and a bountiful buffet breakfast.

Dinner: **Cafe Beaujolais,** 9161 Ukiah Street. (707) 937–5614. Owner Margaret Fox is nationally known for her cookbooks and her creations that are envied (and copied) by other California cuisine restaurants. A Victorian house surrounded by flower and vegetable gardens is the setting for a country-chic, comfortable environment in which breakfast, brunch, lunch, and dinner are served. Picture this: pizza with chicken sausage and pear barbecue sauce, black bean chili omelette, roasted chicken with pecan and brandied prune stuffing, homemade everything. Reserve ahead, days or even weeks ahead. Some people come to Mendocino just for Cafe Beaujolais.

Lodging: Joshua Grindle Inn (see above).

Day 3

Morning

Breakfast: Joshua Grindle Inn.

On a drive north on Highway 1 on the way to the lumbering and fishing town of Fort Bragg, stop at beach and forest parks, and a botanical garden.

Two miles north of Mendocino on Highway 1, **Russian Gulch State Park** (707–937–5804) is known for sea caves, a waterfall, and a beach popular for rock fishing, scuba diving, and swimming in chilly waters. From the headlands in the park you can see the Devil's Punch Bowl, a 200-foot-long tunnel with a blow hole. Inland, the park includes 3 miles of Russian Gulch Creek Canyon, with paved and unpaved trails in dense forest and stream canyons. A hiking trail leads to a 36-foot waterfall and to high ridges where views are breathtaking. A small campground here is particularly lovely and there is a special equestrian campground with riding trails into **Jackson State Forest.** RVs up to 27 feet are allowed.

One mile north of Russian Gulch State Park, turn west into **Jug Handle State Reserve** (707–937–5804), a 700-acre park notable for an "ecological staircase" marine terrace rising from sea level to 500 feet. Each terrace is 100,000 years older than the one above, a unique opportunity to see geologic evolution. The plants and trees change from terrace to terrace too, from wildflowers and grasses to wind-strafed spruce, second-growth redwoods, and pygmy forests of cypress and pine. **Mendocino Coast Botanical Gardens** (18220 Highway 1, 1.5 miles south of Fort Bragg, 707–964–4352) is forty-seven acres of plantings, forest, and fern canyons on a bluff overlooking the ocean— where you can see gray whales during their migrating season—with 2 miles of paths leading through lush gardens. Rhododendrons and roses are rampant with bloom in May. Heathers, succulents, camelias, and literally thousands more plants crowd the gardens.

Lunch: Smack in the middle of the Botanical Gardens, the **Gardens Grill** (707–964–7474) is a scenic spot to have lunch, dinner, or weekend brunch. Try the grilled fresh fish, grilled eggplant salad, mushroom crepe torte, or the apple wood rotisseried game hen.

Just south of Fort Bragg, at the mouth of the **Noyo River, Noyo Harbor** is headquarters for a large fleet of fishing trollers and canneries. Barking and posing, sea lions lounge on the wooden piers, waiting for the return of the boats at day's end. **The Wharf** bar (707–964–4283) overlooking the harbor is a great place for a sundown cocktail and a calamari appetizer.

Based at Noyo Harbor, the *Noyo Belle* is a small, comfortable vessel that cruises along the coastline for whale-watching, sunset viewing, and photo ops of the village of Mendocino (215 South Sanderson Way, Fort Bragg, 707–964–3104).

Dinner: **Coast Hotel Cafe,** 101 North Franklin Street, Fort Bragg. (707) 964–6446. Red-checked tablecloths give no hint of the sophisticated menu and big wine list; oysters, jambalaya, twenty pastas, fresh fish in imaginative sauces, house smoked ribs. Warm and cozy on a cold night, live jazz on weekends.

Lodging: **Grey Whale Inn,** 615 North Main, Fort Bragg. (707)

964–0640. Built as a hospital in 1915, the rooms and public spaces of this three-story landmark are spacious, with high windows looking to the sea or inward through the trees to town. Rooms have sitting areas with armchairs, deep tubs, some fireplaces, lots of books. A penthouse suite with double Jacuzzi tub and private deck with ocean view is the highest point in Fort Bragg.

Day 4

Morning

Breakfast: A big buffet in the Gray Whale's tiny dining room or in your room. Owner Colette Bailey wins prizes at the county fair for her coffee cakes and fruit breads; you'll get to try them along with breakfast casseroles, fresh fruit, bottomless pots of coffee, and big city newspapers.

Walk out the back door of the inn to take a long walk along the waterfront on the **Old Coast Road.**

Heading back to San Francisco, head south on Highway 1 to Albion, then take Highway 128 inland or take the coastal route all the way south to Jenner, then head inland through the Russian River Valley on Highway 116 to Highway 101, and south to the Golden Gate Bridge. The coastal route will take you several hours and the driving is demanding. For rest stops, restaurants, lodgings, and recreation along the way, see Escapes Eight and Nine.

There's More

MacKerricher State Park, 3 miles north of Fort Bragg. (707) 927–5804. A 1,598-acre park with a popular beach play area at Pudding Creek, at the southern end of the park. Horseback riding, mountain biking, and hiking trails are found throughout bluffs, headlands, dunes, forests, and wetlands and on 6 miles of beaches. Developed campsites, RV sites for up to 35-foot vehicles, nonmotorized boating.

Lost Coast Adventures, 19275 South Harbor Drive, Fort Bragg. (707) 961–1143. Kayak tours, mountain bike and skin and scuba diving rentals, boat charters for fishing, diving, and whale-watching.

North Coast Trailer Rentals. (619) 648–7509. Self-contained trailer rentals parked in ocean-view campsites.

Party Boat Patty-C, North Harbor Drive, P.O. Box 572, Fort Bragg 95437. (707) 964–0669. Licensed Coast Guard skipper takes six passengers on daily salmon, cod, bottom fish, and whale-watching expeditions.

Ricochet Ridge Ranch, 24201 North Highway 1, Fort Bragg. (707) 964–7669. Horseback riding on the beach.
Skunk Train, Laurel and Main streets, Fort Bragg. (707) 964–6371. Historic diesel and steam logging trains make round-trips between Fort Bragg and Willits, taking a riverside route through scenic redwood forests; deli foods and snacks available at midpoint. Kids love this.

Special Events

March. Whale Festival, Mendocino. (707) 961–6300. Chowder and winetasting, tours and talks.
March. Fort Bragg Dixieland Jazz Fest. (707) 954–0807.
May. Heritage Days, Mendocino. (800) 726–2780. Parade, film festival, historical activities.
May. Historic House and Building Tour, Mendocino. (707) 937–5791.
June. Mendocino Coast Garden Tour of private gardens, Mendocino. (707) 937–5818.
July. Mendocino Music Festival, P.O. Box 1808, Mendocino 95460. (707) 964–3153. Classical and jazz.
July. World's Largest Salmon Barbecue, Fort Bragg. (707) 964–6598.
August. Art in the Gardens, Fort Bragg. (707) 965–4352. Art, music, wine, and food at the Botanical Gardens.
September. Mendocino Art Center Open Studio Tours. (707) 937–5818.
September. Paul Bunyan Days, Fort Bragg. (707) 961–6300. Parade, arts and crafts, entertainment, games, food, wine, and beer.
December. Fort Bragg Hometown Christmas. (707) 961–0360.
December. Candlelight Tours of Bed and Breakfast Inns, Fort Bragg, Little River, Albion, Mendocino. (707) 961–6300.

Other Recommended Restaurants and Lodgings

Mendocino

Mendocino Hotel, 45080 Main Street. (800) 548–0513. Victorian rooms in the main hotel; luxurious garden suites across the way. Garden cafe and dining room dependably good for breakfast, lunch, and dinner.
Whitegate Inn, 499 Howard. (707) 937–4892. A dream of a Victorian bed-and-breakfast establishment, right in the village.

Glendeven Country Inn and Gallery, 1.5 miles south of Mendocino on Highway 1, P.O. Box 282, Mendocino 95460. (800) 822–4536. Antiques decorate rooms and suites in a gray and white farmhouse, big breakfasts. Walking path to the sea, gardens. Gallery of contemporary, hand-crafted furniture, art, jewelry.

Agate Cove Inn Bed and Breakfast, 11201 Lansing Street. (707) 937–0551. Right in town, garden cottages with fireplaces and private decks, ocean views. Breakfast by the fireplace in the dining room with a wonderful sea view.

Bay View Cafe, 45040 Main Street. (707) 937–4197. Breakfast, lunch, and dinner, indoors or on the deck with a zowie sea view, upstairs in a water tower. Good, simple fare such as burgers, salads, pasta, steak.

Sea Rock Inn, 11101 Lansing Street. (707) 937–0926. One-half mile south of Mendocino in a wild garden, country cottages with kitchens, expanded continental breakfast.

Tote Fête, 10450 Lansing. (707) 937–3383. California cuisine to go: inventive salads, homemade meatloaf, sesame asparagus, white beans with chevre, Chinese chicken salad, focaccia topped with wonderful things, dazzling desserts.

Pacific Resorts. (800) 358–9879. Vacation home rentals by the night or by the week, most with ocean views, fireplaces, and fully equipped kitchens.

Manchester

Victorian Gardens, 14409 Highway 1, just south of Elk. (707) 882–3606. A Victorian ranch inn on ninety-two acres, luxurious rooms and suites, full breakfast. Dining room serves dinners of authentic Italian regional cuisine.

Albion

Albion River Inn, Highway 1 south of Mendocino, P.O. Box 100, Albion 95410. (707) 937–1919. On ten acres overlooking the rugged coastline, ocean-front rooms with spectacular views, fireplaces, spas, contemporary decor. Cliff-top restaurant and bar serving great fresh local seafood.

Huckleberry House, 29381 Albion Ridge Road. (800) 482–5532. A country bed-and-breakfast inn surrounded by redwoods on five acres. Rooms and suites have private decks, fireplaces, full breakfast. Hot tub and massage available.

Elk

Harbor House Inn, 5600 South Highway 1. (707) 877–3203. Classic

Craftsman-style mansion, spectacular cliffside location, notable restaurant, lovely rooms.

Little River

Heritage House, 5200 Highway 1. (707) 937–5885. Rooms and cottages on a bluff above a cove, almost every one with a view of the dramatic seascape. Part of the lodge was built in the late 1800s, and the entire complex looks like New England. This is one of the most desired and best known lodgings in the Mendocino area, making it necessary to book weeks and perhaps months ahead. Rooms include full breakfast and dinner in a sedate and elegant atmosphere, in three lovely dining rooms; almost every table has a view of the sea. Produce for the inventive menus comes from the nearby Anderson Valley. Fresh local fish, Sonoma County poultry, lamb, and cheeses are put together for some of the best food you'll find in the region. Think about fresh Maine lobster bisque, Gewürztraminer-cured gravlax, apricot-stuffed pork chops with sour cherry sauce, pistachio cream cannoli with dark chocolate rum sauce. And for breakfast, brioche French toast and local Dungeness crab omelette.

Decor varies from old-fashioned comfortable to luxurious. Most rooms have fireplaces or wood-burning stoves, some have Jacuzzi tubs and ocean-view decks. Among the vast natural and introduced plantings, you will find Mediterranean, English country, and woodland gardens. Hire a limo here for guided tours of the coast and the Wine Country.

Remember the film *Same Time Next Year,* with Alan Alda and Ellen Burstyn? The entire movie was written and filmed at Heritage House.

Little River Inn, 7751 Highway 1, Little River 95456. (707) 937–5942. In the same family since it was built in the 1850s, a white wedding cake of a house that's expanded to become a sizable resort with one of the best restaurants in the area, a nine-hole golf course in the redwoods, and tennis. The bar is a favorite locals' meeting place. Rooms behind the inn have porches overlooking a beautiful beach and bay.

Fort Bragg

North Coast Brewing Company, 444 North Main Street. (707) 964–BREW. Exotic beers, ales, stouts, local fresh fish, Cajun black beans and rice, ribs, Mendocino mud cake. Voted Mendocino County Restaurant of the Year. Tons of fun and a hearty menu.

Round Man's Smoke House, 137 Laurel Street. (707) 964–5954. A family-operated smoke house where you can buy smoked salmon, tuna, and bass, salmon jerky, German sausage, bacon, and more. All of it is vacuum-packed to last for weeks and they will ship for you.

For More Information

Mendocino Coast Accommodations (inns, hotels, bed-and-breakfast places, cottages, homes). (707) 937–1913.

Mendocino Coast Reservations. (707) 937–5033.

Fort Bragg–Mendocino Chamber of Commerce, 332 North Main Street, Fort Bragg, CA 95437. (707) 961–6300.

Coastal Visitor's Center, 990 Main Street, Mendocino, CA. (707) 937–1938.

California State Park Reservations. (800) 444–7275.

Advice: Driving can be hazardous on the twists and turns of Highway 1, and it's not recommended that you attempt it after dark or during storms. Farm animals and deer in the road can be a scary, and maybe deadly, surprise as you're coming around a blind curve.

Marin Waterfront

A short ferry ride will take you to Angel Island State Park.

Sausalito, Tiburon, and Larkspur

———————————— 1 NIGHT ————————————
Sea views • Waterfront cafes • Mountaintop walks
Wildlife sanctuaries • Island idyll • Boutique shopping

On the north side of the Golden Gate, Marin County is a "banana belt," sunny and warm all summer when San Francisco is socked in with fog. It's nice to get away for a couple of quiet days in Marin's small, seaside towns.

Sausalito tumbles down steep, forested hillsides to the edge of the bay. Sophisticated shops, sea-view restaurants, and marinas lined with yachts and funky houseboats share postcard views of the San Francisco skyline.

A residential community of vintage mansions and luxury condos, Tiburon occupies a spectacular peninsula surrounded by the quiet waters of Richardson Bay, where kayakers paddle and sailboarders fly about. Raccoon Straits, a narrow, windswept channel carefully navigated by sailboats and ferries, runs between Tiburon and Angel Island, which is a state park.

Shopping, walks in the salty air, and fine dining are primary activities on this trip, with a Mount Tamalpais sidetrip on the way home.

Day 1

Morning

You have a wide choice of transportation between San Francisco and **Sausalito.** A new shuttle service makes a loop between 11:00 A.M. and 5:30 P.M., stopping every thirty minutes at the Golden Gate Bridge Vista Point West parking lot, the Sausalito Ferry Landing, the Bay Model, and the Discovery Museum (415–331–7262). A ferry sails between the San Francisco waterfront and both Sausalito and Tiburon (see ferry information below). Golden Gate Transit buses run in San Francisco and throughout Marin County (415–332–6600).

In your car, immediately to the north of the Golden Gate Bridge, take the Alexander Avenue exit, descending down into Sausalito; Alexander becomes Bridgeway, the main street. Turn left at the first light, at **Princess Street;** go up the street and make a U-turn, then a right at the same light, and turn immediately into a public parking lot. Some of the best shops in town are located on Princess. At **Studio Saga,** 16 Princess (415–332–4242), the jewel-like colors of soft, silky handwovens envelop you—sweaters, coats, fringed scarves. **Something Special,** at 28A Princess (415–332–0338), specializes in glass oil lamps, potpourri, and brightly colored stuffed gamebirds.

Breakfast: **Seven Seas,** 682 Bridgeway, Sausalito. (415) 332–1304. From 8:00 A.M. every breakfast specialty you can think of, best in town, indoors or on the patio.

Downtown Sausalito is a National Historic Landmark District and a long-established haven for artists, writers, and craftspeople. The annual **Sausalito Art Festival** attracts 50,000 people over Labor Day weekend.

In midtown, where a hundred or so shops and restaurants are concentrated, is a small city park with palm trees and huge stone elephants with streetlights on their heads, leftovers from San Francisco's

1915 Exposition. Behind the park is a dock where ferries come and go to San Francisco and Tiburon. Across the street the **Village Fair,** 777 Bridgeway, is a four-story, hillside rabbit's warren of shops. The **Bearded Giraffe,** at 1115 Bridgeway (415–332–4503), specializes in books, tapes, art, and crystals "for lighting the inner lamp." **Fine Woodworking,** at 1201 Bridgeway (415–332–5770), exhibits the work of more than fifty Northern California artists and craftspeople. Off Bridgeway the **Armchair Sailor,** at 42 Caledonia (415–332–7505), has books, charts, games, and art for the nautically inspired. Two miles north of midtown, the **Heathware Ceramics Outlet,** 400 Gate 5 Road off Bridgeway (415–332–3732), is worth a stop for seconds from a major producer of stoneware.

Heading north on Bridgeway, watch for the sign for **Bay Model,** 2100 Bridgeway at Spring Street (415–332–3871), a one-and-a-half-acre, hydraulic working scale model of the San Francisco Bay Delta, a fascinating research tool used by the U.S. Corps of Engineers; call ahead to find out when the tides in the model are scheduled for activity. The natural and cultural history of the bay are traced in exhibits—wetlands, wildlife, shipwrecks, antique equipment—plus there are videos to watch and video games to play; kids love it.

Nearby at **Open Water Rowing,** off Bridgeway at 85 Liberty Ship Way (415–332–1091), take a kayaking lesson on Richardson Bay between Sausalito and Tiburon; all ages find it easy to learn and a great way to get a gull's-eye view of wildlife on the bay. Along the Sausalito shoreline in this area is a series of yacht harbors, marinas, and houseboat moorings. The houseboats, permanently located at the north end of town, are a phenomenon in themselves and fun to see. Look out past the huddle of moored houseboats into the middle of Richardson Bay to see Forbes Island, a man-made, private tropical island complete with swaying palm trees, flowers, and a waterfall cave. Within the island is a science-fiction world à la Captain Nemo. Fourteen rooms are filled with antiques, nautical memorabilia, portholes to watch marine life, and an art gallery. Arrangements can be made to visit the island (415–332–5727).

Drive south out of town to Highway 101 to the Tiburon exit, taking Tiburon Boulevard south along Richardson's Bay to **Tiburon.**

Lunch: **Sam's Anchor Cafe,** 27 Main. (415) 435–4527. One of several harborfront restaurants with views of the San Francisco skyline, Belvedere Island, and Angel Island. Ferries, yachts, and seagulls slide by; time slides by, too, as you sip a beer on the sunny deck and tuck into clam chowder, fresh crab, and fish of all kinds. Casual, with a frisky bar crowd at times. Weekend brunches are a reason to spend the day at Sam's.

If you plan to be here on the opening day of yacht season in April, arrive early for a good seat at Sam's or grab enough space for a picnic blanket on the lawns beside the bay. Decorated to the max, hundreds of pleasure craft are blessed, then they sail or motor back and forth while landlubbers engage in vernal behavior, like kite flying and boom-box playing.

Afternoon

From the waterfront on Main, you can walk up the wooded streets of **Belvedere Island**—not an island, just a hill covered with zillion-dollar mansions from several eras. It's an architectural sightseeing adventure to drive or walk the steep, narrow lanes.

Prior to the 1920s, Tiburon was a lagoon lined with houseboats, called arks. When the lagoon was filled in 1940, the arks were placed on pilings. Today, curvy tree-lined **Ark Row,** at the west end of Main, is a charming shopping street. Along with 1-block-long **Main Street,** Ark Row is also chockablock with art galleries. Between the two streets is the **Corinthian Yacht Club;** it's OK to walk in through the gate and take a look at the fancy yachts.

You'll find seascapes and posters at the **Wooden Pelican,** 7 Main (415–435–1407). **Windsor Vineyards,** 72 Main (415–435–3113), will ship gift boxes of wine with your name on the bottles. **Westerley's,** 46 Main (415–435–4233), has old-fashioned penny candy, bubblegum cigars, chocolate sardines, and licorice pipes. The **Designer Watch Shop,** 28 Main (415–435–3732), sells cheapo copies of every name-brand watch; your friends will never know the difference.

On the west side of Ark Row at 52 Beach Road on an inlet of the bay, is the **China Cabin,** a delightful fragment from a sidewheel steamer that plied the trade routes between San Francisco and the Orient in the late 1800s. The saloon was salvaged when the ship burned, and served as a home for decades before becoming a maritime museum furnished with period antiques and elaborate gold-leaf ornamentation. Call for a seasonal schedule (415–435–5633).

There are a number of historic buildings in Tiburon. You can get a walking tour brochure from the Tiburon Peninsula Chamber of Commerce, at the above phone number.

From Main, walk north on Tiburon Boulevard 3 blocks to the **Boardwalk** shopping center, where tucked into an alleyway is **Shore-birds,** 1550 Tiburon Boulevard (415–435–0888), a shop worth searching out. It's a gallery/gift store displaying sophisticated, one-of-a-kind jewelry pieces; locally crafted ceramics and woodware; European toys; paintings; and nautical gifts.

From downtown Tiburon to the north end of Richardson Bay is a beautiful waterfront walk, 2 miles one way, on a flat, paved path; there are benches along the way and a huge lawn for Frisbee tossing and sunbathing. The path is popular with joggers, rollerbladers, bikers, and tykes on trikes. At the north end of the path is the **Richardson Bay Audubon Center and Wildlife Sanctuary**, 376 Greenwood Beach Road (415–388–2524). Thousands of sea- and shorebirds, accompanied by harbor seals in the wintertime, inhabit this 900-acre preserve. A self-guided nature trail and a bookstore are adjacent to **Lyford House**, a lemon-yellow landmark Victorian open to the public.

Reachable by a short ferry ride from Main Street (Red and White Fleet, 415–435–2131), **Angel Island State Park** (415–435–3522) is just offshore. Popular activities here are walking and biking the breezy island paths and roads to get a gull's-eye view of three bridges and the bay. Once a Miwok hunting ground, then a cattle ranch, a U.S. Army base, and a prisoner of war camp, Angel Island owns a unique past and you will see several historical sites. The easy way to learn about the history and get some fresh air is to take the narrated tour in an open-air tram. Historic buildings remain from World War II, when 5,000 soliders a day were processed before leaving for the Pacific. Between 1910 and 1940 hundreds of thousands of Asians were detained on the island, awaiting admission into the United States.

Thirteen miles of hiking trails and 8 miles of mountain-biking roads crisscross the island. Twenty-one–speed mountain bikes are available to rent or you can take sea kayaking tours—even moonlight paddle trips—that are conducted around the perimeter of the island with historical and ecological interpretation (415–332–4465). Less energetic visitors will enjoy sitting on the deck of the cafe with an espresso and a light lunch, watching sailboats and freighters gliding by.

The Angel Island–Tiburon Ferry offers a Sunset Cruise on weekends where you bring your own picnic dinner and enjoy cruising the bay in the early evening (415–388–6770).

Dinner: **Guaymas**, 5 Main, Tiburon. (415) 435–6300. Spectacular waterfront location; nouvelle Southwest/Mexican food; lively bar and outdoor terrace.

Lodging: **Tiburon Lodge**, 1651 Tiburon Boulevard, 94920. (415) 435–3133. The only hotel in town; walking distance to everything; eclectic decor; some suites with spas.

On weekends, dance to live bands at **Christopher's** on the waterfront, 9 Main (415–435–4600).

Day 2

Morning

Breakfast: **Sweden House**, 35 Main. (415) 435–9767. Breakfast by the bay with the denizens of Tiburon. Swedish pastries, eggs, and everything else.

At the west end of Main Street, Belevedere Island is a wooded hilltop almost completely surrounded by water, an exclusive neighborhood of mansions from several eras. It's an architectural sightseeing adventure to drive or walk the steep, narrow lanes; the homes, the gardens, and the ocean views—wow!

From the east end of Main Street, take Paradise Drive around the west side of the Tiburon Peninsula, a narrow, winding road through forestlands on the edge of the bay. After 1 mile, before Westward Drive, watch for the **Nature Conservancy Uplands Nature Preserve,** also known as the **Ring Mountain Preserve,** 3152 Paradise Drive (415–435–6465), a ridgetop, 377-acre piece of wilderness with walking trails and wonderful views. It's less than 1 mile's walk to the summit on a trail edged with knee-high native grasses dotted with wildflowers in the spring. Bay trees, madrones, live oaks, and buckeyes provide shade in meadows inhabited by several endangered plant species, including the **Tiburon Mariposa Lily,** existing nowhere else in the world; blooming all through the spring on a stalk about 2 feet tall, the lily has a tan, cinnamon, and yellow bowl-shaped flower. On the hilltop you'll have a 360-degree view of San Francisco Bay, Mount Tam, and Marin County, across the Richmond–San Rafael Bridge over Berkeley to the East Bay hills.

Proceed on Paradise Drive 2 miles to Highway 101 at Corte Madera, then go north for five minutes to the Larkspur exit, to the west side of the freeway opposite the Larkspur ferry terminal, parking at **Larkspur Landing Shopping Center,** a complex of forty stores and restaurants.

Lunch: **A Clean, Well-lighted Place for Books,** at Larkspur Landing. (415) 461–0171. A casual cafe with a bistro menu, in one of the Bay Area's biggest and best bookstores. Open until 11:00 P.M. on the weekends, ACWLPB is popular for after-the-movies people-watching.

Afternoon

Shop to your heart's content, then drive south on 101 to the Panoramic/Highway 1 exit south of Mill Valley, turning west and winding several miles up on the east side of **Mount Tamalpais State Park** (415–388–2070). You can't miss Mount Tam—it's the 2,500-foot mountain peak that you can see from everywhere in Marin. Park at the Pan Toll Ranger Station and Visitor's Center, get a trail map, and walk a bit on one of several hiking trails that start here; the shortest one is the **"Twenty-Minute Verna Dunshea Trail"** circling the peak. Views are beyond description, and it's often sunny up here when it's foggy everywhere below. Dominating the Marin Peninsula, the mountain looms high above the Pacific Ocean, the Marin headlands, San Francisco Bay, and the rolling hills of the Marin and Sonoma County farmlands. Easily accessible by car or mountain bike or on foot or horseback, Mount Tam's natural wonders are legion—canyons, forests, streams and meadows, waterfalls, and wildflowers—and offer opportunities for wild-and-wooly mountain biking or easy downhill walking.

Perhaps you'll want to stop for a sunset cocktail on the deck at **Mountain Home Inn,** 810 Panoramic Highway (415–381–9000), if you have a designated driver for the trip back to San Francisco.

There's More

Bay Area Discovery Museum, 557 East Fort Baker, Sausalito. (415) 332–9646. A hands-on museum for kids, in turn-of-the-century buildings at East Fort Baker, accessible from the Alexander Road exit just north of the Golden Gate Bridge. Designed to appeal to youngsters ages one to ten, the museum has a multimedia center with CD-Roms, a science lab, a maze of illusions with optical tricks, and a fishing boat to climb aboard. Crawl through an underwater tunnel, make crafts and art projects, develop photos, or go on a nature walk. Interactive science projects and imaginative toys and books are sold in the museum shop.

China Camp State Park, RR 1, P.O. Box 244, San Rafael 94901. (415) 456–0766. North of San Rafael take the Civic Center exit off Highway 101 to North San Pedro Road, heading east. A 1,640–acre waterfront park on San Pablo Bay, with beach, hiking trails, a small museum, and primitive camping. Trails along the ridge offer views of the north Bay Area. Weather at the protected beach level is often warm when fog chills the rest of Marin. Windsurfing is a big deal from May through October, and there is even a special windsurfers' parking lot. Walk-in campsites are in lovely meadows about a mile from parking.

Ferries. Tiburon, Sausalito, and Larkspur are accessible by ocean-going ferry.

Angel Island Ferry. (415) 546–2700.

Blue and Gold Fleet. (415) 781–7877.

Red and White Ferries. (415) 332–6600.

Boating and Bay tours. Bluewaters Ocean Kayak Tours. (415) 456–8956. Birdwatching and natural history kayak trips for beginners.

Cass' Marina, 1702 Bridgeway at Napa Street, Sausalito. (415) 332–6789. Sailboat and yacht rentals, sailing school, junior sailing camp, skipper's course.

Captain Case Powerboat and Waterbike Rental, Schoonmaker Point

Marina off Bridgeway, Sausalito. (415) 331–0444. Boston whalers, tours on the bay, sunset cruises, water taxi, high-tech water bikes to play with on calm Richardson Bay. Water bikes are the latest variation on self-propelled travel. These are two-pontooned, one-person craft with a seat in the center that you pedal with feet and hands, reaching a sizzling top speed of 10 miles an hour. It's so safe that you don't even need to wear a bathing suit.

Commodore Seaplanes, from the north end of Sausalito. (800) 973–2752. San Francisco Bay tours, sunset champagne flights.

Hawaiian Chieftain. (415) 331–3214. 103-foot replica of a 1790 square-rigged topsail ketch, romantic sunset sails, Sunday brunch, sail up the northern coast.

Sea Trek, Schoonmaker Point, Sausalito. (415) 488–1000. Guided kayak tours of the bay, classes, sunset and full moon paddles, Point Reyes tours, Angel Island tour, and more.

Marin Headlands, accessible from Bunker and Conzelman roads west of Highway 101, just north of the Golden Gate Bridge. The north shore of the Golden Gate, 12,000 acres of wilderness with famous views of San Francisco, the Bay, and the Pacific. Scattered throughout the headlands are old military tunnels and bunkers that guarded the Gate from the Spanish-American War through the Cold War. Remains of Forts Barry and Cronkhite, old barracks, the Headlands Center for the Arts, the Pacific Energy Resources Center, the Marine Mammal Center, and more. A visitor's center is located in Fort Barry. If you would like to explore and hike in the headlands, a trail map describing the historical and natural sites, wildlife, and suggested hikes is available by calling (415) 331–1540.

Marine Mammal Center in the Marin Headlands. (415) 289–7325. A rare opportunity to see the largest denizens of the sea at this hospital for orphaned, sick, and injured seals, sea lions, dolphins, otters, and whales from California's 900-mile coast, from ten-pound newborn harbor seals to 600-pound sea lions. Many of the patients are endangered or threatened species. There is never a day when rescued animals are not in residence being fed, treated, and comforted. The twin goals of the center are to ready the animals to return to their watery environment and to create public understanding of and appreciation for our fellow creatures. Call for directions and schedules.

Special Events

April. Opening Day of Yacht Season, Tiburon and Sausalito waterfront. (415) 435–5633. Pleasure craft decorated and blessed; a beautiful and exceedingly high-spirited day on the bay.

June. Humming Toadfish Festival, Bay Model, Sausalito. (415)

332–0505. Entertainment, games, food, in celebration of a famous fish.

June. Floating Homes Tour, Sausalito. (415) 332–1916. A chance to see surprising sophistication and inventive decor in Sausalito's famous houseboats.

September. Art Festival, Bay Model, Sausalito. (415) 332–0505.

October. Bay Area Cajun and Zydeco Music, Dance, and Food Festival, San Rafael. (415) 472–7470.

October. Marin Center Fall Antiques and Art Show, San Rafael. (415) 472–7470.

October. Italian Film Festival, San Rafael. (415) 472–7470.

December. Lighted Yacht Parade, Sausalito. (415) 332–0505.

Other Recommended Restaurants and Lodgings

Sausalito

Scoma's, 588 Bridgeway. (415) 332–9551. On the water at the south end of town, in a baby blue clapboard building. Dependably good seafood.

Sushi Ran, 107 Caledonia. (415) 332–3620. Trendy, contemporary sushi bar and restaurant.

Casa Madrona Hotel and Restaurant, 801 Bridgeway. (415) 332–0502. Circa-1880 landmark inn, luxurious rooms, suites, and cottages with fireplaces, European antiques, garden and harbor views, outdoor Jacuzzi, in-room dining and massage, beautiful gardens, complimentary breakfast and evening refreshments.

Mikayla Casa Madrona, 801 Bridgeway. (415) 331–5888. One of the outstanding restaurants in the San Francisco Bay Area, miraculous murals, unique interior decor and furnishings created by world-famous designer Laurel Burch. Dining terrace with retractable roof and sliding-glass walls, dramatic views of San Francisco Bay and Sausalito yacht harbor. Award-winning California-European cuisine and wine list, Sunday jazz brunch. It's worth the drive to Sausalito just to have lunch or dinner here. One of the Bay Area's finest restaurants.

Golden Gate Youth Hostel, Fort Barry. (415) 331–2777. Single or shared dorms; accessible by public bus.

Alta Mira Hotel and Restaurant, 125 Bulkley Avenue. (415) 332–1350. The breathtaking view from the terrace makes a sunset cocktail or Sunday brunch an event.

Tiburon

New Morning Cafe, 1696 Tiburon Boulevard. (415) 435–4315. Indoors or out, lunch and breakfast, the best.

Larkspur

The Lark Creek Inn, 234 Magnolia Avenue. (415) 924–7767. Internationally famous chef Bradley Ogden, American heartland and nouvelle cuisine, garden patio, vintage architecture.

Good Earth, Larkspur Landing Center. (415) 461–4646. Homemade vegetarian soups, sandwiches, salads, and pastas, California-style Mexican food. Breakfast, lunch, and dinner.

San Rafael

Las Camelias, 912 Lincoln Avenue. (415) 453–5850. Voted the best Mexican restaurant in Marin.

Mill Valley

Mill Valley Inn, 165 Throckmorton Avenue. (800) 595–2100. Sixteen inn rooms around an interior atrium, indoor/outdoor terrace where breakfast and afternoon refreshments are served. Contemporary European ambiance, cottages and guest rooms, balconies or decks, fireplace or wood stove. Beautiful use of salvaged woods and environmentally friendly materials, sundeck overlooking redwoods and Papermill Creek.

Tea Garden Springs, 38 Miller Avenue. (415) 389–7123. Asian-style spa for spending the day in heaven, therapeutic herbs, several varieties of massage, aromatherapy, beauty treatments, tea house, shiatsu, acupressure. A soothing environment of gurgling fountains, elegant treatment rooms, gardens, Jacuzzis, views of Mount Tam. If not now, when?

Gira Polli, 590 East Blithedale Avenue. (415) 383–6040. As many as a hundred chickens at a time spin over a wood fire, emerging crisp and juicy, redolent of rosemary and sage, orange and lemon. Pasta, too, and risotto, antipasti, daily Italian specialties. Take-out and delivery.

Corte Madera

Corte Madera Inn, 1815 Redwood Highway. (800) 777–9670. Nice motel rooms overlooking gardens and lawns, with swimming and wading pools, a laundry, playground, and a good coffee shop. Continental breakfast is free and so is the shuttle to the San Francisco ferry. Can't beat this combo anywhere in Marin.

Book Passage, 51 Tamal Vista. (800) 999–7909. One of the largest independent bookstores in the country specializing in travel guides and mystery novels, and a full-service general bookstore. The in-store cafe has indoor and outdoor seating, opens early, closes late. Movie stars, literary lions, and the most interesting people in Marin County are seen at Book Passage.

Il Fornaio Restaurant and Bakery, 223 Town Center. (415) 927–4400. Contemporary Italian cuisine in an upscale bistro setting. Open early for espresso and pastries.

For More Information

Sausalito Chamber of Commerce, 333 Caledonia Street, P.O. Box 566, Sausalito, CA 94977. (415) 331–7262.

Belevedere-Tiburon Chamber of Commerce, 96 Main, Tiburon, CA 94920. (415) 435–5633.

Bed and Breakfast Exchange of Marin. (415) 485–1971.

Point Reyes and Inverness

McClure Beach is a great place to explore.

The National Seashore

_____ 2 NIGHTS _____

Natural seashore · Beachcombing · Birdwatching
Wildflower walks · Oyster farms · Inns by the sea

More than a few weekends are needed to discover the many joys of the Point Reyes National Seashore, comprising 71,000 miraculous acres on the edge of the continent: two fingerlike peninsulas pointing jaggedly into the Pacific; the long, shallow biodiversity of Tomales Bay; the big curve of Drakes Bay, where the English explorer Sir Francis Drake set foot in 1579; and oyster farms, clamming beaches, tide-pools, and wildlife sanctuaries.

The National Seashore was created in 1962 when President John F. Kennedy signed legislation to preserve the nation's dwindling undeveloped coastline for future generations. Separated from the mainland by the San Andreas Fault, the unique location of the peninsula enables the occurrence of several distinct habitats. Over 45 percent of the bird species in North America have been sighted here, and nearly 20 percent of California's flora are represented.

From February through early summer, the meadows and marine terraces of Point Reyes are blanketed with California poppies, dark blue lupine, pale baby-blue-eyes, Indian paintbrush, and a few varieties of wildflowers existing only here. Dominating the landscape is the green-black Douglas fir forest of Inverness Ridge, running northwest to southeast alongside the San Andreas earthquake fault. The summit of Mount Wittenberg, at 1,407 feet, is reachable in an afternoon's climb.

Subject to summer fogs and winter drizzles, Point Reyes is a favorite destination not only for those who love a sunny day at the beach but for intrepid outdoor types who follow cool-weather nature hikes with cozy evenings by a fireplace in a vintage bed-and-breakfast inn.

Day 1

Morning

Drive north from the Golden Gate Bridge on Highway 101 to the Sir Francis Drake/San Anselmo exit.

Breakfast: **Victoria Pastry,** 292 Bon Air Center, about twenty minutes off the freeway exit. (415) 461–3099. Offspring of a seventy-five-year-old traditional Italian bakery in San Francisco, espresso and pastries, open 7:00 A.M.

Proceed west forty-five minutes on winding, two-lane Sir Francis Drake Boulevard to the **Point Reyes National Seashore Visitor's Center** at **Olema** (415–663–1092). (On the way, 5 miles east of Olema, you will pass **Samuel P. Taylor State Park,** a 2,600-acre piece of forested canyon along Lagunitas Creek, a popular place for mountain bikers, horseback riders, and hikers; 415–488–9897.)

Exhibits, guidebooks, and trail maps at the Point Reyes Visitor's Center will help orient you to the diverse ecosystem and the many destinations within the National Seashore. According to the day's weather, you may choose beachcoming and sunbathing (or fog-bathing) at **Limantour Beach** on Drakes Bay; backpacking to overnight sites; or easy walks or bike rides on popular meadowland paths, such as the 4.4-mile **Bear Valley Trail** to Arch Rock overlook at the beach—a sunny picnickers' meadow and restrooms are located halfway. This is the most popular and one of the most beautiful trails, leading through forest tunnels, along creeks, and through meadows, ending on a bluff 50 feet above the sea.

Birdwatching is excellent in the 500-acre **Limantour Estero Reserve,** west of Limantour Beach. You get to **Drakes Estero,** a much larger saltwater lagoon, from Sir Francis Drake Boulevard on the west side. This rocky intertidal area is a giant tidepool and bird sanctuary, rich with such wildlife as anemones, sea stars, crabs, and even rays and leopard sharks.

Lunch: Picnic on the beach or in a trailside meadow.

Afternoon

Energetic hikers can make the steep but short ascent on Sky Trail to the summit of Mount Wittenberg, and beach bums will choose from many coastal access trails. The long sandy stretch of Point Reyes Beach is accessible in two places by car.

Short, easy walks near the visitor's center include **Kule Loklo,** the Miwok Village, where an ancient Indian site has been re-created, and the **Woodpecker Trail,** a self-guided nature walk leading to the park rangers' Morgan horse ranch and a Morgan horse museum. Horses are bred and trained here on a hundred beautiful acres for the use of the National Park rangers in this park and in Zion and Hawaii Volcanoes National Parks. You can tour a blacksmith's shop, a museum, and the stables.

The **Earthquake Trail,** less than a mile in length, is where you'll see photos of the effects of the 1906 earthquake and signs explaining earth movement.

Dinner: **Station House Cafe,** Main Street, Point Reyes. (415) 663–1515. Eclectic, hearty California food; pot roast, duck breast with cherry sauce, fresh fish, pecan pie; dinner served until 11:00 P.M. in the bar; live entertainment three nights a week. Kick up your heels to country music at the **Western Saloon** on Main Street (415–663–1661).

Lodging: **Point Reyes Seashore Lodge,** 10021 Highway 1, P.O. Box 39, Olema 94950. (415) 663–9000. Just south of Point Reyes. Reminiscent of national park lodges from a century ago, a castlelike re-creation of a large Victorian inn on the exterior, modern California Craftsman–style inside, sweeping lawns above a creek and woods, all bordering the National Seashore. Twenty-two rooms and suites with featherbeds, down comforters, bay windows, fireplaces, Jacuzzi tubs, buffet breakfast.

Day 2

Morning

Breakfast: At the Point Reyes Lodge.

Give your hiking legs a break and spend the morning shopping and cafe lounging in the town of **Point Reyes Station.** Many hundred-year-old buildings remain on the main street of this old narrow-gauge railroad town founded in the 1800s. The train depot is now the post office, the Fire Engine House a community center. Dairy ranches and commercial oyster companies fuel the rural economy.

The **Black Mountain Weavers,** on Main Street (415–663–9130), is a co-op gallery of fine woven rugs, sweaters, and tapestries, plus jewelry and art. The **Borge Gallery,** 221 B Street (415–663–1419), specializes in California landscapes. Equestrians will go into **Cabaline Saddle Shop,** on Main Street (415–663–8303), for English and western saddlery and clothing. Also on Main is **Toby's Feed Barn** (415–663–1223)—fresh flowers, plants, produce, T-shirts, and hay for your horse.

Lunch: From Point Reyes, drive north on Highway 1 along the shoreline of Tomales Bay a few miles to **Nick's Cove,** 23240 Highway 1, Marshall. (415) 663–1033. Rustic, aromatic, on the wetlands of the bay, barbecued oysters and seafood galore, a list of beers as long as your arm, lots of fun. Also in Marshall, **Hog Island Oyster Company** (20215 Highway 1, 415–663–9218) sells the succulent shellfish and provides shucking knives, tables, and BBQ kettles.

Afternoon

Five miles farther north, the mini-town of **Tomales** is a 2-block-long headquarters for crabbing, clamming, and surf fishing. At low tide in the winter, catch a clammer's barge from here out to the flatlands around Hog Island in the bay. Hog Island and nearby Duck Island are private wildlife sanctuaries frequented by harbor seals.

In a wooden false-front, antiques-bedecked building, the **Old Town Cafe** in Tomales is a cozy spot for sandwiches, homemade soup, and fresh fish (707–878–2526).

The town of **Dillon Beach,** 4 miles west of Tomales, is a clutch of Craftsman-style beach cottages from the 1930s. A number of nineteenth-century buildings remain near the intersection of Main Street and Dillon Beach Road. The Church of the Assumption, just south of town, was built in 1860.

Often very windy, Dillon Beach has some of the richest tidepools on the entire coastline. Walk on the dunes or drive a mile south to Lawson's Landing where hang gliders often ride the winds (707–878–2204).

On your way back from Dillon Beach and Tomales to Point Reyes, then around to Inverness, take a walk or swim in the quiet waters of **Heart's Desire Beach** in **Tomales Bay State Park** (415–669–1140). This is the most accessible beach on the bay for windsurfing, kayaking, and clam digging.

A resort village since 1889, Inverness, population 1,000, is a daytripper's reststop and a community of country cottages on steep wooded slopes at the northern end of **Inverness Ridge** overlooking Tomales Bay. There are seafood cafes, bed-and-breakfast inns, a small marina, and not much else but eye-popping scenery.

Discovered by Spanish explorers in the 1600s, Tomales Bay is 13 miles long, 1 mile wide, and very shallow, with acres of mudflats and salt- and freshwater marshes. Commercial oyster farms line the western shore. More than one hundred species of resident and migrating waterbirds are the reason you'll see anorak-clad, binocular-braced birdwatchers at every pullout on Highway 1. Perch, flounder, sand dabs, and crabs are catchable by small boat. The San Andreas earthquake fault runs beneath Tomales Bay; in 1906, 20 feet of the peninsula dropped beneath the bay waters.

Dinner: **Manka's Inverness Restaurant,** 30 Calendar Way, Inverness. (415) 669–1034. A 1917 fishing lodge nestled under the pines; game and fresh fish grilled in an open fireplace, house-cured meat and poultry, homegrown produce; comfortably cozy, candlelit atmosphere, notable chefs; reservations essential.

Lodging: **Ten Inverness Way,** (same address), Inverness. (415) 669–1648. Country-style inn with five rooms filled with quilts, lace curtains, comfort, and light. Common room with big stone fireplace, lovely gardens, hot tub, full breakfast, walk to hiking trails.

Day 3

Morning

Breakfast: At the inn.

Drive north on Sir Francis Drake Boulevard to the Pierce Point Road; take a right and park in the upper parking lot at **McClure Beach.** It's a 9-mile round-trip around **Tomales Point** and along the coastline. Spring wildflowers float in the meadows; whales spout December through February. A herd of elk live in the grassy fields of **Pierce Ranch** on the tip of the peninsula. These windswept moors remind some visitors of Scotland.

McClure Beach is wide, sandy, backed by high cliffs, and dotted with rocks and great tidepools. Bluffs framed by groves of Bishop pine look like Japanese woodcut prints; these pines are found only in a few isolated locations on the California coast.

Point Reyes Lighthouse, at the end of Sir Francis Drake Boulevard, 15 miles south of Inverness, is reachable by 400 steps leading downhill from a high bluff. Many shipwrecks occurred off the **Point Reyes Headlands** until the lighthouse was built in 1870. Below the dramatic cliffs are miles of beaches accessible from Sir Francisco Drake Boulevard. Exposed to the full force of storms and pounding surf, these beaches are unsafe for swimming or surfing, although the intrepid are sometimes seen holding forth in the waves. The headlands, the tidepools, sea stacks, lagoons, wave-carved caves, and rocky promontories are alive with birds—endangered brown pelicans, cormorants, surf skooters, sandpipers, grebes, terns—and sea life such as giant anemones and sea palms, urchins, fish, and even the occasional great white shark offshore of Tomales Point.

At **Drakes Beach** are a visitor's center, picnic tables, and a great sandy beach. During whale-watching season, December through spring, a shuttle bus may be operating between the lighthouse and the beach. Some 20,000 California gray whales travel the Pacific coastline going south to breed in Mexican waters, and then return with their babies to the Arctic.

Lunch: **Barnaby's by the Bay,** 12938 Sir Francis Drake Boulevard, 1 mile north of Inverness at the Golden Hind Inn. (415) 669–1114. Two decks overlooking a marina, fresh fish, salads, barbecued oysters and chicken, and ribs from the applewood smoker, jazz on weekends; you'll be tempted to stay here for the rest of the day.

Head back to the Bay Area.

There's More

Horseback riding. Five Brooks Trailhead. (415) 663–8287. Three miles south of Olema.

Bear Valley Stables. (415) 663–1570.

Mount Vision hike. From downtown Inverness walk up Inverness Way, past the school and through the pedestrian gate; bear right at the Y and left through a gate at the next Y. You'll reach the summit in about ninety minutes; dizzying views of Tomales Bay all along the way and views of the ocean and the world at the top!

Oysters. Tomales Bay Oyster Company, 5 miles north of Point Reyes Station on Highway 1. (415) 663–1242. Founded in 1914; fresh oysters and other live shellfish.

Special Events

July. Coastal Native American Summer Big Time, Point Reyes National Seashore. (415) 663–1092. Demonstration of crafts, skills, music, dancing.
October. Acorn Festival, Point Reyes. (415) 663–1092. Celebrations and festivities of the Miwok Indians.

Other Recommended Restaurants and Lodgings

Point Reyes Station

Chez Madeleine, 10905 Star Route 1. (415) 663–9177. Very French, very wonderful dining; cassoulet, roast chicken, fresh fish, escargots.
Holly Tree Inn and Cottages, 3 Silverhills Road. (415) 663–1554. On nineteen acres of lawns, gardens, and wooded hillsides, common rooms in French provincial decor, antiques, fireplaces, French doors open to the meadows. Four guest rooms. Cottages have hot tubs and fireplaces.
Thirty-nine Cypress, 39 Cypress Road. (415) 663–1709. With wonderful views of the Point Reyes Peninsula, a redwood country inn with three guest rooms. Private patio, hot tub, common rooms with oriental rugs, library, antiques, fireplace. Includes breakfast.

Inverness

Inns of Point Reyes, P.O. Box 145, 94956. (415) 485–2649. Referral service for several inns.
Point Reyes Hostel. (415) 663–8811. Off Limantour Road, 6 miles from Bear Valley Road in the National Seashore.
Blackthorne Inn, 266 Vallejo. (415) 663–8621. Five charming rooms. In a wooded canyon, a treehouse with decks, hot tub, fireman's pole, spiral staircase, glass-sided "eagle's nest," handcrafted from redwood, cedar, and a 180-foot Douglas fir. Includes buffet breakfast.
Dancing Coyote Beach B and B, P.O. Box 98. (415) 669–7200. Four Southwest-style cottages, decks, views, fireplaces, kitchens.
Golden Hind Inn, 12938 Sir Francis Drake Boulevard. (415) 669–1389. Bay view and poolside rooms, some fireplaces, kitchens, fishing pier, restaurant, bar; reasonable.
Gray Whale Pizzeria and Bakery, 12781 Sir Francis Drake Boulevard. (415) 669–1244. The view from the wisteria arbor is of Tomales Bay and the hills beyond. Espresso, homemade soups, salads, desserts, pizza, pasta.

Olema

Olema Ranch Campground, .25 mile north of Highway 1 and Sir Francis Drake Boulevard. (415) 663–8001. RV facilities, tent sites, forest and meadow setting, gas, store. Campfires allowed.

San Anselmo

Bed and Breakfast Exchange of Marin, 45 Entrata. (415) 485–1971.

For More Information

West Marin Chamber of Commerce, P.O. Box 1045, Point Reyes Station, CA 94956. (415) 663–9232.

Audubon Canyon Ranch. (415) 383–1644. A private, nonprofit research organization that owns Olema Marsh and other nature preserves.

South Coast Marin

There's always time for a relaxing stroll on the beach.

Stinson Beach, Bolinas, Olema

——————————— 1 NIGHT ———————————

Sandy beaches · Hiking trails · Seafood cafes · Wildlife preserves

It's a short drive to the 3-mile-long sandy shores of Stinson Beach, often warm and sunny when the Bay Area is fogged in. Nearby is the quiet village of Bolinas, at the southern end of the Point Reyes National Seashore trail system. Extensive lagoons and wetlands in the area support hundreds of species of sea- and shorebirds and ducks. Beachcombing, nature hikes, cafe sitting, and photo snapping are your main activities on this overnight escape.

Day 1

Morning

Drive north from the Golden Gate on Highway 101, turning west at the Stinson Beach/Highway 1 exit just south of Sausalito. You'll connect with Panoramic Highway, a winding two-lane road over **Mount Tamalpais,** the "Sleeping Maiden" whose 2,600-foot profile dominates western Marin County. A series of wilderness trails connecting the Marin Headlands with Muir Beach and Mount Tamalpais, the **Coastal Trail** has a trailhead at Stinson and near Steep Ravine Cabins. Maps are available at ranger stations on Mount Tam, at Rodeo Beach, and at other locations. You can hike 5.5 miles up from the cabins to Mountain Home Inn (see below) on the east summit of the mountain and stay overnight. Golden Gate Transit buses make San Francisco/Mountain Home Inn/ Stinson Beach runs on the weekends.

Weekends only, have breakfast on the top of the world at **Mountain Home Inn,** 810 Panoramic Highway (415–381–9000). The road drops steeply from here, through oak and evergreen forests, down to the tiny burg of **Stinson Beach,** headquarters for daytripping and vacationing at the beach on **Bolinas Bay** in the **Golden Gate National Recreation Area** (415–868–0942). One of the state's first home subdivisions founded the summer vacation colony in 1906, the year of the big one in San Francisco.

Lunch: **Stinson Beach Grill,** 1 block from the beach on Highway 1. (415) 868–2002. Fresh seafood, pasta, Southwest cuisine; fifty varieties of beer. Dine indoors or on the sunny deck; breakfast, lunch, and dinner.

Afternoon

The waters off Stinson are surprisingly warm in the winter, due to a unique rising to the surface of the tropical undercurrent. In a protected mini–banana belt, the beach and the town enjoy a Mediterranean climate all year. Resting in eucalyptus and Monterey pines, thousands of monarch butterflies like the winters here, too. Surfboards, boogieboards, and wetsuits can be rented, and bathing suits purchased, at **Live Water Surf Shop,** 3450 Highway 1 (415–868–0333). If nude sunbathing is your choice, **Red Rock** beach is the place to go

(1 mile south of Stinson Beach, watch for a parking area off the highway below reddish cliffs, access by steep trail).

Among the galleries and shops is **Claudia Chapline Gallery,** at 3445 Highway 1 (415–868–2308), showing a wide variety of locally produced fine art. **Stinson Beach Books,** 3455 Highway 1 (415–868–0700), has regional guidebooks, maps, and best-sellers for beach bums.

Dinner: **The Sand Dollar,** Highway 1 at Stinson Beach. (415) 868–0434. People come all the way out here just for dinner; small, friendly, crowded; superb fresh seafood and more; bar.

Drive north on Highway 1 for 5 miles to Bolinas. At the north end of the lagoon, watch for a left turn—there will be no sign—onto Olema/Bolinas Road, skirting the west side of the lagoon. Wharf Road is the main street of town.

Lodging: **Thomas' White House Inn,** 118 Kale Road, Bolinas 94924. (415) 868–0279. Be sure to call for directions. Bed-and-breakfast accommodations in a New England–style clapboard house; wonderful sea views from rooms and garden. Just two rooms on the second floor. First floor is a living room with fireplace, sun porch, aviary, open kitchen. Beautiful gardens.

Day 2

Morning

Breakfast: Bountiful continental breakfast at Thomas' White House Inn and/or unforgettable organic-ingredient pastries, breads, pies, and espresso at **Bolinas Bay Bakery and Cafe,** 20 Wharf Road, Bolinas (415–868–0211).

Lost in the 1960s, Bolinas is a quiet country village inhabited by artists, craftspeople, and weekenders. Some nineteenth-century buildings remain from a summer colony in the 1800s. On the 2-block-long main street, part of Smiley's Bar dates from 1852, and St. Mary Magdalen Catholic Church from 1878.

Bolinas Lagoon is 1,200 acres of saltmarsh, mudflats, and calm seawaters harboring myriad wildlife. Great blue herons and egrets, migrating geese and ducks—as many as 35,000 birds have been spotted in a single day. Harbor seals hang out at the mouth of the lagoon.

Drive through Bolinas on the road to **Duxbury Reef,** a mile of shallow tidepools that are exposed at low tide on the Bolinas Bay shoreline. In this vast intertidal area you will see gooseneck barnacles, ochre and pink sea stars, purple and giant red anemones, chitons, and more exotic sea life. This is a marine reserve and not a thing may be removed. At the north end of the reef is **Agate Beach,** a small county park. Beware of the swift incoming tide.

Drive 4 miles northwest from Bolinas on Mesa Road to the **Point Reyes Bird Observatory** and field station (415–868–1221) to see research projects, a small museum, and a short self-guided nature trail. You are welcome to observe the activities here, which include banding rufous-sided towhees, song sparrows, and other birds.

One mile farther on Mesa Road is **Palomarin Trailhead,** at the southern end of Point Reyes National Seashore; this trail leads to four freshwater lakes that are waterfowl habitats, as well as to the small **Double Point** bay, where harbor seals breed and tidepools are inviting to look into; you're not allowed to touch. The rocks around Double Point are important feeding and roosting sites for cormorants, grebes, and pelicans. Three miles from the trailhead, watch for **Bass Lake,** a secret swimming spot.

Lunch: The **Olema Farm House Restaurant,** Highway 1 at Sir Francis Drake Boulevard, Olema. (415) 663–1264. Fifteen minutes north of Bolinas on Highway 1. Seafood, steak, pasta, espresso—indoors or out.

Afternoon

Headquarters for hikers, horseback riders, and campers heading for Point Reyes National Seashore, Olema has a few structures remaining from the mid-1800s. Nearby, forty-acre **Olema Marsh** (415–868–9244), a birdwatchers' mecca, is privately owned but can be enjoyed from the side of the road.

Head back south on Highway 1 and stop just south of the Bolinas exit for a visit to **Audubon Canyon Ranch** (415–868–9244), an educational and research center open to the public from March through July on weekends and holidays. In the tops of redwoods and pines in deep, wooded canyons, herons and egrets make their nests, and hundreds of thousands of monarch butterflies spend the winter here in a grove of eucalyptus trees. A short trail leads to fixed telescopes for nest-watching; you can also walk on two nature trails. Watch for newts, frogs, foxes, deer, and quail. The ranch is a magical place and you will want to spend at least a couple of hours here. There are exhibits, a bookshop, and picnic tables adjacent to a circa-1870 house.

Retrace your route back to the Golden Gate Bridge, or drive back on Highway 1 (see below).

There's More

Muir Beach. An alternate route to or from Stinson is on Highway 1 around the base of Mount Tamalpais, a supercurvy, spectacular seacoast road providing access to Muir Beach and, on the slopes of the mountain, Muir Woods National Monument (see below). Located at Redwood Creek lagoon, a spawning stream lined with maples and alders, the often windy beach is long and sandy with tidepools; a World War II gun emplacement, the Muir Beach Overlook is now a county park.

Muir Woods National Monument, 3 miles north of Highway 1 on Muir Woods Road. (415) 388–2595. The only remaining old-growth redwood forest near San Francisco, it is a popular tourist destination, so try to arrive early in the day. Beneath the towering redwoods, on the forest floor, are western azalea, huckleberry, and violets. Lady ferns and sword ferns and colorful fungi are seen in the wetter areas. A short wheelchair-accessible nature trail and other trails enter **Mount Tamalpais State Park.** There is a visitor center, a gift shop, and a snack bar.

Slide Ranch, 2025 Shoreline Highway, Muir Beach. (415) 381–6155. A few miles south of Stinson, 2.2 miles north of Muir Beach, on a hillside overlooking the sea lies a ranch built in the early 1900s. Now, it's an environmental education center where children can milk a goat, harvest veggies, bake bread, and learn how to care for animals and nature. Special days are scheduled for ocean exploration and for children under five. You can take away a packet of Slide Ranch activities to play at home. Call ahead for a reservation.

Bolinas Museum for the Art and History of Coastal Marin, 48 Wharf Road, Bolinas. (415) 868–0330. Artifacts of Marin's earliest inhabitants.

Other Recommended Restaurants and Lodgings

Stinson Beach

Steep Ravine Cabins. Simple, rustic buildings from the 1930s, sleep up to five people, woodburning stoves, bunks, water, no electricity. Rented through the state park (800–444–7275).

Casa del Mar, 37 Belvedere Avenue. (415) 868–2124. A Mediterranean villa in an exotic terraced garden that was once used as a demonstration garden for the UC Berkeley School of Landscape Architecture. Small inn, each room with private bath and balcony with views of the sea or Mount Tamalpais, down comforters. Full breakfast in the dining room or on the courtyard.

A few yards from the inn is the trailhead for the Matt Davis Trail, a 6-mile climb though a Douglas fir forest across grassy hills and down into a coastal redwood forest.

Olema

Olema Inn Restaurant and B&B, Sir Francis Drake Boulevard and Highway 1. (415) 663–9559. Garden setting, historic inn at the entrance to the National Seashore. Rooms with private baths. Lunch and dinner.

Bear Valley Inn, 88 Bear Valley Road. (415) 663–1777. Two-story Victorian ranch house built in 1899, three guest rooms, antiques, down comforters. Common parlor with woodstove, includes breakfast.

Roundstone Farm, 9440 Sir Francis Drake Boulevard. (415) 663–1020. On a ten-acre horse ranch, a cedar farmhouse, five guest rooms with fireplaces, armoires, down comforters. Common room with woodburning stove, deck overlooking pond and pasture. Includes breakfast.

Muir Beach

Pelican Inn, several miles south of Stinson Beach on Highway 1. (415) 383–6000. Re-creation of a sixteenth-century English country inn; small, comfy rooms; full breakfast.

Bolinas

Blue Heron Inn and Restaurant, 11 Wharf Road. (415) 868–1102. Two lovely rooms with private bath, owned by a family who also owns The Shop, a local cafe, where inn guests take their complimentary breakfasts.

155 Pine, P.O. Box 62 94924. (415) 868–0263. A private cottage overlooking the ocean; short walk to the beach.

For More Information

Bed and Breakfast Exchange of Marin. (415) 485–1971.

Southbound Escapes

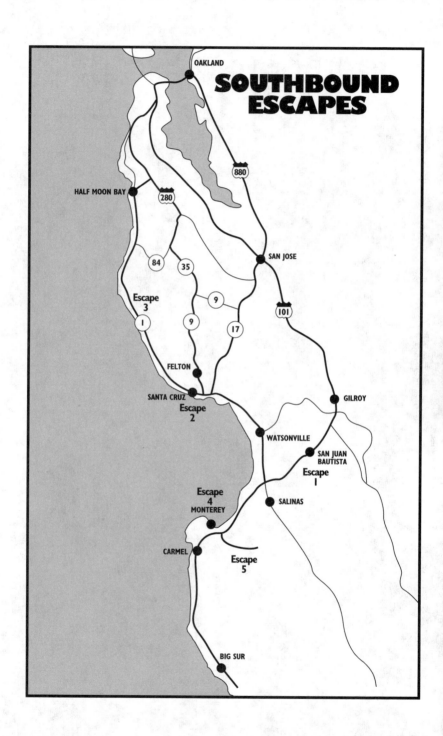

SOUTHBOUND ESCAPES

OAKLAND

880

HALF MOON BAY

280

84

35

Escape
3

9

9

17

FELTON

SANTA CRUZ

Escape
2

SAN JOSE

101

GILROY

WATSONVILLE

SAN JUAN
BAUTISTA

Escape
1

Escape
4
MONTEREY

SALINAS

CARMEL

Escape
5

BIG SUR

Old California, the Central Valley

The Mission San Juan Bautista, the largest of all California mission churches.

San Juan Bautista and the Pinnacles

_____ 1 NIGHT _____

Mission town · Antiques · Nature trails, rocky climbs
Mexican food · Garlic galore · Salinas Valley

Between the tawny Gabilan Mountains on the east and the coastal range of the Santa Lucias on the west, vegetable fields surround a handful of small farming towns in the Salinas Valley. The Salinas River curls and twists around the valley, finally relaxing into Monterey Bay. Meadows and foothills are carpeted with lupines and poppies in the spring, turning to knee-high yellow mustard, then to golden grasses all summer.

Here John Steinbeck lived and wrote of the struggles and romances of early farm families. Father Junípero Serra founded his largest mission, around which grew a town that's not much changed in a hundred years. Thrusting dramatically up in rocky spires, Pinnacles National Monument goes lush and green when winter rains reinvigorate the waterfalls and rushing streams.

Day 1

Morning

From the Oakland Bay Bridge, drive south on Highway 880 to Highway 101, for about ninety minutes, to Gilroy, edging out of the smog into the oak-studded, rolling hills of San Benito County. Wisping in over the coast range, morning fogs cool the dusty summer heat of the valley.

The scent of fresh garlic announces **Gilroy,** home of the **Gilroy Garlic Festival,** attended each July by 150,000 lovers of the stinking rose. About 10 miles south of the Highway 152 junction, watch for a huge red barn on your left. On weekends here there's a big flea market and farmer's market, a barbecue, and an antiques fair.

Take the Highway 156 exit to **San Juan Bautista,** often called San Juan, a Spanish village since the late 1700s, in the arms of the Gabilan Range. Park at the first available space. The little town consists of a large state historic park, one of the most beautiful of California's missions, and a few charming streets of antiques shops and Mexican restaurants shaded with pepper trees, mimosa, and black walnuts. Everything is within walking distance. Go to the grassy plaza on the north side of town and start at the heart and soul of San Juan, the magnificent **Mission San Juan Bautista,** at Second and Mariposa streets (408–623–2127). Founded in 1787, it's the largest of all California mission churches, with three aisles and a glorious 40-foot-high ceiling of grayed beams in traditional viga-latilla formation. Light floods the cathedral, making vibrant the rust-and-blue painted decoration, most of it created in 1816 by a Boston sailor who worked at the mission in exchange for room and board. It's OK to stand at the back, near the giant entry doors, before and during the masses, when local families mingle and chat, little girls flit about in their ruffled best dresses, and their brothers jet up and down the aisles. The soft singing voices of the congregation float out the open door into the sunshine of the plaza.

Many original statues, paintings, and carvings remain. The carving of St. John the Baptist behind the main altar was brought from Mexico in 1809, a superior example of the style. Surrounding the cathedral are a series of rooms, once living quarters for the padres, housing a museum of early Indian, Spanish Colonial, and Victorian artifacts, including one of the best collections of Mission furniture in the world. You'll see a small kitchen with iron pots in an open firpelace, from which 1,200 people were fed three times a day.

The mission gardens are dense with old cacti, aromatic lavender, and climbing roses. Behind the church under ancient olive trees, 4,300 Indians and early pioneers are buried. The cemetery and the plaza overlook vast, flat fields and the **San Andreas earthquake fault,** here at the south end of the Santa Cruz Mountains. A seismograph sits in a glass box, recording every tremor.

Lunch: **Jardines de San Juan,** 115 Third Street. (408) 623–4466. A Mexican restaurant with a big, popular garden patio. Guitarists strum, breezes ruffle the fig and maple trees, people-watching is excellent; it's tempting to stay for a second margarita. Lunches and dinners are served at umbrella tables or indoors in art-filled dining rooms.

Afternoon

The plaza is circled by historic buildings open to inspection. The **Plaza Stable,** a barn museum of horse-drawn carriages and wagons, dispatched coaches for seven stage lines in the 1860s. San Juan was on a main route between San Francisco and Los Angeles, with silver and gold miners trading, resupplying, and traveling through town; as many as eleven coaches a day arrived, with about seventeen passengers each.

Restored and completely furnished, the **Plaza Hotel** was the first place the dusty travelers headed, to get a beer or something stronger in the bar and to book a room for the night. The owner of the hotel, Angelo Zanetta, built himself a magnificent dwelling on the plaza; the structure now houses an outstanding collection of early California furnishings and personal items—the **Zanetta House.**

The red-tile–roofed **Castro House** was owned by a family from the Donner party who struck it rich in the Gold Rush; behind the house is a 150-year-old pepper tree shading lovely gardens. Fat-trunked pepper trees, mimosa, and black walnuts shade the few streets constituting the village; lushly overgrown old-fashioned gardens romp and ramble around the buildings.

Twelve antiques stores await discovery, plus small shops of every description, delightfully untrendy. At the **San Juan Crate and Packing Company,** 404 Third Street (408–623–4159), are regional gourmet food products, garlic braids, and wreaths; the establishment will pack and mail for you. **Buchser Farms,** 318 Third Street (408–623–4430), sells wine and antiques, a great combination. **Tops,** 5 Second Street (408–623–4441), offers semiprecious stones and rare rocks in a museumlike store. And **Kushi Weaving Mission Gallery,** 35 Muckelemi Street (408–623–2051), is a source of miraculous woven clothing and gifts.

Dinner: **Cademartori's,** 600 First Street. (408) 623–4511. For decades, a family-owned and -operated Italian restaurant, casual, homemade pasta, wonderful ravioli, steak, traditional Italian specialties, indoors or on the garden patio.

Lodging: **Country Rose Bed and Breakfast Inn,** 455 Fitzgerald Avenue. (408) 842–0441. Drive ten minutes north on Highway 101 to San Martin, taking the Masten exit west to three mailboxes, turning right to reach the inn. Beneath gigantic spreading oaks, Rose's place is a shady five-acre oasis in the middle of vegetable fields, a stone's throw from the western side of the Santa Cruz Range. Five quiet, private, spacious rooms with baths, some fireplaces; the largest is a suite with Jacuzzi tub and steam shower.

Day 2

Morning

Take a morning walk on nearby country lanes; explore the five-acre farmyard.

Breakfast: In the garden terrace dining room, with a merry blaze in the fireplace when it's cool, Rose serves you Dutch apple pancakes, fresh local fruits, and stories of her celebrity guests. If you stayed overnight in San Juan, the best place in town for breakfast is **Donkey Deli,** 322 Third Street (408–623–4521), serving cappuccino and homemade Danish on the garden patio. (*Sidetrip:* From Rose's, it's just a half-hour over a beautiful mountain road, Highway 152, to the Monterey coast.)

It's an hour's drive from Rose's—through Hollister on Highway 25—to **Pinnacles National Monument,** Paicines (408–389–4485). Spires and crags rising dramatically out of the valley are what's left of an ancient volcano; the other half of the volcano lies 195 miles to the southeast, thanks to the San Andreas Rift Zone. All through the winter and spring, and in the fall after the rains have come, the 1,600-acre wilderness park attracts rock climbers, hikers, cave explorers, and picnickers. Short, easy paths make ferny creeks and mountain views accessible. At the visitor's center, a jewel of a stone building constructed in the 1930s by the Civilian Conservation Corps, pick up trail maps and chat with the rangers. They'll head you toward the Bear Gulch waterfalls, a swimming hole, and a short trail to spooky caves. Midsummer can be extremely hot and dry, with temperatures in the hundreds. A nice private campground at the entrance to the park has a swimming pool: **Pinnacles Campground** (408–389–4462).

Lunch: **La Casa Rosa**, 107 Third Street, San Juan Bautista. (408) 623–4563. A taste of old Spanish days in San Juan; hearty American food in an antiques-filled, pink clapboard house built in 1858. Try the Old California Casserole and the chicken soufflé. Famous treats to take home—chutney, preserves, pickles.

Don't leave town without a loaf of Portuguese bread, panetone, brownies, and a pie from **San Juan Bakery,** 319 Third Street (408–623–4570).

Afternoon

Head back to the Bay Area, stopping along the way to buy wine at **Mirassou Winery,** 3000 Aborn Road, San Jose (408–274–4000), owned by America's oldest winemaking family. Dozens of wineries are located in the Salinas, Gonzales, and Soledad areas. A directory and map of the Salinas Valley/Monterey wine country is available by calling (408) 375–9400.

Still in the mood to shop? Take Highway 680 or 880 from San Jose to Milpitas to the **Great Mall of the Bay Area,** the largest factory outlet center west of the Mississippi, with more than 200 outlet and off-price retailers (447 Great Mall Drive, off the Montague Expressway, 800–945–4022). Dedicated shoppers can get lost in 1.5 million square feet of discount outlets while nonshoppers are entertained in four travel-themed venues: Great Autos, Great Planes, Great Railroads, and Great Ships, each outfitted with antique forms of transport and hands-on play equipment. At a giant sports store, you can "test drive" a baseball batting cage mimicking the pitches of famous hurlers, hit a few on a computerized golf course, shoot a few baskets, and climb a vertical treadmill wall. At a discount sportswear store, a children's play area has three TV screens with first-run kids' movies and a big play area stocked with toys.

The biggest attraction in the mall (besides the stores) is Wonderpark, 30,000 square feet of high-tech arcade games, a carousel, a roller coaster, bumper cars, pinball machines, and *more.*

There's More

Steinbeck House, 132 Central Avenue, Salinas. (408) 424–2735. The perfectly preserved, turreted Victorian where Steinbeck was born and raised, a mecca for his devotees. Unfortunately, not open to the public except for lunch Monday–Friday; small gift shop open seven days. An annual Steinbeck Day includes walking tours of the town and a special lunch at the house.

Christopher Ranch, 305 Bloomfield Avenue, Gilroy. (408) 847–1100. The ultimate source for garlic.

Golf. Ridgemark Golf and Country Club, 3800 Airline Highway, Hollister. (408) 637–8151. Golf, tennnis, lodging, restaurant.

Hollister Hills State Vehicular Recreation Area, 7800 Cienega Road, Hollister. (408) 637–3874. Some 2,400 acres and campground for motorcycles, four-wheel-drive vehicles, and their operators.

San Luis Reservoir State Recreation Area, 30 miles from San Juan, on Highway 152. (209) 826–1196. Three lakes for fishing, swimming, and waterskiing. Most fish species found in the Sacramento Delta are found at San Luis. Windsurfing is very good from March through September.

California Antique Aircraft Museum, San Martin. (408) 683–2290. Many planes from 1928 to the 1950s, such as a Sopwith Pup, a Bowlus Albatross, and a Benson Gyrocopter.

Special Events

May. American Indian Spring Market, San Juan Bautista. (408) 623–2379.

June. Early Days in San Juan. (408) 623–2454. Celebration of the founding of the State Historic Park.

July. Gilroy Garlic Festival, Gilroy. (408) 842–1625. Huge food fair featuring garlic dishes, entertainment, arts and crafts, even garlic ice cream.

July. California Rodeo, Salinas. (408) 757–2951. America's best cowboys and cowgirls compete.

August. Annual Flea Market and Antiques and Collectible Show, on the streets of San Juan. (408) 623–2454.

August. Downtown Micro Brewery and Antique Collectibles Festival, Salinas. (408) 842–6964.

August. Hispanic Cultural Festival, San Juan Bautista. (408) 848–5780.

September. All-Indian Market, San Juan Bautista. (408) 623–2379.

September. Fine Arts and Crafts Show, San Juan Bautista. (408) 623–2454. Some 300 artisans and crafters.

September. Casa DeFruta Wine Festival, Hollister. (408) 842–9316.

October. Halloween at Hecker Pass, Hecker Pass Road, Gilroy. (408) 842–2121. Three weekends of food, rides, haunted tunnel, pumpkin patch, entertainment.

December. Candlelight processions, La Posada, San Juan Bautista. (408) 623–2454.

Other Recommended Restaurants and Lodgings

San Juan Bautista

Felipe's Restaurant and Bar, 313 Third Street. (408) 623–2161. Where the locals go for the best Mexican and Salvadorean food in town. Live music on weekends.

Dona Esther Restaurant, 25 Franklin Street. (408) 623–2518. Authentic Mexican food, bar, live entertainment on weekends.

Betabel RV Resort, 9664 Betabel Road. (408) 623–2202. Nicely landscaped, full hook-ups, heated pool, mini-mart.

Posada de San Juan Inn, 310 Fourth Street. (408) 623–4030. Fireplaces and whirlpool baths in every room.

Mission Farm RV Park, 400 San Juan–Hollister Road on the southeast corner of town, 95045. (408) 623–4456. Old barns, a store, all facilities, simple surroundings in a walnut orchard.

San Juan Inn, 410 Alameda Street. (408) 623–4380. A forty-two-unit motel.

For More Information

San Juan Bautista Chamber of Commerce, 402A Third Street, P.O. Box 1037, San Juan Bautista, CA 95045. (408) 623–2454.

Advice: Midsummer temperatures in San Juan can reach a hundred degrees or more, so bring a hat. Evenings are cool, as sea breezes rise and fog creeps in from the coast.

Santa Cruz, a California Beach Town

The waterfront restaurants of Capitola.

Blue Water Getaway

——————————— 1 NIGHT ———————————
Beaches · Bikes · Butterflies · The Boardwalk
Wineries · Redwoods · Shopping

The resort town of Santa Cruz is famous for more than 20 miles of wide, sandy, warm-water beaches and an old-fashioned waterfront boardwalk with rides and concessions. Here at the top end of Monterey Bay, the climate is mild, surf's up every month of the year, and the attitude is young and healthy, due to a large population of university students and residents who love outdoor recreation.

Rebuilt and restored completely since a major earthquake in 1989, the town has many fanciful Victorian homes and a variety of architectural styles such as Queen Anne, Gothic Revival, Mission Revival, and California bungalow. Pacific Avenue, the main street, is a tree-shaded boulevard with outdoor cafes and dozens of shops. Musical performances take place on Pacific all summer long.

The University of California at Santa Cruz and Cabrillo College are located here and the collegiate community is culturally oriented, with a large contingent of artists and musicians in residence, and a lively annual schedule of arts events and music festivals.

Even if you are not a beach person, there is much in the way of outdoor recreation and sightseeing to enjoy, and not just in the summer. Near the city of Santa Cruz and in the **Santa Cruz Mountains** are country roads that meander through ancient redwood groves and along the banks of the San Lorenzo and Santa Cruz rivers. Walking and biking trails and campgrounds are liberally scattered throughout the region. If kids are along on your escape, don't miss **Roaring Camp,** an 1880s loggers' village with a steam train in the Santa Cruz Mountains.

Day 1

Morning

Drive south from San Francisco on Highway 280 to Highway 1 to **Santa Cruz,** about a one-and-a-half-hour drive, unless it's late Friday afternoon, when it will be a longer trip.

A good way to orient yourself in Santa Cruz and get right to the ocean views is to continue on Highway 17 northwest when you reach the junction with Highway 1 at Santa Cruz, then take the Natural Bridges exit on the north side of Santa Cruz and drive south along West Cliff Drive to **Mark Abbott Memorial Lighthouse** at Lighthouse Point Park overlooking Monterey Bay and the city. Walkers, bikers, joggers, and passengers in baby strollers love the city, sea, and sea lion views from West Cliff Drive. Go into the lighthouse to see a small surfing museum, the only one in the world (408–429–3429).

Almost every day there are surfers in "Steamers Lane" below. In June, the **Longboard Invitational** is held here and hundreds of surfers from all over the world compete (408–684–1551). If there is a surfer in your family, he or she will be blown away by the great surfing in the Santa Cruz area. **Club Ed** at **Cowell Beach** is the place for lessons and board rentals (408–462–6083). A service of the Santa Cruz City Beach Lifeguards, the Surf Report gives weather and water conditions from Memorial Day through Labor Day (408–429–3460). **Twin Lakes State Beach** below East Cliff Drive is where the windsurfers go. There are fire rings here, outdoor showers, and, nearby, wild bird sanctuaries (408–688–3241) at **Schwan Lagoon** and **Schwan Lake.** Prowl around (watching out for poison oak) to see Virginia rail, chickadees, swallows, and belted kingfishers, among dozens more species of birds and waterfowl. You can kayak and canoe on the lake and there is a birdwatching platform.

The main Santa Cruz beach at the boardwalk and the pier, Cowell Beach (408–429–3747) is the most popular piece of sand on the central coastline for sunning, swimming, and volleyball. A special beach-going wheelchair is available from the lifeguard.

Proceed on West Cliff Drive to Pacific Garden Mall, the main street. Almost completely flattened by an earthquake in October of 1989, downtown Santa Cruz arose from the splinters and piles of brick into twenty-nine blocks of new and reconstructed boutiques, sidewalk cafes, coffeehouses, and galleries, over 200 stores in all. The tree-lined, flower-bedecked boulevard is loved by the browser and the coffeehouse sitter. Book lovers should make a beeline to the restored St. George Hotel building at Pacific and Front to **Bookshop Santa Cruz** (408–423–0900), one of the largest bookstores in Northern California. Destroyed in its previous incarnation, the store survived in a tent and reopened in these vast new digs to become, once again, the hub of Pacific Avenue for local and visitor alike. Scattered throughout are benches, stools, and armchairs, comfortable spots to peruse the books and the huge variety of domestic and international magazines and newspapers. There is a cafe in the store, also.

A unique cafe downtown (1415 Pacific, 408–429–8484), **Memphis Minnie's,** with lace curtains, a pressed-tin ceiling, and lazily revolving fans, is a bit of New Orleans presided over by a brilliant young chef who turns out crawfish and andouille gumbo, catfish with black-eyed peas, and sweet potato pie.

At the corner of Pacific and Cooper, **Pacific Wave** is headquarters for surfboards, skateboards, and all the cool accessories and clothing to go with them (408–458–9283).

An example of how the shops on Pacific are now upscale, even chic, compared to the old days when the businesses catered to street-people and students, **Shen's Gallery** (1368 Pacific, 408–425–0525) is seductive with exotic scents, flute sounds, and Asian antiques and art. They have a large collection of one-of-a-kind tiny ceramic teapots from mainland China, "shard" boxes, and beautiful tea chests. Notice the storefront of **Bead It** (1325 Pacific, 408–426–0779)—bead appetizers, bead entrees, bead desserts.

Step into **Zoccoli's** for a deli sandwich or just smell the Italian meats, cheeses, and pastries (1534 Pacific, 408–423–1711).

The **Santa Cruz Art League,** nearby at 526 Broadway (408–426–5787), has three galleries and a shop selling fine arts and crafts.

Lunch: **Costa Brava,** 1222 Pacific Avenue. (408) 425–7871. An urban oasis with exceptional Latin American cuisine, black granite tables, banquettes, open kitchen. A Culinary Institute of America–trained chef creates applewood- and mesquite-smoked entrees such as Peruvian prawns brochette with Mandarin orange glaze, ribeye steak in garlic-cilantro butter, world-class flan. Sunday afternoon live jazz makes this a place to linger.

Afternoon

Proceed to the foot of Beach Street for a walk on mile-long **Santa Cruz Beach** or go to the **Santa Cruz Beach Boardwalk,** the only beachside amusement park on the West Coast, to indulge in some of the twenty-five rides, the old-time arcade, the shops, and restaurants (408–423–5590). The classic 1911 carousel and the Giant Dipper roller coaster are National Historic Landmarks. At Neptune's Kingdom, an indoor miniature golf course, volcanos erupt, pirates threaten, cannons fire. If you hear screaming, it's probably coming from the $5 million roller coaster, the Hurricane, guaranteed to make you forget your name. Get rid of your spare cash in the Casino Arcade or just sit on the boardwalk and watch the bikinis and the sailboats glide by.

Within sight of the boardwalk, **Santa Cruz Municipal Wharf** (408–429–3628) is all about fishing off the pier, shopping in tourist traps, browsing the fresh fish markets, eating chowder and shrimp cocktail in waterside cafes, and watching the sea lions, the pelicans, and the passing boats. Deep-sea fishing trips and bay cruises start from here.

On the south side of Santa Cruz, **Santa Cruz Harbor** (408–475–6161) and its beach are where the locals go to escape the tourists. You can kayak and sail, and have a sandwich at **Aldo's Harbor Restaurant** on the sunny dockside deck (408–426–3736).

Drive south 4 miles from the Santa Cruz Wharf on East Cliff Drive to **Capitola Village** (or, take the quicker, less-winding route, Highway 1). An oceanside resort since 1861, Capitola remains a quaint artists' colony, one-tenth the size of Santa Cruz. Swimmers, waders, and sunbathers flock to **Capitola Beach,** sheltered by two high cliffs. A riparian shelter for birds and ducks, **Soquel Creek** rushes right through town into the sea. Restaurants with outdoor patios are lined up at beachfront on the Esplanade and there are a few blocks of boutiques, art galleries, and beachwear shops.

Dinner: **Shadowbrook Restaurant,** 1750 Wharf Road, Capitola. (408) 475–1511. On the banks of Soquel Creek, reached by self-operated cable car down a flower-bedecked hillside or by a winding pathway. Romantic, live music, reservations absolutely necessary. Winner of many awards for continental and California cuisine, outdoor terrace. Sunday brunch, too.

Lodging: **Inn at Depot Hill,** 250 Monterey Avenue, Capitola. (408) 462–3376. Eight suites with fireplaces, featherbeds, marble bathrooms, private garden patios, hot tubs, European traditional furnishings, and antiques. Award-winning luxury and service. Wonderful breakfasts, walking distance to Capitola Beach.

Day 2

Morning

Breakfast: **Zelda's,** #203 on the Esplanade at the beach. (408) 475–4900). Sit by the window or on the deck while the early morning sea turns from rosy to silver-blue as it laps Capitola's scruffy old fishing pier. Home-fry scramble, blackened snapper with eggs. Zelda's is a fun hangout any time of day, live jazz on the weekends.

Capitola Beach and most public beaches in the area are cleaned nightly; even in the summer they start out trash-free and pearly white every day.

The shops and galleries near the beach are touristy but fun. **Draginwood** (216 Capitola Avenue, 408–475–0915) sells crystals and magical chotchkes. **Capitola Dreams** (118 Stockton Avenue, 408–476–5379) has an eye-popping collection of bikinis and wild beachwear. Painted wood gewgaws and jewelry from Thailand are featured at **Oceania** (204 Capitola Avenue, 408–476–6644). For a hundred stores in an indoor mall, go up the hill to the Capitola Mall on Forty-first Avenue (408–476–9749).

Capitola Beach sports a small fishing pier; licenses are not required. Join in a volleyball game on the beach or walk south to **New Brighton Beach** (408–475–4850). There is a nice campground here where cypress and pines provide a sense of privacy between campsites. Surf fishing and clamming are good, and from here a continuous stretch of sandy beach runs 15 miles, all the way south to the **Pajaro River.**

The next beach south of New Brighton, **Seacliff State Beach** at **Del Mar** has almost 2 miles of shoreline backed by steep sandstone cliffs. A 500-foot wooden pier and the wreck of a concrete ship are roosting spots for birds, and you can fish off the pier. There is a campground and a small visitor's center where you can sign up for walking tours to see the fossilized remains of multimillion-year-old sea creatures lodged in the cliffsides (408–688–7146).

Just south of Capitola at **Aptos, Rio Del Mar Beach** is a wide stretch of sand with a jetty and lifeguards. Shopping and restaurants are within walking distance (408–688–3241).

Accessed from the next little town south of Aptos, La Selva Beach, **Manresa State Beach** is popular with surfers and campers (408–761–1795).

On the north side of Highway 1, just south of Capitola, the village of Aptos is where you'll find **Aptos Antiques,** behind the Bay View Hotel on Soquel Road (408–662–2421). This is a big antiques collection in a huge old barn, a place for losing track of time.

Lunch: **The Veranda at the Bay View Hotel,** 8041 Soquel Drive, Aptos. (408) 685–1881. In a huge Italianate mansion, California cuisine, corn fritters with Smithfield ham, shiitake mushroom ravioli, Southwest ceasar salad, roast pork and chicken, fresh fish. The Bay View has nice bed-and-breakfast rooms upstairs (800–422–9843).

Afternoon

A cool, green place to take a walk in the highlands near Santa Cruz is the **Forest of Nisene Marks State Park,** a densely forested 10,000-acre wilderness on **Aptos Creek** (408–335–9145). Popular with runners, bikers, horseback riders, hikers, and picnickers, the park ranges in elevation from 100 to 2,600 feet. Unpaved roads and trails lead to a wide variety of mixed evergreen woods and creekside willows and ferns. Walk-in camping is permitted, as are horseback riding and steelhead fishing in certain areas.

Near the entrance to the park, **Mangels House** is a bed and breakfast in a wedding-cake-white circa-1880 mansion, with six rooms (408–688–7982).

A beautiful beach that makes a nice stop on the way home from Santa Cruz is **Natural Bridges State Beach,** a few minutes north of Santa Cruz on Highway 1 (408–425–4609). Named for dramatic sandstone arches, Natural Bridges has tidepools rich with sea life; guided tidepool tours are often conducted. A short boardwalk from the beach parking lot leads through a eucalyptus forest to the **California Monarch Butterfly Preserve.** Depending on the time of year—early October through March is best—you'll see hundreds of thousands of butterflies hanging in the trees and moving about in great golden clouds. A .75-mile self-guided nature walk begins at the Monarch trail and heads for Secret Lagoon, where blue herons, mallard ducks, and more freshwater and seagoing birds live.

Long Marine Laboratory and Aquarium, a University of Santa Cruz research facility near Natural Bridges, is open to the public (408–459–2883). In addition to the aquarium are an eighty-five-foot blue whale skeleton and "touch tanks" where kids can pick up sea animals.

If you have time to spare on your way back to San Francisco, dawdle in the Santa Cruz Mountains among ancient redwood groves, on sunny river banks, and in quiet little resort towns affording peaceful getaway days. Discover rustic boutique wineries, known for their dark Pinots and German varietals. Take a ride on a rollicking steam train, chugging up into redwood country or all the way down to the beach (more on the mountains, below).

Retrace your route back to San Francisco.

There's More

Henry Cowell State Park, 101 North Big Trees Park Road, Felton. (408) 335–4598. Eighteen hundred acres of stream canyons, meadows, forests, and chaparral-covered ridges along the meandering San Lorenzo River and Eagle Creek. Short, easy trails, such as **Redwood Grove Nature Trail** to the **Big Trees Grove,** offer a rare opportunity to see first-growth redwoods. Besides BIG redwoods and pines, you'll see sycamore, elders, madrone, manzanita, California poppies, doves, quail, waterfowl, deer, and maybe poison oak. The redwood-dotted campground in the park has over a hundred tent and RV sites, for vehicles up to 24 feet, with no hook-ups (408–438–2396).

Felton Covered Bridge. Built in 1892, this is the tallest bridge of its kind in the country and one of the few left in the state.

Antonelli Brothers Begonia Gardens, 2545 Capitola Road between Capitola and Santa Cruz. (408) 475–5222. This is a showplace of more hanging begonias, ferns, and indoor plants of all kinds than you can imagine, at their blooming best in late summer and fall. There are picnic tables in the Hanging Begonia Room.

Wilder Ranch State Park, 1401 Coast Road, 2 miles north of Santa Cruz. (408) 423–9703. A 5,000-acre working ranch since the 1800s. Stroll in and out of the old barns, homes, and gardens.

Big Basin Redwoods State Park, off Highway 236 near Boulder Creek in the Santa Cruz Mountains. (408) 338–6132. Thousand-year-old redwoods, fern canyons, the Bay Area's most wonderful waterfalls; a round-trip hike to the falls takes four to five hours. There are 50 miles of shorter trails. The Sea Trail drops from mountain ridges to

Waddell State Beach through dense woodlands, along Waddell and Berry creeks; waterfalls, sea and mountain views, 11 miles one-way. Bike, horse rentals.

Roaring Camp and Big Trees Narrow-Gauge Railroad, just south of Felton on Graham Hill Road in the Santa Cruz Mountains. (408) 335–4484. A re-creation of an 1880s logging town, complete with covered bridge, general store, and a wonderful narrow-gauge steam train that you can ride up through forests of giant redwoods to the summit of Bear Mountain on the steepest railroad grade in North America. A second route runs along the San Lorenzo River down to Santa Cruz Beach. A chuckwagon barbecue serves charcoal broiled steak and chicken burgers in a forest glade, or you can have your own picnic on the mountain.

Wineries in the Santa Cruz Mountains: David Bruce Winery, Bear Creek Road east of Boulder Creek. (408) 354–4214. One of California's gold-medal makers of Pinot Noir and Chardonnay. Open for tasting on the weekends, by appointment during the week.

Byington Winery and Vineyard is on Bear Creek, too, with dizzying views of Monterey Bay from the picnic grounds (408–354–1111).

Bonny Doon Vineyard, 10 Pine Flat Road, 8 miles west of Bear Creek Road via the beautiful Felton-Empire Road. (408) 425–3625. The winemaker has made his wines famous with crazy labels like Clos de Gilroy, Le Cigare Volant, Big House Red, and Old Telegram. Hang out in the redwood grove on Soquel Creek and try his European "ice wines," produced in just a handful of American wineries.

Hallcrest Vineyards, Felton-Empire Road. (408) 335–4441. Specializing in organic Gewürztraminers, Rieslings, and grape juices.

Wineries near Santa Cruz: Devlin Wine Cellars, at the end of a country road, 3801 Park Road off Soquel Drive just south of Soquel. (408) 476–7288. Luscious dessert wine, Muscat Canelli, and several other varieties. Picnickers are welcome amid thirty acres of redwoods.

Bargetto Winery, 3535 North Main Street, Soquel. (408) 475–2258. Overlooking Soquel Creek, a scenic spot where you can buy homemade fruit wines and vinegars—raspberry, olallieberry, and apricot.

Von's Garden, 2701 Monterey Avenue, Soquel. (408) 462–4255. Fresh and dried flowers, orchids, exotic plants, vegetables, and herbs.

Apple Barn, 1765 Hames Road, Aptos. (408) 724–8119. Seventeen kinds of apples, fresh juice and cider.

Santa Cruz County Cycling Club, 414 Soquel Avenue, Santa Cruz. (408) 423–0829. Day trips, map of area bikeways.

Boating: Chardonnay Sailing Charters, 704 Soquel Avenue, Santa Cruz. (408) 423–1213.

Pacific Yachting, 790 Mariner Park Way, Santa Cruz. (408) 476–2370. Day tours.

Kayak Connection, 413 Lake Avenue, Santa Cruz. (408) 479–1121. Tours, lessons, rentals, no experience necessary.

Golf: Pasatiempo Golf Club, 18 Clubhouse Road, off Highway 17 near Santa Cruz. (408) 459–9155. One of the top one hundred courses in the United States. Top-notch restaurant.

Boulder Creek Golf and Country Club, 16901 Big Basin Highway, Boulder Creek. (408) 338–2121. Eighteen beauiful holes in the redwoods, restaurant, tennis.

Aptos Seascape Golf Course, 610 Clubhouse Drive, Aptos. (408) 688–3213. Eighteen holes by the sea.

DeLaveaga Golf Course, Upper Park Road at DeLaveaga Drive, Santa Cruz. (408) 423–7212. Eighteen holes.

Special Events

February. Migration Festival, Natural Bridges State Beach, Santa Cruz. (408) 423–4609. The monarchs are celebrated at the largest butterfly colony in the west.

March. Carnaval Santa Cruz, Civic Auditorium, Santa Cruz. (408) 429–1324. Brazilian and Caribbean festival, music, dancing, refreshments.

April. Amazing Egg Hunt, Roaring Camp. (408) 335–4484. Ten thousand eggs.

May. Art and Wine Festival, Boulder Creek. (800) 833–3494.

May. Civil War Memorial, Roaring Camp. (408) 335–4484. Re-enactment of Civil War battles and camp life, the largest encampment in the United States.

May. Longboard Invitational, Steamers Lane, Santa Cruz. (408) 684–1551. Hundreds of surfers compete. Watch from Cliff Drive.

June. Redwood Mountain Faire, Felton. (800) 833–3494.

June. Art on the Wharf, Santa Cruz Municipal Wharf. (408) 429–3477. Art show and live jazz.

June. Japanese Cultural Fair, Mission Plaza, Santa Cruz. (408) 429–3778. Celebration of Japanese-American culture, arts, foods, and entertainment.

July. Jumpin' Frog Contest, Roaring Camp. (408) 335–4484.

August. Artist's Weekend, Soquel. (800) 833–3494.

August. Cabrillo Music Festival, 9053 Soquel Drive, Aptos. (408) 662–2701. On the Cabrillo College campus, an internationally acclaimed two-week musical extravaganza.

September. National Begonia Festival, Capitola. (408–476–3566). Residents vie for awards for their spectacular waterborne floats that are maneuvered perilously down Soquel Creek into town; you've never seen a watery parade like this one

October. Roaring Camp Harvest Fair. (408) 335–4484. 1880s crafts, demonstrations, pumpkin carving, free pumpkins.

October. Brussels Sprout and Italian Heritage Festival, Santa Cruz. (408) 423–5590.

November. Christmas Craft and Gift Festival, Santa Cruz. (408) 423–5590.

December. Children's International Holiday Gift and Food Faire, Santa Cruz Civic Auditorium, Santa Cruz. (408) 429–3765.

Other Recommended Restaurants and Lodgings

Santa Cruz

Babbling Brook Inn, 1025 Laurel Street. (800) 866–1131. Country French bed-and-breakfast inn, lovely gardens, full breakfast. Ask for a room near the creek.

Indian Joze, 1001 Center Street. (408) 427–3554. Indoor/outdoor cafe in leafy surroundings. Middle Eastern, Mediterranean, and Asian specialties of the day might include calamari saté, red snapper in curry, pecan pie. Decor is bright and light, featuring squid mobiles and folk art.

Beach Street Cafe, on the corner of Beach and Cliff streets across from the boardwalk. (408) 426–7621. The walls are literally covered with prints by Maxwell Parrish, a famous pre–art deco artist. Bistro food, espresso.

Chateau Victorian, 118 First Street. (408) 458–9458. Hidden away on a side street, just a half-block from the beach and boardwalk, a hundred-year-old passionate purple Victorian with a sunny garden and seven small rooms with fireplaces. Interiors are opulently of the era, the big continental breakfast is satisfying, and proprietors Franz and Alice-June are charmers (be sure to ask them how they met). Over late afternoon wine and hors d'oeuvres, Alice-June will fill you in on sights and restaurants.

Chaminade at Santa Cruz, 1 Chaminade Lane. (800) 283–6569. An executive retreat, resort, and a restaurant in a eucalyptus forest on a hill overlooking Monterey Bay on the south side of Santa Cruz. Fitness center, lighted tennis courts, pool. Suites are often available and this is a good place for families to stay. Sunday brunch here is legendary.

Casablanca, 101 Main Street. (408) 426–9063. Overlooking beach and boardwalk, elegant, candlelit, fresh seafood, notable wine list, winetasting dinners.

Cliff Crest, 407 Cliff Street. (408) 427–2609. A Queen Anne mansion built in 1887 with five guest rooms, antiques throughout, four-poster beds, claw-foot tubs. On a quiet street 2 blocks from the sea and the boardwalk.

Villa Vista, 2-2800 East Cliff Drive, ten minutes from downtown. (408) 866–2626. Two perfectly wonderful condo units with living rooms, each with three master bedrooms with baths, gourmet kitchen, seaview patio, home entertaiment center, and laundry facilities. Great for several couples or a large family.

Santa Cruz Brewing Company, 516 Front Street. (408) 429–8838. A microbrewery with tours and tastings of porter, lager, root beer, and seasonal brews.

Capitola

Seafood Mama, 820 Bay Avenue at the Crossroads Center, 1 block from Highway 1. (408) 476–5976. A casual cafe with a juke box and charcoal grill. The menu is printed every day with a huge variety of fresh seafood.

Gayle's Bakery and Rosticceria, 504 Bay Avenue, on the corner of Bay and Capitola avenues. (408) 462–1127. Homemade pasta, salad, pizza, sandwiches, spit-roasted meats. The bakery is famous for pies, cheesecake, breads, and pastries.

Capitola Venetian Hotel, 1500 Wharf Road. (800) 528–1234. On the beach, a 1920s Mediterranean pink stucco motel, unassuming eclectic/eccentric decor, kitchens. Reasonable rates for families and groups.

El Salto Resort, 620 El Salto Drive. (408) 462–6365. In a luxurious garden overlooking Monterey Bay, beautifully furnished Victorian guestrooms, cottages, and apartments. Continental breakfast.

Aptos

Broken Egg and Crepe Cafe, 7887 Soquel Drive, Aptos. (408) 688–4322. Indoor or outdoor breakfast, lunch, and dinner, a favorite for more than two decades.

Seascape Resort, 1 Seascape Resort Drive off San Andreas, south of Santa Cruz. (800) 929–7727. Studio, one-, and two-bedroom condos for up to eight people, restaurant with a bay view. Swimming pool. Adjacent to Aptos Seascape Golf Course and the Sports Club with tennis courts, Olympic pool, and gym.

Cafe Sparrow, 8042 Soquel Drive. (408) 688–6238. Country French ambiance with floral cotton ceiling and tablecloths, baskets of fresh flowers. Lunch, dinner, and weekend brunch. Salads, fresh seafood, vegetarian specialties, lamb, and filet mignon, everything created in-house.

Boulder Creek

Boulder Creek Lodge and Conference Center, 16901 Big Basin Highway, a few minutes west of Boulder Creek on Highway 236. (408–338–2111). Condo units, eighteen-hole golf course, tennis, swimming pools, in a glorious redwood forest setting.

Big Basin Redwood State Park, 21600 Big Basin Way. (800) 444–7275. One hundred forty-seven camp sites, thirty-six tent cabins, showers, snack bar, store, trails. No hookups.

Watsonville

Santa Cruz KOA Kampground, 1186 San Andreas Road off Highway 1. (408) 722–0551. Two hundred forty tent and RV sites, cabins, pool, store, hot tubs, all facilities, lively atmosphere, near beaches.

Pajaro Dunes, 2661 Beach Road, just south of Santa Cruz. (800) 675–8808. Condos and homes to rent on a long, sandy beach.

Ben Lomond

Tyrolean Inn and Cottages, 9600 Highway 9. (408) 336–5188. Seven simple cottages, walking distance to town and river, German/American restaurant.

Felton

Griffin's Fern River Resort, 5250 Highway 9. (408) 335–4412. Nice little red housekeeping cabins, some fireplaces, on four acres of lawns, trees, and fern gardens, private sandy river beach, adjacent to Cowell Park and Roaring Camp.

Henry Cowell Redwood State Park, 101 North Big Trees Park. (408) 438–2396. One hundred twelve camp sites in the mountains, hiking in the redwoods, trailers to 24 feet, campers to 31 feet, no hook-ups.

For More Information

Santa Cruz Visitors Bureau, 701 Front Street, Santa Cruz 95060. (408) 425–1234.

San Lorenzo Valley Chamber of Commerce, Boulder Creek. (408) 335–2764.

Santa Cruz Mountains Winegrowers, P.O. Box 3000, Santa Cruz 95063. (408) 479–WINE. Free brochure and map describing nineteen wineries.

MISTIX. (800) 444–7275. State campground reservations.

Half Moon Bay

Waterfront at Pillar Point Harbor in Half Moon Bay.

Harbor Lights, Tidepool Treasure

_____ 2 NIGHTS _____

Beaches, bikes, hikes, fishing • Lions of the sea
Art and antiques • Flower marts, veggie farms

The small Victorian town of Half Moon Bay and the beaches and harbors nearby hold several days' worth of discoveries. Accessibility to the San Francisco Bay Area, good weather, sea air, and the outdoor fun to be had here are what create bumper-to-bumper traffic at times on summer weekends. Weekdays and off-season are the times to come, although you can get pleasantly lost and alone in the redwoods or on the beach any day of the year.

Besides commercial ocean fishing, the important endeavor in Half Moon Bay is flower and vegetable growing. The annual Pumpkin and Art Festival and Great Pumpkin Parade in October draw hundreds of thousands of revelers and their children.

Within huge greenhouses and in the fields around them, flowers such as carnations, roses, tulips, and irises are grown for shipment all over the world, and you can buy plants and flowers—and Christmas trees—at several places along the highways.

A stroll through the town of Half Moon Bay turns up Western saloons, country stores, fancy boutiques, galleries, and hundred-year-old hotels and homes, many on the National Register of Historic Places.

At the north end of the big curve of the bay, Pillar Point Harbor is a good place to escape the tourist mania. You can watch fishing boats and yachts go in and out of the marina, fish for flounder and rockfish from the wharf, or go shelling on the little beach west of the jetty. South along the coast within an hour of Half Moon Bay, beaches, nature preserves (including one of the most unusual in the world), and two tiny old villages await the visitor.

Day 1

Morning

Drive south from San Francisco on Highway 1, along the Pacific Coast through **Pacifica** to **Moss Beach,** an hour's drive. This estimated time does not account for heavy weekend and holiday traffic.

South of Pacifica after San Pedro Beach, the road narrows and clings precariously to the steep cliff for a mile or so, dropping off 2,000 feet on the sea side to rocks and surf. This is **Devil's Slide,** where earthquakes and heavy rains have historically destroyed the road from time to time, as recently as the winter of 1995. You are perfectly safe now, but in the near future, a new road or a tunnel will replace this spectacular but fragile piece of roadway.

The **Fitzgerald Marine Reserve** in Moss Beach (415–728–3584) is a good place to get out and stretch your legs. A walking trail loops through meadows and along a bluff above some of the richest tide pools on the Pacific Coast. At low tide, a kaleidoscope of sponges, sea anemones, starfish, crabs, molluscs, and fish emerges. With a special fishing license, you can take abalone and some rock fish. For the best tidepooling, call ahead to find out when the low tides are scheduled. Docent tours are available.

The best place to stay in Moss Beach is the **Seal Cove Inn,** a big yellow mansion in an English garden on the edge of the Marine Reserve (415–728–7325). Built and operated by a long-time writer of guidebooks on bed-and-breakfasts inns, the inn is a classic, with spacious, luxurious public rooms and guest rooms, all with garden views, woodburning fireplaces, and traditional furnishings. A full breakfast and afternoon wine and hors d'oeuvres are served.

Between the inn and the Marine Reserve are a wild English garden and wildflower meadows. From here, you can walk to the beach and walk, bike, or drive on country roads a couple of miles south to **Pillar Point Harbor** at Princeton-by-the-Sea, a picturesque harbor busy with a fleet of more than 200 fishing boats and yachts. Park in the harbor parking lot and walk on trails to beaches and marshlands on both the north and south sides of the harbor. Pillar Point Marsh is a favorite birdwatching site. Due to the confluence of both fresh- and saltwater, and a protected environment, nearly 20 percent of all North American bird species have been sighted here, including great blue herons, snowy egrets, and red-winged blackbirds.

Fishermen cast their lines into the ocean from the rocky jetty; to the west of the jetty is a seashell-scattered beach.

From December through April, whale-watching boats depart from the wharf. You are almost guaranteed to see California gray whales on their 4,000-mile migration from the Arctic to Baja. **Captain John's** (415–726–2913) and **Huck Finn Sportfishing** (415–726–7133) are charter companies based at the harbor that offer regular fishing and whale-watching expeditions. Huck Finn also has a bait-and-tackle store here that sells fishing licenses. Rock fishing is year-round, salmon fishing seasonal, and whale-watching is in the wintertime.

Just south of the harbor, Surfer's Beach is popular not only for surfing but for ocean kayaking, boogie boarding, wind surfing, and jet skiing.

Two fish markets at the harbor sell a huge variety of fresh, locally caught seafood, and there are several small cafes and bars frequented by locals who wouldn't be caught dead in the trendy downtown establishments of nearby Half Moon Bay.

Lunch: **Ketch Joanne and the Harbor Bar,** 25 Johnson Pier, Pillar Point Harbor, Princeton. (415–728–3747). A bowl of clam chowder in a booth next to the wood stove can be a warm experience. The fish is fresh daily from the Ketch Joanne Fish Market.

Afternoon

Save at least half a day for browsing Main Street in Half Moon Bay, a few blocks of buildings built early in the century that are now inhabited by upscale, country-chic shops, cafes, and galleries. On the south end of the street at 604 Main in a terra-cotta–colored enclave called **La**

Piazza are several shops of note and a popular bakery serving coffee drinks and pastries in a streetside cafe (**Moonside Bakery,** 415–726–9070). **Sterling Road Silversmiths** here has the most eye-popping collection of hand-wrought silver belt buckles and jewelry this side of Santa Fe (415–712–0643). **Calico Barn** specializes in teddy bears and quilting fabrics and kits (415–726–9646).

At La Piazza and at the William Adams Simmons House at 751 Kelly Avenue, the **Joan Baker Gallery** shows realistic and impressionist works by leading California contemporary artists (415–726–3888).

Other shops on Main include **Quail Run** (412 Main, 415–726–0312), a nature-oriented emporium with elaborate bird mansions for the feathered few and butterfly gardens for kids; the **Coastal Gallery** (424 Main in a garden alley, 415–726–3859), with rooms full of prints, oil paintings, and watercolors by regional artists, including the regionally famous Thomas Kinkade; and **Native American Arts** (444 Main, 415–726–6723), which will lure you in with bright rugs hung all the way up a stairway, leading to a large gallery of Native American jewelry, kachinas, clothing, and fetishes. If you have time to visit only one shop on Main Street, go to **Cedanna,** a gallery store loaded with one-of-a-kind avant garde artisans' inventions such as iron furniture, mirrors, handmade cards, jewelry, photo frames, prints, and painted fantasies (400 Main at Mill, 415–726–6776).

One of the oldest established businesses in town, **Cunha's** (448 Main, 415–726–4071) is a grocery with a large deli and perfect fruits for picnics, their own line of homemade packaged gourmet foods, and, upstairs, Western boots, hats, souvenirs, hardware, and T-shirts. On the corner across from Cunha's, the city has set up a nice picnic table area.

At the north end of Main, **The Tinnery** is another indoor mall crammed with small shops and cafes, including a sushi bar, a coffee cafe, a card shop, and a gallery.

Dinner: **San Benito House,** 356 Main Street, Half Moon Bay. (415) 726–3425. A renowned European country–style place in a historic building serving Mediterranean cuisine, named by *National Geographic Traveler* as the finest restaurant on the coast between San Francisco and Monterey. Garden patio.

Lodging: **Half Moon Bay Lodge,** 2400 South Cabrillo Highway (Highway 1) on the south end of Half Moon Bay. (800) 368–2468. Eighty spacious rooms with small patios or balconies overlooking lovely gardens and lawns, traditional furnishings, comforters, some fireplaces; swimming pool, large, enclosed spa. Many extras such as borrowable best sellers, free coffee, personalized luggage tags, down pillows, beach blankets.

Adjacent to the lodge is one of the best golf courses in the state.

Ask about Golf Getaway packages. Less than five minutes from here, you can walk or bike a coastal trail that runs along the bluffs above the beaches several miles to Princeton-by-the-Sea. The easiest part of the trail is a 3-mile path between Kelly Avenue at Half Moon Bay and Mirada Road in Miramar. Beaches are accessible all along the way.

Day 2

Morning

Breakfast: **Main Street Grill,** 435 Main at Kelly, Half Moon Bay. (415) 726–5300. Cajun sausage, artichoke omelettes, and homemade waffles and muffins. Also good for lunch: grilled sandwiches, thick milkshakes, microbrewed beers, and a juke box.

South from Half Moon Bay along Highway 1 are a string of beaches, wildlife preserves, and two tiny historic towns. It's 15 miles to the **Pescadero State Beach,** one of the prettiest, duniest, tidepooliest places you could spend an afternoon (415–726–6238). On the inland side of Highway 1, **Pescadero Marsh** is 588 acres of uplands and wetlands, an important stop on the Pacific Flyway. Over 200 species of waterfowl and shorebirds make this a must-see for avid birders, or for anyone wishing to walk the trails through the marsh (415–726–6238). Thousands of birds rest and feed here. Great blue herons nest in the blue gum eucalyptus trees, egrets walk stiffly in the shallow waters, northern harriers glide above, marsh wrens follow you around. Late fall and early spring are the best times to see the birds.

It's 2 miles from Highway 1 on Pescadero Road to **Pescadero,** a block or so of clapboard buildings and steepled churches, circa 1850. On weekend afternoons and evenings and on Sunday mornings, Duarte's Tavern is busy, as it has been for over fifty years, with diners going for the cioppino, the fresh seafood specialties with a Portuguese accent, artichoke soup, deep fried calamari, and the ollalieberry pie (202 Stage Road, 415–879–0464).

A half-mile beyond the town on Pescadero Road, park under the giant oak and get out your camera at **Phipps Ranch** (415–879–0787), a combination produce market, farm, plant nursery, and menagerie of exotic birds and farm animals. Among the cacophony of sounds are parrots' squawks, green and orange canaries' songs, and peacocks' trumpetings. There are fancy chickens, big fat pigs, a variety of bunnies, and antique farm equipment. You can pick your own berries or buy them at the produce stand.

A real sleeper of a park and campground, **Butano State Park** off Pescadero Road is a lush piece of the earth, with magnificent redwood groves freshened by creeks and ferny glades (2 miles past Pescadero, turn right onto Cloverdale Road, 5 miles to park entrance, 800–444–7275). From small, pretty campsites you can walk streamside paths or take a challenging mountain hike on an 11-mile loop to the **Año Nuevo Island** lookout.

Back on the highway, proceed south; it's 22 miles to **Davenport,** where you'll have lunch. On the way are the 115-foot tall **Pigeon Point Lighthouse,** which houses a unique youth hostel, and a scattering of beautiful beaches, tide pools (best ones just north of the lighthouse), wind-bent cypress, wildflower meadows, and fields of vegetables.

Proceed to the village of Davenport for lunch (36 miles south of Half Moon Bay).

Lunch: **New Davenport Cash Store Restaurant and Inn** on Highway 1 at Davenport (408–425–1818). Tuck into grilled chicken sandwiches, homemade soup, omelettes with homemade chorizo, big killer brownies, fresh fruit from nearby farms. The gift shop sells guidebooks and a top-notch array of African masks, Turkish jewelry, Mexican crafts, and Santa Fe jewelry. Breakfast and brunch are very popular here on the weekends, and definitely worth the wait. Upstairs is a casually comfy bed-and-breakfast operation.

Afternoon

If art glass is one of your interests, don't miss the **Lundborg Studios** (down the road a block or so—ask for directions), a mecca for aficionados of Tiffany-style lamps and art deco paperweights (408–423–2532).

Across Highway 1 from the restaurant are a short walking path on the bluffs and a nice beach.

Returning north 9 miles, stop at **Año Nuevo State Reserve,** which may turn out to be the highlight of your trip on the Central coast (415–879–0595). On 1,200 acres of dunes and beaches, the largest groups of elephant seals in the world come to breed from December through April. A .5-mile walk through grassy dunes brings you to an unforgettable sight: dozens of two-ton animals lounging, arguing, maybe mating, cavorting in the sea, and wiggling around on the beach. As many as 2,500 seals spend their honeymoons here and there's lots of other wildlife to see, too. During the mating season, it is necessary to reserve spaces in guided interpretive tours (800–444–7275). At other times, you can wander around on your own, but are not allowed to come too close to the animals.

Dinner: **Duarte's Tavern,** 202 Stage Road, Pescadero. (415) 879–0464. See description above.

Lodging: Half Moon Bay Lodge. See above.

Day 3

Morning

Breakfast: **Cafe Classique,** corner of Granada and Sevilla, across the road from Pillar Point Harbor. (415) 726–9775. Big cappucinos, monster muffins, and croissants, breakfast and lunch.

Before leaving the Half Moon Bay area, stock up on some of the fresh fruits, veggies, plants, and flowers that are grown here. **The Lemos Family Farm** (12320 Highway 92, Half Moon Bay, 415–726–2342) not only sells flowers, vegetables, and Christmas trees, they keep kids busy with a petting zoo, pony rides, and hayrides, with live music in the fall and special annual events. Since 1926, the **Andreotti Family Farm** has sold fresh-picked fruits and veggies, juices, eggs, garlic, and vinegars year-round (Kelly Avenue on the way to the beach, 415–726–9151). **Cypress Flower Farm,** open on the weekends, sells fresh and dried flowers, wreaths, and other home accessories made of dried flowers (333 Cypress Avenue off Highway 1, near Seal Cove Inn, 415–728–0728).

Lunch: On your way back to San Francisco on Highway 1, have lunch at the **Moss Beach Distillery** (Beach and Ocean, Moss Beach, 415–728–5595). Said to be haunted by the Blue Lady, who wanders the nearby cliffs where she died mysteriously in the 1930s. On a spectacular hilltop overlooking a cove, with an outdoor patio and indoor dining room and bar with sea views, luscious fresh local seafood for lunch, dinner, and weekend brunch.

There's More

Bach Dancing and Dynamite Society, P.O. Box 302, El Granada 94018, at Miramar Beach, 2.5 miles north of Half Moon Bay. (415) 726–4143. Begun in a private home years ago, Sunday afternoon jam sessions evolved into big name jazz and classical concerts with catered lunches and dinners. These long, lazy, musical afternoons by the sea, across from the very strollable Miramar Beach, are popular; purchase tickets in advance.

Purissima Creek Redwoods, Higgins Purissima Road, a mile south of Half Moon Bay. (415) 691–1200. On the western slope of the Santa Cruz Mountains, a redwood preserve with hiking, biking, and equestrian trails, some handicapped-accessible trails. Wildflowers, ferny creeks, giant redwoods, maples, and alders.

Burleigh Murray State Park, Mills Creek Ranch Road off Higgins Purissima Road, a mile south of Half Moon Bay. (415) 726–8820. Century-old dairy barn, said to be the only one of its kind remaining in the state. Past the barn, a pretty creekside trail ambles for about a mile.

Spanishtown Arts and Crafts Center, San Mateo Road and Highway 92, Half Moon Bay. (415) 726–9971. Local and regional artisans sell a wide variety of wares.

Bicyclery, 432 Main Street, Half Moon Bay. (415) 726–6000. Rentals, accessories, service.

Sea Horse and Friendly Acres Horse Ranches, Highway 1 at Half Moon Bay. (415) 726–2362. Ride on your own or guided rides on the beach and trails; hayrides; picnic area.

Half Moon Bay Golf Links, 2000 Fairway Drive off Highway 1, Half Moon Bay. (415) 726–4438. Rated number 4 in the state by the PGA, a championship course designed by Arnold Palmer, typical links challenges of breezes, coastal weather, barrancas, and bluffs.

Special Events

June. Pasta, Chili and Chowder Cook-off, Pillar Point Harbor. (415) 726–8380.

July. Cross Ranch Rodeo, Cross Ranch, Pescadero. (415) 726–2925.

July. Tours des Fleurs, tours of coastside nurseries and flower farms. (415) 726–8380.

August. Pescadero Arts and Fun Festival, Pescadero. (415) 726–8380.

September. Harbor Day at Pillar Point Harbor. (415) 726–5202. Crafts booths, music, fantastic seafood barbecue.

October. Pumpkin and Art Festival, Half Moon Bay. (415) 726–5202. Great Pumpkin Parade, entertainment, contests—carving, pie-eating, biggest pumpkin. The town is mobbed.

October. Blue Grass Festival, Princeton Harbor. (415) 726–0552.

November. California Coast Air Show, Half Moon Bay Airport. (415) 726–3417. Antique and modern aircrafts displayed, stunning air show.

December. Harbor Lighting Ceremony, Pillar Point Harbor. (415) 726–5202. Boat owners compete with gloriously lighted and decorated boats.

Other Recommended Restaurants and Lodgings

El Granda

Harbor View Inn, at Pillar Point Wharf. (415) 726–2329. A contemporary Cape Cod–style motel, large rooms with bay windows.

Half Moon Bay

San Benito House, 356 Main Street. (415) 726–3425. English garden bed-and-breakfast inn built at the turn of the century. Fresh flowers throughout, twelve rooms with antiques and brass beds. European country–style restaurant with garden patio, the most celebrated in the region.

Half Moon Bay Campgrounds, 95 Kelly Avenue. (415) 726–8820.

Princeton

Pillar Point Inn, 380 Capistrano Road at Pillar Point Harbor. (800) 400–8281. Small, romantic, New England–style inn with sea views, overlooking the harbor. Fireplaces, featherbeds, steam baths, great breakfast.

Shore Bird, 390 Capistrano Road overlooking Pillar Point Harbor. (415) 728–5541. For over twenty-five years, a Cape Cod–style restaurant serving wonderful seafood for lunch, dinner, and weekend brunch.

Miramar

Miramar Restaurant and Bar, 131 Mirada Road, 2.5 miles north of Half Moon Bay. (415) 726–9053. Lunch, dinner, and weekend brunch across the street from Miramar Beach, fresh seafood specialties, lively bar crowd, sometimes live music.

Cypress Inn, 407 Mirada Road. (415) 726–6002. On 5 miles of beach, eight contemporary-design, luxury rooms and suites, sumptuous breakfasts and afternoon wine, a few steps from the beach. Fireplaces, private decks, sea views, skylights, in-house massage therapist!

Montara

Point Montara Lighthouse AYH Hostel, Sixteenth Street and Highway 1. (415) 728–7177.

Pescadero

Old Saw Mill Lodge, 700 Ranch Road West. (800) 596–6455. On sixty wooded acres, five new bed-and-breakfast rooms, indoor pool and spa, hiking trails, full gourmet breakfast, afternoon wine, sea and forest views.

Pigeon Point Lighthouse AYH Hostel, Highway 1. (415) 879–0633.

For More Information

MISTIX. (800) 444–7275. State campground reservations, Año Nuevo tour reservations.

Half Moon Bay Coastside Chamber of Commerce, P.O. Box 188, 520 Kelly Avenue, Half Moon Bay, CA 94019. (415) 726–5202.

Harvest Trails, 765 Main Street, Half Moon Bay. Map of where to buy and pick local produce.

Monterey and Big Sur

A serene scene along the Monterey Peninsula.

Spanish History, Wild Coastline

_____ 3 NIGHTS _____

Museums, mansions, mountains · Beachcombing · A golfer's dream
Shopping, biking, hiking · Chowder and cioppino

Arriving on the Monterey Peninsula in the mid-1500s, Spanish explorers saw dark cypress trees, like sentries along a rocky shoreline. Rivers and streams rushed down from a rugged mountain range. Otters, seals, and whales played in the bays. In the late 1700s the Spanish returned in force to stay for a century or so, using Monterey as headquarters for their huge Baja and Alta California domains, and Father Junípero Serra built one of his largest and most beautiful missions. Then Mexico took a turn as occupier of Monterey for more than twenty years.

This rich Hispanic heritage remains in the thick-walled adobes and Spanish Colonial haciendas of Monterey and in the gnarled old olive trees and courtyard gardens planted by the early conquistadores.

In stark contrast to the historic neighborhoods and sophisticated atmosphere of today's Monterey, Big Sur is a sparsely developed stretch of wilderness running 90 miles south to San Simeon, a series of cliffs and river valleys hemmed in by a high mountain range on one side and a largely inaccessible, spectacular seacoast on the other. A long-time resident of Big Sur, author Henry Miller, said of the area, "It is a region where extremes meet, a region where one is always conscious of weather, of space, of grandeur, and of eloquent silence."

Indeed, the weather, the sky, and the sea are constantly changing in Big Sur, from clear, bright winter days to summertime's fog rolling in through the dark redwood groves. You might see a hawk, an eagle, or an osprey circling. Owls hoot at night, coyotes howl, and mountain lions moan on the far ridges. The sea boils hundreds of feet below, stretches lazily out on a rocky beach, and swells beyond the breakers to dark kelp beds where sea creatures hide.

Day 1

Morning

From the Oakland Bay Bridge, take Highway 880 south to Highway 17, connecting with Highway 1 at Santa Cruz, heading south to Monterey; it's about two hours from the Oakland Bay Bridge to Monterey. Park downtown at one of the parking garages—you'll want to walk everywhere or take public transportation; "The Wave" shuttlebus stops at several parking garages. Pick up a walking-tour map at the **Monterey Peninsula Visitor's Bureau,** Camino El Estero at the foot of Franklin Street, between Fremont and Del Monte avenues.

Walk south on Alvarado, turn right onto Jefferson to Pacific, and spend a couple of hours strolling in and out of the historic buildings and garden courtyards on the "Path of History." Dominating the grassy knolls of **Friendly Plaza** is **Colton Hall,** at Pacific and Jefferson, a museum in an old school. Notice the small plastered-adobe homes in back of Colton Hall, some of the first built in California.

Part of the Monterey State Historic Park complex, **Cooper Store,** on Polk Street (408–649–2836), sells antique toys, postcards, and souvenirs. Go through the store to the museums and gardens behind; a spectacular cypress towers overhead. In the heart of the Historic District is the **Monterey Peninsula Museum of Art,** 559 Pacific Street (408–372–7591), with a fine collection of Western and Asian art and photography.

The new **Maritime Museum of Monterey** at the waterfront is 18,000 feet of exhibits focused on the Monterey Peninsula's long seagoing history (408–373–2469). Priceless marine artifacts include the 16-foot-tall, 10,000-pound lens that once operated atop the Point Sur Lighthouse. When you are ready to get off your feet for twenty minutes, take in the historical film here—it's free.

Lunch: **Abalonetti's,** 57 Fisherman's Wharf, Monterey. (408) 373–1851. Sit indoors or on the wharf; calamari, Italian antipasto, pizza, seafood pasta; for forty years one of the best fish cafes on the wharf. *Look* at the dessert tray.

Afternoon

Somehow avoiding the architectural upgrade and commercial development that destroyed an "Old Town" ambience once found on Cannery Row, **Fisherman's Wharf** still smells of salt spray and carmel corn. Fishing boats bob in the harbor, seagulls squawk and wheel overhead, and salty breezes blow between slightly seedy boardwalk cafes and tourist-trap shops.

Walk along the waterfront **Monterey Peninsula Recreational Trail** that runs from the wharf all the way along Cannery Row and around Pacific Grove, a distance of 5 miles, if you care to walk that far. It's fun to dodge brown pelicans and watch sea lions barking to get your attention. You can even rent a pedaling vehicle, powered by two adults in back, with room for two little kids in front.

The walking trail from Cannery Row to **Asilomar State Beach** is part of an 18-mile trail connecting the greenbelts and parks on the coast, encompassing historic landmarks. Along the way are drinking fountains, benches, picnic sites, and bike racks.

Dinner: **Fishwife,** 1996 Sunset Drive, Pacific Grove. (408) 375–7107. Casual, popular, reasonably priced cafe at Asilomar Beach. Wide variety of fresh fish, Cajun blackened snapper, Salmon Alfredo, key lime pie; reservations a must.

Lodging: **Monterey Plaza Hotel,** 400 Cannery Row, Monterey. Unassuming from the street, spectacular inside, in an unbeatable bayside setting over the water with wide views of the bay from nearly every public space and from more than half of the 285 rooms. Corner rooms on the upper floors have two walls of glass and balconies, separate work areas with modem ports. Once settled in at the hotel, you don't need a car to enjoy Monterey. "The Wave" public shuttles and bike, roller-blade, and kayak rental companies are within a few steps of the hotel, and the aquarium and myriad shops are nearby.

Open to the public, big-name summer jazz concerts are held on the outdoor decks of the hotel, with kayaks, yachts, and otters in attendance offshore.

Warm and clubby, at the same time romantic, is the hotel dining room, the Duck Club, with big picture windows on the water and outdoor dining (408–646–1706). Fresh seafood, pasta, and wood-roasted specialties—duck, beef, and lamb—are prepared in an open kitchen. Try the seared Muscovy duck breast with ginger green peppercorn sauce, Dungeness crab cakes, hot apple cobbler. Breakfast, lunch, and amazing weekend brunch also served here.

Day 2

Morning

Breakfast: **Fifi's Cafe and French Bakery,** 1188 Forest Avenue, Pacific Grove. (408) 372–5325. French bistro and spa cuisine, pastries, espresso, omelettes.

Don't miss a visit to the **Monterey Bay Aquarium,** 886 Cannery Row (408–648–4888). In the summer and on weekends and holidays, it's important to arrive here at Monterey's most popular attraction when it opens at 10:00 A.M., otherwise you'll stand in a long line (an alternative is after 3:00 P.M.). Restored smokestacks and boilers on the behemoth of a building create an architectural cross between a sardine cannery and a contemporary masterpiece. Some 6,000 sea creatures reside here in giant tanks. The three-story Kelp Forest is the world's tallest aquarium exhibit, so huge that it feels as if you're swimming around in there with the sharks and the schools of silvery fish. The Monterey Bay Habitats exhibit is 90 feet long, full of fascinating reef life. Playful sea otters and bat rays have their own watery homes, and it's fun to watch them during their feeding time. There are frequent live videos from a research submarine prowling Monterey Bay, as deep as 3,000 feet. On the aquarium's decks overlooking the harbor, you can peer down and watch the otters and seals peering back at you.

A new wing of the aquarium opened in early 1996, exhibiting creatures of the open ocean never before seen by the public. A million gallons of seawater behind the largest window on the planet, the Outer Bay exhibit contains species that the world's aquariums have not dared to exhibit, such as 10-foot-tall, 1.5-ton sunfish, pelagic stingrays, green sea turtles as big as dining room tables, vast schools of yellowfin tuna, and species of sharks too big for aquariums, until now.

Also in the new wing, The Drifters gallery contains the largest permanent collection of jellyfish species in the United States and the largest-scale jellies exhibit in the world. Otherworldly music and a dreamlike design for the jellies venue transfix viewers before the pulsing, drifting, rainbow-hued beings.

One of the most biodiverse marine environments in the world, Monterey Peninsula waters attract divers from all over the world to Monterey and Carmel bays and to the **Monterey Bay National Marine Sanctuary,** encompassing 4,000 nautical square miles of kelp forests and rocky reefs inhabited by a miraculous variety of creatures such as leopard shark, bright nudibranches, anenomes, eels, giant schools of fish, and hundreds more species, plus the everpresent otters, dolphins, whales, and even sharks. *Scuba Diving* magazine chose Monterey Bay as the "Favorite Shore Dive in the U.S." and the Bay has also been in the top five "Favorite Beginner's Dive Destinations."

The **Monterey Bay Dive Center** (225 Cannery Row, 408–655–3483 and 598 Foam Street, 408–655–1818) is a PADI dive center where you can rent complete diving equipment, take a guided dive tour, and arrange to get certified as a diver.

Lunch: **Montrio,** 414 Calle Principal, Monterey. (408) 648–8880. Euro-American urban bistro in a 1910 landmark firehouse. From the display kitchen come Dungeness crab cakes, grilled marinated salmon with fennel ratatouille, cannoli with raspberry coulis, homemade pasta; from the wood-burning rotisserie comes rosemary and garlic chicken, Black Angus ribeye.

Afternoon

Stroll about and shop on **Cannery Row.** Once a few blocks of weathered cannery buildings with funky shops and cafes, the waterfront promenade is now rampant with elegance and élan. Steinbeck and sardines were replaced by upscale boutiques and fancy hotels. The seals, otters, swaying kelp beds, and sailing yachts of Monterey Bay remain.

At the north end of Cannery Row, near the aquarium, are the **American Tin Cannery** factory outlet stores (408–372–1442)—more than fifty of them.

Shopping is primo on Cannery Row and on a few adjacent streets. **Cannery Row Antique Row** at 471 Wave Street (408–655–0264) is over 20,000 square feet housing the antiques and collectibles of a hundred dealers. At 700 Cannery Row is a complex of almost three dozen shops and galleries plus a wax museum, a winery, and cafes. Located here is **A Taste of Monterey,** where you can enjoy a panoramic view of Monterey Bay, wine and food tasting, exhibits, and a multimedia show about the region (408–646–5446).

Drive to the Spanish Bay entrance to the **17-Mile Drive,** at Asilomar near the Fishwife restaurant; you'll pay a $6.00 per car entry fee that's well worth it, even on a foggy day. Ghostly cypress forests and red lichen-painted rocks frame the many vista points. Stop and explore the beautiful beaches and many tidepools; walk or jog on the winding waterfront path. If you're a golfer, this is a chance to see three of the most famous and most difficult courses in the world. Watch for erratic traffic; everyone slows down to ogle the mansions and seaside estates.

At the southernmost point of the 17-Mile Drive (also the southernmost point of the Pebble Beach Links golf course), you can enter the town of Carmel through the Carmel toll gate, or take a sharp left, continuing on the Drive through Pescadero Canyon, exiting the Drive at the Carmel Hill Gate and driving north on the W. R. Holman Scenic Highway back to Pacific Grove, where you will turn left on Sinex Avenue and right on 17th Street to find the restaurant, Fandango.

Dinner: **Fandango,** 223 Seventeenth Street, Pacific Grove. (408) 373–0588. By the fire in the dining room, on the glass-domed terrace, or on the garden patio, European country–style cuisine in a Mediterranean setting. Wood-burning grill, pasta, paella, seafood, cassoulet. Full bar, exceptional wine list.

Lodging: Monterey Plaza Hotel.

Day 3

Morning

Breakfast: The Duck Club at the Monterey Plaza Hotel. Drive south on Highway 1 to Big Sur, about 30 miles of driving on a two-lane, winding mountain road. The brooding mountain shoulders of the **Santa Lucia Mountains** loom to your left, and to your right it's a sheer 1,000-foot drop to a rocky, mostly inaccessible coastline pierced by the small valleys of the Big and Little Sur rivers. Several river and forest parks are here in the **Los Padres National Forest** (408–385–5434), where you'll also find good campgrounds and walking and hiking trails. Shielded by tremendous cliffs, Big Sur is a banana belt, with higher temperatures than Carmel and Monterey, getting more inches of rain but more sunny days. In wintertime you'll often find clear blue skies here when it's drippy just a few miles north.

You'll cross the **Bixby Creek Bridge,** also known as the Rainbow Bridge, a 260-foot-high single-spanner constructed in 1932. Just north of the bridge, take a short sidetrip into the National Forest; turn left onto Old Coast Road and follow it a few miles, returning to Highway 1 at **Andrew Molera State Park** (408–667–2315). The **Big Sur River** flows down from the Santa Lucias through this 4,700-acre park, falling into the sea at a long sandy beach. One of many hiking trails runs along the river, through a eucalyptus grove where monarch butterflies spend the winter, to the rivermouth, where you can see a great variety of sea- and shorebirds.

Besides ancient redwoods, you will see the Santa Lucia fir, found only here, and possibly the endangered Peregrine falcon and bald eagles. For trail maps and information, write in advance to the U.S. Forest Service, 406 South Mildred, King City 93930 (408–385–5434).

One of the most unforgettable ways to see Big Sur is on horseback. **Molera Trail Rides** offers daily two-hour rides, each featuring a different perspective, such as the beach, redwood groves, mountain ridges, and sunset excursions (408–625–8664).

Lunch: **Nepenthe,** Highway 1 just south of Ventana Inn. (408) 667–2345. For decades a favorite destination for visitors to the Big Sur area. The stone patios of the restaurant are perched on a magical promontory at the edge of the continent, with a bird's-eye view of a long shoreline. Just offshore are natural arches and seastacks, rocky remnants of an ancient coastline. Try the ambrosia burger or the fresh fish.

Afternoon

Drive through **Big Sur Valley,** not a town, really, but a handful of river resorts and campgrounds on both sides of the highway. **Pfeiffer Big Sur State Park** (408–667–2171) is another place to hike, picnic, and fish in the Big Sur River. Docent-led nature walks are given in the summer; one trail leads to **Pfeiffer Falls,** in a fern canyon.

Just inside the entrance to the park, the casual restaurant at **Big Sur Lodge** overlooks the river (408–667–2171). Cottage-style lodge rooms are in big demand during vacation season (800–4–BIG–SUR) The nearby Post Ranch Inn (P.O. Box 219, Big Sur 93920, 408–667–2200) is a luxurious, visually stunning inn with fireplaces, spa tubs, a renowned restaurant, and complete privacy for guests.

Ten miles farther down the coast, **Julia Pfeiffer Burns State Park** is 2,400 acres of undeveloped wilderness. Trails along McWay Creek lead to a waterfall that plunges into the ocean (408–667–2315). The **Partington Creek** trail goes through a canyon and a 100-foot-long rock tunnel to **Partington Cove** beach, where sea otters play in the kelp beds.

The two-lane Big Sur highway south from here to San Simeon is crossed by thirty bridges over deep canyons and stream-cut valleys— breathtaking scenery, but probably too unrelentingly curvy for younger children. About half-way to San Simeon, **Jade Cove** is actually a string of coves, where Monterey jade is found at low tide and following storms.

Dinner: **Ventana Big Sur Country Inn Resort,** 30 miles south of Carmel on Highway 1. (408) 667–2331. After dark, the walk up lighted outdoor stairs through a forest is a romantic beginning to a romantic evening in the four-star restaurant, which services lunch and dinner. Indoors, a warm, woodsy atmosphere; outdoors, a stone patio floating high above the sea.

Lodging: Ventana Big Sur Country Inn Resort. Rustic country-luxe, a private, quiet resort on a hillside between the sea and mountain ridges, a compound of several pine buildings, each with canyon or ocean views. High-ceilinged, wood-paneled luxury suites with fireplaces and a feeling of isolation. Decor is of stone, wood, soft earth-toned fabrics.

Two lap pools, Japanese hot baths, sauna, massages on your own completely private deck. Afternoon elaborate wine and cheese buffet in the main lounge. Wild gardens abloom with native flowers and vines, oceans of clematis and jasmine pour over balconies, tree ferns, canopy shady glades.

The Inn also operates a private campground here in a forty-acre redwood grove.

Day 4

Morning

Breakfast: At the Ventana Inn, a big breakfast buffet in the sunny dining lounge, outside on a choice of several garden patios or in your room. Fresh berries, melons, tropical fruits; homemade coffeecakes, croissants, muffins, yogurt, granola.

After a morning exploring the meadow and mountainside trails that start at Ventana Inn, head back to the Bay Area.

There's More

Mopeds, bikes, kayaks. Moped Adventures, 1250 Del Monte, Monterey. (408) 373–2696.

Bay Bikes, 640 Wave Street, Monterey. (408) 646–9090.

Monterey Bay Kayaks, 693 Del Monte Avenue, Monterey. (408) 373–KELP.

Point Lobos State Reserve, 2.5 miles south of Carmel on Highway 1. (408) 624–4909. A rocky point surrounded by a protected marine environment; otters, whales, harbor seals, sea lions; scuba-diving; spectacular landscape; picnicking, walking, photo snapping.

Esalen Institute, 15 miles south of Big Sur. (408) 667–3000. World-famous center for the development of human potential; workshops, seminars, hot tubs; open infrequently to the public.

Golf. Old Del Monte Golf Course, 1300 Sylvan Road, Monterey. (408) 373–2436. Eighteen holes, public, oldest course west of the Mississippi.

Laguna Seca Golf Course, end of York Road off Highway 68, Monterey. (408) 373–3701. Eighteen holes, public.

Pacific Grove Golf Course, 77 Asilomar Boulevard, Pacific Grove. (408) 648–3177. Eighteen holes, public, links-style.

The Links at Spanish Bay, 17-Mile Drive, Pebble Beach. (408) 647–7500. Less than a decade old, the Links at Spanish Bay already appears on "Greatest Resort Courses" and "Best Golf Resorts in America" lists. All but four of the holes flank the sea, and, in true Scottish fashion, the course is marked by waves of low, sandy mounds, fescue grass fairways, pot bunkers, and few trees. Pitch-and-run, staying low to the ground to avoid the steady wind, is the order of the day on eighteen and on most of Spanish Bay.

Poppy Hills Golf Course, 3200 Lopez Road, 17-Mile Drive, Pebble Beach. (408) 625–2154. Eighteen holes, public.

Spyglass Hill Golf Course, Stevenson Drive and Spyglass Hill, Pebble Beach. (408) 647–7500. Semiprivate, eighteen holes.

Pebble Beach Golf Links, 17-Mile Drive, Pebble Beach. (408) 624–3811. Legendary site of U.S. Opens, PGA Championships, and the Crosby Clambake (now the AT&T Pro-Am). Pebble rides the headlands over Stillwater Cove as it has since 1919, when a rippling figure-8 design was laid down on a series of jagged palisades and sandy moors. Eight holes are within sight and sound of the pounding surf. The notorious combination of swirling winds and misty hazes, long tee shots over gaping crevasses, and tiny greens remains a golfing challenge equaled by few courses in the world. Barking harbor seals seem to laugh from the rocks offshore, while gangs of sweet-faced sea otters float, unconcerned, on their kelp beds, knock-knocking on abalone shells.

Monterey Peninsula Golf Packages, P.O. Box 504, Carmel Valley 93924. (408) 659-5361. During high season this may be your best bet.

Playground. Dennis the Menace Park, in Monterey on the south side of Del Monte Avenue, across from Monterey State Beach and adjacent to little Lake El Estero. Designed by the cartoonist who created Dennis, fantastic structures such as a steam locomotive, a giant swing ride, a roller slide, and a special play area for the handicapped. (408) 646–3866.

Monterey Rent-A-Roadster, 229 Cannery Row, Monterey. (408) 647–1919. Authentic reproductions of 1929 Model A's, easy to drive and fun for an open-air cruise along the coast.

Carmel Candy Chocolate Factory, 1291 Fremont Boulevard, Seaside (just north of Monterey off Highway 1). (408) 899–7963. Tours of

the factory and free samples of gourmet chocolates, Monday through Friday. You can even choose your chocolates right from the conveyor belts. See chocolate tunnels, slabs, chunks, rivers, oceans.
Monterey Bay Whale and Nature Cruises, P.O. Box 52001, Pacific Grove 93950. (408) 372–0671. Three-hour winter and spring cruises to see gray whales and dolphins. In summer and fall, longer cruises with varying itineraries.

Special Events

January. AT&T Pebble Beach National Pro-Am. (800) 541–9091. Formerly the Bing Crosby Clambake.
March. Dixieland Monterey. (408) 443–5260.
March. Hot Air Affair, Monterey. (408) 649–6544. Four hundred balloons compete in events and generally turn the sky into a rainbow; many events in the early morning. Public rides in tethered balloons and helicopters. Skydiving exhibition.
March. Monterey Wine Festival, P.O Box 1749, Monterey 93942. (408) 656–WINE. Held at several locations in Monterey, a wine and food extravaganza with celebrity chefs, winetasting, winery tours, golf, workshops, demos, dinners, galas, auction.
April. Adobe Tour, Monterey. (408) 372–2608. Twenty-five adobes and gardens, period costumes.
June. U.S. Open Golf Championships, Pebble Beach. (408) 626–1992.
July. Monterey Bay Blues Festival. (408) 394–2652. Big names.
July. Monterey National Horse Show. (408) 372–1000.
August. Scottish Festival and Highland Games, Monterey. (408) 899–3864.
August. Monterey County Fair. (408) 372–1000.
August. Pebble Beach Concours D'Elegance and Christie's Auction. (408) 625–8562.
August. NCGA Championship, Pebble Beach. (408) 625–4653.
September. Monterey Jazz Festival. (408) 648–5354. Big names.
October. Octoberfest, Monterey. (408) 649–6544.

Other Recommended Restaurants and Lodgings

Coastal Hotel Group. (800) 225–2902. Reservations for two upscale Monterey hotels and a bed-and-breakfast inn.

Big Sur

Post Ranch Inn, Highway 1. (408) 667–2200. Luxury resort in beauiful forest and meadow surroundings on a bluff with zowie views of the coastline; just thirty "treehouse" contemporary design suites. One of the most private, romantic places to stay in California. The Sierra Mar restaurant has floor-to-ceiling glass walls with sea views, and topnotch cuisine and wine list.

Big Sur Lodge, just inside the entrance to Pfeiffer Big Sur State Park. (408) 667–2171. Casual lodge dining room with patio overlooking the river, California cuisine, pasta, local seafood. Cozy, simple cottages in a forest, kitchens, fireplaces, lovely views, pool.

Deetjen's Big Sur Inn, 1 mile south of Ventana Lodge on Highway 1. (408) 667–2377. Quaint, rustic Norwegian-style inn in a redwood grove 2 miles from the coast, twenty simple redwood cottages, fireplaces or wood-burning stoves, down comforters, each cottage has two or three separate guest rooms with shared bath (choose your unit carefully, as some can be noisy). Restaurant serves good American food.

Ripplewood Resort, Highway 1. (408) 667–2242. Breakfast, lunch, Mexican dinners.

River Inn, Pheneger Creek. (408) 667–2700. Eighteen queen rooms and family suites with balconies overlooking the river, simple, rustic accommodations. Restaurant and bar, swimming pool, general store, near state parks.

Pacific Grove

Asilomar Conference Center, 800 Asilomar Boulevard. (408) 372–8016. A secret: When space is available, individual travelers may rent hotel rooms here, some rustic, some deluxe, at very reasonable rates, including full breakfast; wonderful seaside location.

Centrella, 612 Central Avenue. (408) 372–3372. Three-story, elegant Victorian bed-and-breakfast establishment; romantic; quiet.

El Cocodrilo, 701 Lighthouse Avenue. (408) 655–3311. Tropical seafood specialties, fun, colorful; Jamaican curry crabcakes, West Indian ribs, Bahamian seafood chowder.

Pasta Mia, 481 Lighthouse Avenue. (408) 375–7709. Voted Best Italian Restaurant, homemade pasta, veal, grilled fish, country-chic decor, moderate prices.

Lighthouse Lodge, 1150 Lighthouse Avenue. (409) 655–2111. In a seacoast environment of its own on Point Pinos, twenty-nine suites with ocean views, fireplaces, Jacuzzi tubs, full breakfast, afternoon refreshments. Casual, with plenty of space to walk, popular with families.

Monterey

Old Monterey Inn, 500 Martin Street. (408) 375–8284. A vine-covered Tudor mansion in a forest of low-hanging gnarled oaks. Patios are abloom with wisteria, aromatic jasmine, and hundreds of hanging baskets and pots, a combination English country and Japanese garden. Understated European country-house decor, fireplaces galore, many elegant extras, extraordinary service. Two honeymoon cottages, one Safari-luxe, one a blue oasis with a canopy bed. Full breakfast by the fire in the elegant dining room.

Spindrift Inn, 652 Cannery Row. (800) 841–1879. On the water, forty-one luxury rooms, half with ocean views, all with fireplaces, down comforters, marble baths, window seats or private balconies.

Victorian Inn, 487 Foam Street. (800) 232–4141. Sixty-eight charming rooms and suites, marble fireplaces, private balconies or patios, some with living rooms and kitchenettes, hot tub, breakfast buffet and afternoon refreshments, walking distance to Cannery Row and the Wharf.

Tarpy's Roadhouse, Highway 68 and Canyon Del Rey, near the Monterey airport. (408) 647–1444. Originally a ranch house built in the 1920s, stone walls trailing with vines on the outside, covered with art on the inside, large wine cave, garden courtyard dining, updated versions of old-fashioned comfort foods such as polenta with wild mushrooms, Cajun prawns, fresh local seafood, grilled meats, honey mustard rabbit with apples and thyme.

Vacation Centers, 401 Alvarado Street. (408) 655–3920. Eco-sports packages combine accommodations, aquarium tickets, kayak and horseback tours, hang gliding, race car training at Laguna Seca Raceway.

Lone Oak Motel, 2221 North Fremont. (408) 372–4924. Best-kept secret for inexpensive lodgings.

The Clock Garden, 565 Abrego. (408) 375–6100. Glorious garden terrace; notable food for decades.

Pebble Beach

The Lodge at Pebble Beach, 17-Mile Drive. (800) 654–9300. For over seventy years one of the world's great hostelries, Pebble feels like a private club. Those in the know call it "the Lodge." One hundred sixty-one luxury rooms and suites, all quite spacious, most with private balcony, sea or garden views, large dressing and sitting areas, some with fireplace. Guests may play golf not only at Pebble Beach Golf Links—California's most famous course—but at nearby Links at Spanish Bay, Spyglass Hill, and Old Del Monte. Pool with sea view, fourteen tennis courts, fitness club, equestrian center, several outstanding restaurants and cafes. Spectacular is too small a word to describe the seascapes at Pebble Beach.

Inn at Spanish Bay, 2700 17-Mile Drive. (800) 654–9300. In the lee of the dark, brooding Del Monte cypress forest, the luxurious resort hotel lies a few hundred feet from the shoreline on world famous 17-Mile Drive. Two hundred seventy contemporary-design rooms and suites, each with private patio or balcony, overstuffed sofas and chairs, plush comforters, marble bathrooms, some fireplaces, sitting rooms. One of the top tennis complexes in the country, fitness club with complete spa facilities and beauty treatments, several restaurants and upscale shops.

Surrounded by the Links at Spanish Bay, the inn is a mecca for golfers who play here and at nearby Pebble Beach (see "Golf" above).

Fabulous sea views, glamorous blond art deco decor, and world-class Euro-Asian cuisine make Roy's at Pebble Beach at the inn a special occasion restaurant (408–647–7423): cilantro shrimp cakes with pineapple chili salsa, blackened ahi tuna with hot soy mustard sauce, hibachi salmon, lemon grass crusted swordfish with cucumber won ton salad and Thai basil peanut sauce.

Located at the inn, the Ansel Adams Gallery (408–375–7215) shows a huge collection of Adams's photos and the works of other well-known nature photographers, plus Native American jewelry and fine crafts. Camera Walks are conducted from the gallery for small groups a few days a week.

For More Information

Monterey Visitor's Bureau, P.O. Box 1770, Monterey, CA 93942. (408) 649–1770.

Pacific Grove Chamber of Commerce, P.O. Box 167, Pacific Grove, CA 93950. (408) 373–3304.

Big Sur Chamber of Commerce, P.O. Box 87, Big Sur, CA 93920. (408) 667–2111.

MISTIX. (800) 444–7275. State campground reservations.

Carmel Valley Sunshine

Golf courses and sunshine are a given in Carmel Valley.

Home on the Ranch, Shopping Mecca

————————— 2 NIGHTS —————————

Cowboy days · Tennis, golf, horseback rides · Beach walks
Serra's mission · Boutique binge · Art galleries

The Carmel River ambles over the valley floor between two mountain ranges through horse farms, ranch resorts, and meadows liberally sprinkled with spreading oaks. Just a few miles from the Pacific Coast, but a world away, the tawny climate of Carmel Valley is warm and dry. Except for a big shopping and restaurant complex at Highway 1 and Carmel Valley Road, the valley has little commercial development. Your choices are golf, horseback riding, hiking, biking, tennis, or lying in the sun by a swimming pool.

Once settled in the peace and quiet and sunshine of the valley, it may be difficult to leave, but you will enjoy forays to the ocean beaches and to the artist's colony and shopping mecca of Carmel, a square-mile village of rustic country cottages and shingled beach houses in an idyllic forest setting. Carmel's winding lanes are shaded with ancient oaks and cypress, and everyone in town, it seems, is an avid gardener. Hanging baskets and blooming window boxes are everywhere.

Shopping at the literally hundreds of boutiques and art galleries is the main activity of visitors to Carmel. Originally a Bohemian artists' and writers' colony, the town has over seventy-five art and photography galleries.

Day 1

Morning

Take Highway 101 south to Highway 156 at Castroville, heading west to Highway 1 south to **Moss Landing,** about 1.75 hours from San Francisco. You can't miss Moss landing. Just look for the twin 500-foot boiler stacks of the second largest fossil fuel thermal electric plant in the world. When you see a bright pink building with blue awnings, that's the **Whole Enchilada** (408–633–3038), an excellent Mexican restaurant. Turn west at the restaurant into the community of Moss Landing on Elkhorn Slough, where you will find twenty-five antiques shops in Western false-front buildings, a marina of fishing boats, and a boat graveyard. Elkhorn Slough is home to thousands of sea and shore birds and animals. You can walk on 4 miles of easy trails in the mudflats and salt marshes of the **Elkhorn Slough National Estuarine Research Reserve** and visit the **Moss Landing Marine Laboratory,** which is operated by nine California state universities (408–728–2822). A vast stretch of tidal wetlands, extending more than 7 miles inland, the slough shelters over 260 species of birds, including thousands of migrating ducks and geese in the winter and spring. A California record was set here for the most species of birds seen in a day. You may see herons, teals, plovers, golden eagles, terns, peregrine falcons, and dozens more wading and flying birds. On the north bank of the slough, more than 5,000 brown pelicans congregate in the summer and fall. Kayaking and canoeing are some of the best ways to birdwatch. To rent boats, call 408–728–2822. At **Moss Landing State Beach,** you can fish, surf, and horseback ride (408–649–2836). **Moss**

Landing Oyster Bar at the south end of Moss Landing Road is a casual, popular cafe serving fresh fish and homemade pasta (408-633-5302).

Continue on Highway 1 to Carmel, another half hour. Take the **Carmel Valley** exit on the south end of Carmel, and head east into the valley. Drive out Carmel Valley Road about twenty minutes to **Carmel Valley Village.**

Lunch: **Bon Appetit,** 7 Delfino Place, Carmel Valley Village. (408) 659-3559. Sit outdoors under an umbrella, watch the passing scene of the village, and enjoy bouillabaisse, paella, mesquite-grilled fresh fish, gourmet pizzas, and a notable wine list.

Afternoon

Stretch your legs on some of the 5,000 acres at **Garland Ranch Regional Park** with a hike, stroll, or bike ride along the **Carmel River,** across the forested hillsides and up on the high ridges overlooking the valley (408-659-4488). An easy, flat 1-mile walk is the Lupine Loop in the lower meadow, a pleasant, wildflowery route in the winter and spring, but hot and dry in the summertime and fall, unless it has recently rained. The Waterfall Trail is lush with ferns, rushing streams, and beautiful falls that run winter through spring; even when the fall is dry, it's a cool, green trail . Other trails take you to breezy hilltop meadows and ponds where birds and ducks reside.

Just a few steps from the parking lot, picnic sites beside the river are pleasant. John Steinbeck wrote in *Cannery Row,* "The Carmel [River] crackles among round boulders, wanders lazily under sycamores, spills into pools, drops in against banks where crayfish live . . . frogs blink from its banks and the deep ferns grow beside it. The quail call beside it and the wild doves come whistling in at dusk. It's everything a river should be."

Plan to arrive at your valley lodgings early enough to enjoy a late afternoon swim or a game of tennis or perhaps golf.

Dinner: **Robles Del Rio Lodge,** 200 Punta Del Monte (off Carmel Valley Road on the east side of Carmel Village). (408) 659-3705. A long-established award winner, one of the best continental restaurants on the Monterey Peninsula. Book a table for the sunset hour and ask for a window table.

Lodging: Robles Del Rio Lodge. Built in the 1920s, the lodge was a favorite getaway of movie stars in the early days. It's a country resort in a beautiful oak forest with astonishing views of the valley from the restaurant and from most of the rooms and cabins. You will feel far away from the world here in a relaxed, homey atmosphere. Decor is simple and comfortable, knotty-pine, quilts, ceiling fans, old-fashioned bathrooms. The swimming-pool garden terrace is the heart of the place. The bad news is that daytrippers spend the day here. The good news is that the pool is only busy on summer weekend afternoons, it's large enough to accommodate everyone, and, if you are staying on the coast and the weather is foggy and cool, you can come out here and play in the sun for only $5.00 a day.

Day 2

Morning

Breakfast: Robles del Rio. A sumptuous buffet breakfast is served in a glass-enclosed dining room with a fireplace.

The best way to experience the wilderness and the views of the Carmel Valley is from the back of a horse. You can take a trail ride with **J K Corral** into Garland Park. They're based here at the lodge, and the front desk will book for you or you can make your own arrangements (408–659–3370). (Trail rides are also available in the east end of the valley.) You can also take tennis lessons at the lodge, including a special "learn to play" three-hour program.

Another choice for two-hour rides, all day picnic rides, and/or lessons is the **Holman Ranch,** a private 400-acre estate in the valley (408–659–2640). You will likely be the only riders on the Holman Ranch trails.

From Carmel Valley Village, head back on Carmel Valley Road to the shopping complex near Highway 1, turn left into the complex on Carmel Rancho, then right onto Rio Road and across Highway 1 to the **Mission San Carlos Borromeo del Rio Carmel,** one of the most impressive in California's chain of missions and the burial place of Father Junípero Serra, the founder of the missions (408–624–1271). Star-shaped stained-glass windows, cool colonnades, and beautiful courtyard gardens and fountains make this a good place to spend a couple of hours. A warren of thick-walled rooms, restored from original mission buildings, holds a magnificent museum collection of early Indian, religious, and historical California artifacts. Inside, the cathedral, cool and silent even on the hottest days, is sienna, burnt umber, and gold, with soaring ceilings and heavy wooden pews.

Continue on Rio Road 2 blocks to Santa Lucia, turning left and following this street to the waterfront, bearing left to the north end of **Carmel River State Beach** (408–624–4909) adjacent to **Monastery Beach** and the **Carmel River Bird Sanctuary.** Frequented by a wide variety of waterfowl and shorebirds, these two beaches are visited by fewer people than Carmel Beach. Wander over the dunes that form a "plug" for the Carmel River most of the year. Pick up driftwood and shells or make a 4-mile round-trip run or walk. You may see scuba divers getting ready to descend into the kelp forests of the **Carmel Bay Ecological Reserve** offshore.

With the picturesque Carmelite Monastery as a backdrop, Monastery Beach is fine for picnicking but heavy surf can make it unsafe for swimmers.

Four miles south of Carmel on Highway 1, **Point Lobos State Reserve** was named for the sea lions who lie about on offshore rocks (408–624–4909). A rocky, forested point surrounded by a protected marine environment, the park's spectacular landscape includes several miles of trails, pebbled beaches, and one of only two naturally occurring stands of Monterey cypress (the other is at Pebble Beach). In the late 1800s, Robert Louis Stevenson called it the "most beautiful meeting of land and sea on earth."

From 6 miles of coastline, whales, harbor seals, and otters are often seen, as well as storms of pelicans, gulls, and cormorants. In the meadows, mule deer tiptoe through purple needlegrass and wild lilac. Point Lobos is completely protected—the land, the marine life on the beach and in the tidepools, and the flora and fauna underwater. Not a thing may be removed or disturbed, dogs are not allowed, and visitors are required to stay on hiking trails or beaches. Sea Lion Point is accessed by an easy half-hour walk to Headland Cove where sea lions bark and you can see the otters. It will take a half-day to enjoy all the sights of Point Lobos and you are advised to come early on weekends. Guided interpretive walks are conducted by park rangers.

Lunch: **Thunderbird Bookshop and Restaurant,** at the Barnyard, Highway 1 and Carmel Valley Road, Carmel Valley. (408) 624–1803. Indoor or outdoor dining on the site of a big, bountiful bookstore, a fixture in the valley for decades. Healthy salads, grilled sandwiches, homemade soups, monster desserts. Cozy by the fireplace in wintertime and during the week when tourists have gone and Carmelites take their valley back.

If you are in the mood for Southwestern-style food, look for the **Rio Grill** in the adjacent shopping center (408–625–5436). Santa Fe–style decor, butcher-paper–covered tables with crayons for the creative, and tons of awards such as "Best Restaurant in Monterey County" make this a top choice. A wood-burning grill and an oak-wood smoker produce fresh fish, meat, and poultry specialties.

Afternoon

The Barnyard (408–624–8886) is a rambling complex of fifty shops and restaurants in barnlike buildings. If you're a garden fancier, this could be a highlight of your trip. In every nook and cranny, around, under, alongside, and hanging from the buildings are riots of blooming native perennials, thousands of flowers, shrubs, and trees, and oceans of bougainvillea, rivers of begonias, streams of California poppies. A horticulturalist leads a guided tour of the gardens on Fridays (408–624–8886).

Thomas Kinkade, a regionally famous painter of land- and seascapes, has a gallery here, one of several Kinkade galleries in the region (408–622–0939). In a storybook forest at **Twiggs** (408–622–9802) are gnomes, trolls, racoons, bunnies, twittering birds, and fantastical creatures. The fanciest store for dogs and cats you're ever likely to encounter, **Enchanted Tails** has decorated collars, stuffed animals for animals, cushy mats and sleeping baskets, and an array of dog biscuits and treats, such as veggie hearts, liver unicorns, and banana bears (408–625–9648).

What is a crumpet? Find out at the **Carmel Crumpet Company,** where they also sell scrumptious scones, sandwiches, and coffee drinks (408–625–8165). From a glassed-in, heated outdoor deck overlooking the mountains and the Barnyard gardens, the **Sherlock Holmes Pub and Restaurant** holds forth with a British and American pub menu and exotic ales and beers (408–625–0340). Several more restaurants in the Barnyard include a Japanese open-hearth grill, a Chinese place, and a pizzeria.

Dinner: **Oaks Restaurant** (408–626–2533). **Carmel Valley Ranch Resort,** 1 Old Ranch Road, Carmel Valley. (408) 625–9500. Get a table beside the picture window, with a view of the valley and the Santa Lucia Mountains. Award-winning wine list, regional California cuisine.

Lodging: Carmel Valley Ranch Resort. One of California's great luxury resorts, on an oak-studded hillside overlooking a golf course and the valley. An outdoor dining and cocktail terrace looks onto a spectacular pool and gardens. Fireplaces are in the museumlike lobby lounge and the elegant dining room, and one or two fireplaces are found in the super-spacious suites (one or more bedrooms). Suite decor includes wood, leather, subtle fabrics, fine art, fresh flowers. Suites are private and quiet, secluded in the treetops, each with a valley view and a deck, some with outdoor spas. Twelve tennis courts with full-time pros and a clubhouse restaurant. Open only to club members and resort guests, the Pete Dye championship golf course is one of the most challenging and beautiful on the Monterey Peninsula, with a clubhouse restaurant.

Day 3

Morning

Breakfast: Carmel Valley Ranch Resort, room service breakfast on your private deck overlooking the valley or breakfast on the garden terrace.

Take a dip in the pool, play a game of golf, then lace up your walking shoes, warm up your credit cards, and get thee to Carmel for a day of shopping and gallery-hopping. (Park in the parking garage at the top of town, at Junipero and Ocean. Finding a legal parking place on village streets can be difficult.)

On San Carlos between Fifth and Sixth is the Visitor's Bureau, upstairs in the Eastwood Building, where you can pick up a walking tour map and schedule of events (408–624–2522). From the balcony, look down into an indoor/outdoor cafe with pretty good food, the **Hog's Breath** (408–625–1044), owned and occasionally visited by Clint Eastwood, former town mayor.

If time is short, stroll down one side of Ocean Avenue and up the other. With time on your hands, wander the side streets, the courtyards, and alleyways. Even those allergic to shopping will enjoy the mix of architecture, everything from English country cottage to California Mission style.

Lunch: **The General Store,** corner of Fifth and Junípero. (408) 624–2233. At an umbrella table under the oaks or inside by the fireplace, casual, rustic, fresh fish, burgers, salads, bar. Open until 2:00 A.M.

Afternoon

A few notable places to visit: the **Carmel Art Association** at Dolores between Fifth and Sixth (408–624–6276), a co-operative with a wide-ranging collection of the works of top artists; the **Weston Galleries** at Sixth and Dolores (408–624–4453) where three generations of famous photographers are represented; the **Mischievous Rabbit** (Lincoln between Ocean and Seventh, 408–624–6854) is a warren of Peter Rabbit–inspired treasures—handpainted baby clothing, rabbit videos and books, carrot surprises. You will often find **Howard Lamar** painting in his studio on Dolores between Ocean and Seventh (408–626–6725). The famous Dzigurski seascapes are on view at **New Renaissance Galleries** on San Carlos between Fifth and Sixth (408–624–7422.)

Gardeners like **Devonshire,** the English garden shop at Ocean and Monte Verde (408–626–4601). Francophiles go to **Pierre Deux** for fantasties created with famous French country fabrics (408–624–8185).

The **Scotch House** on Ocean (408–624–0595) is a mecca for cashmere sweater collectors. You'll find contemporary-design enameled jewelry by a local celebrity artist at **Laurel Burch Galleries** at Ocean and Monte Verde (408–626–2822). The **Carmel Doll Shop** in the

Court of the Golden Eagle (408–624–2607) is a fairyland of antique European dolls, teddy bears, and Victorian gewgaws. Garden sculpture and topiaries are the specialties of **The Dovecote** in a landmark Carmel cottage at Ocean Avenue south of Dolores (408–626–3161).

If you have time to browse in only one shop, make it **African Odyssey,** a large, spectacular gallery shop showing some of the finest wood sculpture and furniture created on the continent of Africa (408–626–8090).

Many of the inns and hotels in Carmel are historic landmarks, such as **La Playa Hotel** at Eighth and Camino Real, a pink Mediterranean mansion built in 1904 (408–624–6476). Take a peek at the luscious gardens blooming beneath a canopy of Angel's Trumpet trees. The lobby is a museumlike world of heirloom furnishings, hand-loomed rugs, and contemporary art. Rooms are upscale traditional, with views of the sea, the gardens, or the village, and the hotel has cottages hidden away in a pine and cypress grove, with kitchens, fireplaces, and private terraces.

Before leaving town, take a late afternoon walk on **Carmel Beach** at the foot of Ocean Avenue—truly white, powdery sand, truly memorable sunsets.

Drive north on Highway 1 to Highway 156, connecting with Highway 101 north to San Francisco. If you have extra time, continue on Highway 1 to Moss Landing (see below).

There's More

Tor House and Hawk Tower, 26304 Ocean View Avenue, Carmel. (408) 624–1813. Medieval stone house and tower, the former home of poet Robinson Jeffers. Tours Friday and Saturday.

Mission Trail Park, Carmel. Thirty-five acres of native vegetation, 5 miles of trails. Enter and begin wandering at Mountain View and Crespi, at Eleventh Street and Junípero, or on Rio Road across from the Mission.

Golf. Rancho Canada Golf Course, Carmel Valley Road, 1 mile from Highway 1. (408) 624–0111. Two beautiful eighteen-hole public courses with mountain backdrop and valley views. On both the East and the West courses, you must negotiate over the Carmel River, it seems an endless number of times, thread the needle between tall cottonwoods, and watch out for the mature pines and oaks throughout every fairway.

Golf Club at Quail Lodge, 8000 Valley Greens Drive, Carmel Valley. (408) 624–2770. Eighteen stunning holes for lodge guests or members of other private clubs. Robert Muir Graves's long-established hilly layout is famous for close-up views of the rugged Santa Lucia Mountains, a demanding array of bunkers, and water, lots of water. You can see the course from every room of the rustic but luxurious Spanish-style lodge resort. Luckily, you are not required to take a cart, all the better to enjoy the 840 acres of wild countryside and elaborate landscaping.

Carmel Valley Ranch Resort, 1 Old Ranch Road, Carmel Valley. (408) 625–9500. Pete Dye designed the Carmel Valley Ranch course in the late 1980s and returned to rearrange the holes with exciting (some say alarming) results. The tees on the eleventh hole float into the stratosphere 100 feet above a teensy bit of fairway. The green on the 330-yard fourteenth makes an interesting target, about 30 feet wide and 90 yards long. The Carmel River runs cheerily along beside several holes, and Dye's amusing deep sand and grass bunkers are magnetic to golf balls. Deer, fox, and wild turkey are often seen peering shyly at golfers from the rough.

Monterey Peninsula Golf Packages, P.O. Box 504, Carmel Valley, 93924. (408) 659–5361.

Special Events

May. Carmel Art Festival, Carmel. (408) 659–4000. Gallery Walk open house and entertainment, meet the artists at dozens of Carmel galleries, gala party and auction, sculpture in the park, many events over four days.

May. California Cowboy Show, Carmel Valley. (408) 659–4000.

June–August. Outdoor Forest Theatre Season, Carmel. (408) 626–1681.

July. Carmel Bach Festival. (408) 624–1521. Internationally acclaimed, two weeks of concerts and classes.

July. Annual Antique and Flea Market, Moss Landing. (408) 633–5202.

August. Carmel Valley Ranchers' Days, Carmel Valley Trail and Saddle Club. Horned steers herded through town, rodeo, 300 roping teams. (408) 659–4000.

September. Carmel Shakespeare Festival. (408) 649–0340.

September. Carmel Mission Fiesta. (408) 624–1271.

September. Sand Castle Building Contest, Carmel Beach. (408) 624–2522. Architects and amateurs vie for biggest, best, most outrageous sand structure.

November. Carmel Homecrafter's Marketplace. (408) 659–5099.

Other Recommended
Restaurants and Lodgings

Carmel Valley

Los Laureles Lodge, 313 West Carmel Valley Road. (408) 659–2233. Behind white picket fences, a ten-acre horse ranch from the 1930s transformed into a country inn and restaurant with a pool, gardens, bar with live music. Ask for a unit away from the road. Special events include BBQs and country music.

Thai Bistro, 55 West Carmel Valley Road. (408) 659–5900. Owned by a French couple from Thailand, exceptionally delicate and sophisticated versions of classic Thai dishes, with an emphasis on fresh seafood.

Wills Fargo, Carmel Valley Road and El Caminito, Carmel Valley Village. (408) 659–2774. Steak by the pound, casual Western atmosphere, dependably good and fun for years and years.

Quail Lodge Resort and Golf Club, 8205 Valley Greens Drive. (408) 624–1581. Upscale, full-service resort with a spectacular golf course at the foot of the mountains.

Carmel Valley Inn, at Carmel Village Road and Las Laureles Road, P.O. Box 115, Carmel Valley 93924. (408) 659–3131. Casual, reasonably priced, simple rooms and suites, tennis; nice pool area open to the public for small fee.

Valley Lodge, 8 Ford Road, P.O. Box 93, Carmel Valley 93924. (800) 641–4646. Small, quiet, pretty patio rooms and cottages, reasonable.

Riverside RV Park, a mile off Carmel Valley Road on Schulte Road. (408) 624–9329. Small, shady sites, some on the Carmel River.

Adjacent to Riverside Park and operated by the same people, the Saddle Mountain Recreation Park also has tree-shaded RV sites, most with nice views of the valley. Here is an attractive swimming pool terrace with picnic tables under oak trees; day use includes the pool and barbecues.

Carmel Country Spa Health Resort, 10 Country Club Way. (408) 659–3486. Weight-loss and lifestyle programs, gourmet restaurant with spa menu, Olympic pool, yoga and water workouts, aerobics, health treatments, nicely decorated, comfortable rooms, seven acres of gardens and grounds.

Carmel

Highlands Inn, 4 miles south of Carmel on Highway 1. (408) 624–3801. Since 1917, wonderful accommodations at a full-service five-star resort with glorious ocean views. The renowned restaurant,

Pacific's Edge, has spectacular sea views from big windows, and a California/French menu to match: grilled Monterey Bay salmon on braised small artichokes and tangy onion-rosemary sauce, grilled swordfish with carmelized Maui onions, chocolate raspberry parcel with vanilla bean ice cream. *Gourmet* magazine calls it the most satisfying place to dine on the *entire* California coast. Twenty-seven thousand bottles of wine in the cellar.

The casual California Market cafe at Highlands Inn is a fun place to have lunch on the way to Big Sur—a table on the deck overlooking the coast or indoors by the pot-bellied stove, pasta, salads, sandwiches.

Luxurious rooms have wood-burning fireplaces, outdoor decks, or balconies. Suites have Jacuzzi tubs, kitchens, and special amenities like terry robes and large dressing areas. Heated pool, spa.

Carmel Mission Ranch, 26270 Dolores Street. (408) 624–3824. Overlooking the Carmel River with views of Carmel Bay and Point Lobos, cowboys and cowgirls kick back and eat steak, local fresh fish, California cuisine in casual surroundings.

Fabulous Toots Lagoon, Dolores and Seventh. (408) 625–1915. Pasta, ribs, salads, seafood, lively bar crowd.

Piatti, Sixth and Junípero. (408) 625–1766. Dependably terrific California Italian food, homemade pasta, rotisserie chicken, oakwood oven pizza, fresh fish and meats on the mesquite grill.

Vagabond House Inn, Fourth and Dolores. (408) 624–7738. Half-timbered English Tudor country inn, blooming courtyard gardens, walking distance to everything in the village, elegant, traditional decor, continental breakfast.

Katy's Place, Mission between Fifth and Sixth. (408) 624–0199. French toast with strawberries and nine kinds of eggs Benedict, a million omelettes, dine indoors or out.

Village Corner, Dolores and Sixth. (408) 624–3588. For more than fifty years, inside and on the patio, locals have been meeting here to complain about how Carmel isn't like it used to be. Breakfast, good sandwiches, salads, less expensive than most.

Cactus Jacks, San Carlos and Fifth. (408) 626–0909. Best Mexican food in town, outdoor patio.

The Cottage, Lincoln between Ocean and Seventh. (408) 625–6260. Granola parfait, cottage oatmeal, panettone French toast for breakfast, artichoke soup and chicken stew in a sourdough basket for lunch, lemon chicken for dinner.

Lincoln Green Inn, Carmelo between Fifteenth and Sixteenth. (408) 624–1880. In the true spirit of Carmel-quaint, sweet cottages at south end of Carmel near Carmel River Beach.

Inns by the Sea. (800) 433–4732. Reservation services for several inns.

Resort Time Roomfinders. (408) 646–9250.

For More Information

Carmel Business Association (visitor's bureau), San Carlos between Fifth and Sixth, P.O. Box 4444, Carmel, CA 93921. (408) 624–2522.

Carmel Valley Chamber of Commerce, Oak Building, Carmel Valley Road, Carmel Valley 93924. (408) 659–4000.

Eastbound Escapes

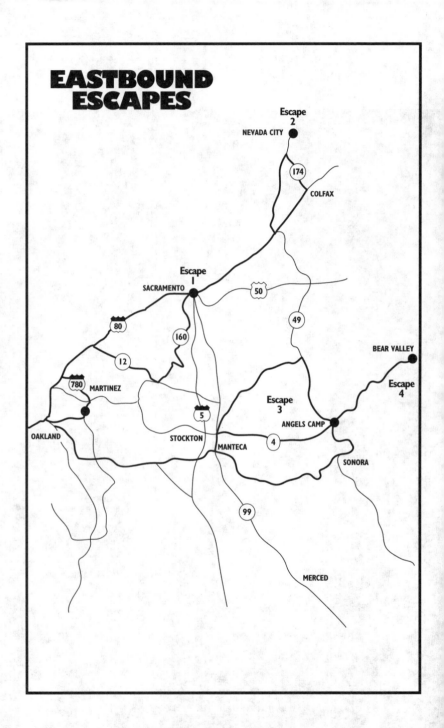

Sacramento Delta Loop

Tour Old Town by carriage and bicycle.

Levee Towns and Old Sacramento

_____ 1 NIGHT _____

Exploring the delta · Old Town shopping · Railroad museum
The Capitol · Crawdads and California history · Cruising the river

Wide, cool, and green, fringed with overhanging trees and plied with
fishing boats and waterskiers, the mighty **Sacramento River** slides
through the metropolitan capital of Sacramento and heads south,
spreading out into a vast delta scattered with ramshackle river towns,
where life remains slow and sweet. Boats and ferries, sailboards and

houseboats ply miles of meandering waterways. Blue herons silently stalk the lagoons and sloughs, home to thousands of birds and ducks, a birdwatcher's mecca. Small towns were abandoned by the Chinese workers who built the levees a hundred years ago, but crawfish cafes, scruffy saloons, and a few inns remain for weekenders seeking quiet getaways.

You'll hang out on the boardwalks of the old port of Sacramento, where ships sailed in for supplies and refreshment in the wild days of the Gold Rush—as many as 800 vessels in 1849. The look and feel of Forty-niner days has been re-created by the miraculous refurbishment and rebuilding of original hotels, saloons, restaurants, firehouses, and establishments of questionable reputation. There are upscale and down-home restaurants, paddlewheelers for river cruises, dozens of shops, and several world-class museums highlighted by the largest and finest railroad museum in the United States.

Topping off your Sacramento delta weekend is a tour of the magnificent state capitol building and grounds.

Day 1

Morning

Drive north on Highway 80 from the Oakland Bay Bridge for about an hour. Two miles south of Fairfield, turn east on Highway 12, past the Jelly Belly factory, through the flat cattle country of Solano County, to **Rio Vista** on the Sacramento River, a 25-mile trip.

Before crossing the Rio Vista bridge, go north along the river 2 miles to the ferry to **Ryder Island,** one of the last remaining ferries in the delta; it's free. Prowl around the island a little, then return to the bridge taking Highway 160 north, the levee road.

On the east side of the river is the **Brannan Island State Recreation Area** (916–777–6671), where campers and boaters enjoy fishing and swimming in the Sacramento and a couple of sloughs. There are tent and RV camps, boat-in campsites, a public beach, and picnic sites.

Breakfast: At **Isleton** bear right at the Y to **Ernie's,** 212 Second Street (916–777–6510). Seems like Ernie's restaurant and bar has been here forever, serving crawfish for breakfast, lunch, and dinner.

Isleton consists of a down-at-the-heels collection of tinfront and falsefront Western buildings. Antiques shops nearby are worth a browse.

You'll drive through **Walnut Grove,** a quiet community on both sides of the river, with a ghostly, empty Chinatown. At **Locke** turn right, leaving the highway, at Yuen Chong grocery; go 1 block down the hill and park. Just 1 block long, Locke is the only surviving rural community built and lived in by Chinese early in this century. Now it's a maze of creaky wooden buildings connected by a boardwalk. The **Dai Loy Museum,** open on the weekends, is a spooky former gambling hall and opium den. **Al the Wop's** bar and cafe is dustily atmospheric and frequented by farmhands and fishermen. **Locke Ness** buys junque and sells antiques.

Along the levee road are farmhouses and mansions from several eras, in various states of repair. If you spy tall palm trees, that's usually where the houses are located, surrounded by overgrown gardens. Slow down just north of Hood to see a particularly genteel Victorian. In the summertime keep your eyes open for **Eagle Point Orchards** (916–744–1120), where you can buy tomatoes and wonderful Bartlett pears.

Lunch: **Courtland Docks** at the Courtland Marina, Highway 160 at Courtland. (916) 775–1172. Burgers, salads, homemade soup, and apple pie.

Afternoon

At Freeport are several seafood restaurants and bars attracting daytrippers from Sacramento. It's just 9 miles farther to **Sacramento,** where you'll connect with I–5 north, proceeding for a few minutes to the J Street/Old Sacramento exit; there are parking garages on the east side of Old Town.

Top off the day with a late-afternoon cruise on the river. The *Spirit of Sacramento* paddlewheeler departs from the L Street landing in Old Sacramento for one-hour sightseeing trips (916–552–2933).

Sacramento was a simple homesteader's fort that became a boomtown during the Gold Rush in the mid-1800s, and the first link in the transcontinental railroad. At the confluence of the American and Sacramento rivers, with a deepwater connection to San Francisco Bay and the world, the fortune-seeker's town of the 1800s is now a modern metropolis and a gathering place for state representatives. Summer days average in the nineties, with many days over a hundred degrees, but this is a city of more than a million trees, and ready access to the water, so relief is never far away.

Dinner: **Crawdad's River Cantina,** 1375 Garden Highway. (916) 929–2268. On the levee near I–5; Cajun popcorn, fresh fish, steaks, salads, lively atmosphere. Several excellent marinas, with restaurants and boat tie-ups, are found along the Garden Highway on the north edge of the city.

Lodging: **Radisson Hotel Sacramento,** 500 Leisure Lane, Sacramento. (916) 922–2020. Five minutes from Old Town, a comfortable oasis of a resort hotel with swimming pools, fitness center, par course, access to the 35-mile-long biking and walking trail along the American River (bike rentals here), eighteen acres of gardens surrounding a small lake, and several restaurants with garden patio seating. Each room or suite has a balcony or patio, most overlooking the gardens. The nightclub is a popular spot for night owls who like to dance. Families like the comfort and spaciousness of the suites, which offer separate sleeping areas. The business center is state-of-the art, with a full range of services and equipment, including laptops, pagers, mailing and secretarial services, an ATM, plus airport shuttle.

Day 2

Morning

Breakfast: **Whistle Stop Cafe,** Front Street, Old Town Sacramento. (916) 446–4445. From 6:30 A.M., Belgian waffles, homemade cinnamon rolls, steak and eggs.

Take Sixteenth Street into **Old Town Sacramento.** Cool early mornings are the best time to prowl the boardwalks, taking photos of the wooden falsefronts, and climbing around on antique railcars.

Opening at 10:00 A.M., the **California State Railroad Museum,** on the north end of Old Town (916–448–4466), comprises 100,000 square feet housing three dozen locomotives and railcars in pristine condition. One of the engines weighs a mere million pounds. The Canadian National sleeping car rocks back and forth as if on its way down the track. Sound effects, snoozing passengers, and compartments that look as if they're occupied give you a taste of vintage train travel. Retired conductors in their dark blue uniforms are available to answer questions and pose for photos. On the second level is a dream of a toy train running through tiny towns and over bridges; to start the action, push the red button. The **Railroad Museum Gift Shop** next door has fabulous train-related toys, books, and souvenirs.

Now that you're a railroad aficionado, step over to the depot and take a short trip up the tracks along the river to the Port of Sacramento.

Nearby, the **Sacramento History Center** (916–449–2057) contains five galleries of Sacramento area history.

Explore the ***Delta King,*** 1000 Front Street (916–444–KING), a huge Mississippi riverboat permanently moored here at the waterfront. Now a forty-four-stateroom hotel and restaurant, the *Delta King* has small but comfortable cabins with windows overlooking the river; the bars and restaurant have fine river views and are popular, although somewhat touristy, for brunch, lunch, and dinner. Next to the *Delta King* is the **Visitor Information Center,** 1104 Front Street (916–442–7644).

Based primarily in Old Town, the annual **Sacramento Jazz Jubilee** at the end of May is the largest traditional jazz festival in the world, with more than a hundred American and international bands playing in indoor and outdoor venues for thousands of fans. If you love Dixieland and can handle the crowds, make your hotel reservations early, get a program of events from the Jazz Society, and put on your dancing shoes (916–372–5277).

April brings a big **Festival de la Familia** to Old Town (916–326–5520), a day of live outdoor entertainment, an open-air market, and foods from more than two dozen Latin countries.

Lunch: **California Fat's,** 1015 Front. (916) 441–7966. A New Age offshoot of the famous Victorian-style Fat City establishment next door. A contemporary jade, fushia, and royal blue cafe decor seems aquariumlike as you step downstairs into the narrow dining room; subtle sounds of a 30-foot waterfall mask everyone's conversation but your own. On the menu are *nouvelle* Chinese specialties and fresh fish, Peking duck pizzas, grilled crab sandwiches, salads, and banana cream pie; exotic drinks include a Sacramento Slammer and Electric Lemonade.

Afternoon

A hundred or so shops await your discovery in old town. The **Artists' Collaborative Gallery,** 1007 Second (916–444–3764), is a large space displaying paintings, ceramics, weavings, and jewelry by local artists, the best gallery in Old Town. Navajo rugs and Native American turquoise and silver jewelry are the specialty of **Gallery of the American West,** at 121 K Street (916–446–6662).

Mike's Puzzle Store, 1009 Second Street (916–444–0446), has hundreds, maybe thousands, of puzzles, mostly jigsaws. **Two Crows,** 1003 Second Street (916–444–3616), specializes in fascinating nature and wildlife items. **Brooks Novelty Antiques,** 1107 Front (916–443–0783), is a delightfully musty, crowded place filled with old records, jukeboxes, weird TVs, radios, vintage bikes, magazines, and posters.

Decorated to the max for every holiday and smelling like chocolate heaven, the **Rocky Mountain Chocolate Factory,** 1039 Second Street (916–448–8801), lures you in with hand-dipped ice cream bars, caramel apples, chocolate-covered strawberries, and freshly made candy. You could be in trouble here.

Fanny Ann's, 1023 Second Street (916–441–0505), is five floors of crazily antiques-crammed restaurant and bar; it's a fun place to take the kids during the day, while an adult crowd gathers here at night. **Sticky Fingers,** at 1027 Second Street (916–443–4075), holds forth on the second floor of an old building, serving up ribs, chicken, and seafood while entertaining passersby with live Dixieland and jazz from the veranda.

Walk or drive the few blocks to the **California State Capitol,** Tenth and Capitol Mall (916–324–0333), for a tour of the remarkable double-domed building and surrounding grounds. Updated and re-modeled over many decades, a hodgepodge of eras and styles, the capitol building was treated to a $70 million complete restoration in the 1970s; everything was demolished and removed except the out-side walls and the domes. Furnishings, art, ballustrades, chandeliers, and myriad bits and pieces were located or replicated and reinstalled, re-creating the original architectural masterpiece of the 1870s.

A guided tour provides background on the magnificently carved staircases, elaborate crystal chandeliers, marble parquet floors, historic artwork, and zillions of columns, cornices, and friezes decorated in gold. The "Historic Rooms" tour focuses on artifacts and interesting stories of politicos from the past. You'll learn about California lawmak-ing, and you may even be able to sit in on a legislative session.

Take a tour of the grounds, or stroll around on your own through forty acres of specimen plants and trees, many planted in the 1870s. Springtime in Capitol Park brings waves of blooming camellias, aza-leas, and dogwood, and rivers of tulips and daffodils.

It's 90 miles from Sacramento to San Francisco on Highway 80.

If you want to stop for a meal or to stretch your legs, the **Nut Tree** on Highway 80 at Vacaville, about half-way between Sacramento and San Francisco, has been welcoming travelers since the 1930s when it was just a fruit stand (707–448–8435). Little kids like the big wooden rock-ing horses in the patio, the real carousel, and the little open-air train, which makes an exciting fifteen-minute run through the orchards to the airport and back. In the huge Nut Tree store are a bakery, a gourmet foods section, guidebooks, souvenirs, semiprecious gem and mineral collections, an art gallery, an aircraft store, and a pleasant restaurant.

The large, colorful Nut Tree restaurant is very good, but you will save money and get through your meal faster across the freeway at the **Coffee Tree** (707–448–8435). You may also wish to browse in the hundred-plus discount factory stores located across the street from the Coffee Tree.

There's More

Train. Amtrak passenger trains from Oakland to Sacramento. (800) USA–RAIL.

Antiques. Several large shops at Del Paso Boulevard and Arden Way, and a dozen in the 800 block of Fifty-seventh Street, Sacramento. Pick up a booklet here to locate other shops in Sacramento.

Bike and Surrey Rentals of Old Sacramento, 916 Second Street.

(916) 441–3836. An easy way to get around Old Town or ride 26 miles of paved bike paths on the Jedediah Smith Memorial Bicycle Trail, which follows the American River Parkway, or 23 miles of scenic pathway from Old Town to Folsom Lake, in the foothills of Gold Country. Guided walks on the parkway are available through the Effie Yeaw Nature Center (916–489–4918).

California Citizen-Soldier Museum, 1119 Second Street, Old Sacramento. (916) 442–2883. Some 30,000 papers, documents, and memorabilia tracing California's rich militia and military history.

Crocker Art Museum, Third and O streets, Sacramento. (916) 264–5423. A gigantic restored Victorian sheltering the oldest public art museum in the West, European paintings and drawings, nineteenth-century art.

Towe Ford Museum, 2200 Front Street, Sacramento. (916) 442–6802. The world's most complete antique Ford auto collection—150 vehicles, an almost complete chronology of Henry Ford's genius, from 1903 until the early 1950s. You can climb up behind the wheel of a Model T flatbed truck and get up close to a number of the old beauties. A few other exotic autos are also exhibited here, such as Alexander Haig's armoured Cadillac.

Victorians. A rich trove of magnificent Victorian mansions can be seen on a drive in downtown Sacramento, from Seventh to Sixteenth street, between E and I. Outstanding examples are the Heilbron House, at 740 O Street, and the Stanford House, at 800 N Street.

Grizzly Island State Recreation Area, south of Highway 12 between Fairfield and Rio Vista. (707) 425–3828. Vast marshes inhabited by tule elk and thousands of fresh- and saltwater birds; a million birds spend the winter here. Hunting and fishing with permits in season.

Waterworld USA, 1600 Exposition Boulevard, Sacramento. (916) 924–0555. The biggest wave pool in Northern California, with 4-foot waves and dozens of other water-oriented play venues: the Cliff Hanger, a 65-foot near-vertical slide; the six slides of the California Scream Machine; a tubing river; and a special 100-foot slide for kids three to six years old.

Special Events

February. Mardi Gras, Sacramento. (916) 443–8653.
March. Camellia Festival, Sacramento. (916) 442–8166.
May. Sacramento County Fair, Sacramento. (916) 924–2076.
May. Sacramento Jazz Jubilee. (916) 372–5277. Many bands, lots of people, dawn-to-midnight Dixieland in Old Sacramento and other venues.

June. Folsom Rodeo, a half-hour from Sacramento in Folsom. (916) 985–2698. Major rodeo with many events, bull riding, steer wrestling, barrel racing, bronc riding, carnival, fireworks, arts and crafts, and more.

June. California Railroad Festival, Old Sacramento. (916) 445–7387.

June. Sacramento Renaissance Faire. (916) 966–1036.

June–July. Shakespeare Festival in the Park, Sacramento. (916) 558–2228.

July–August. Sacramento Light Opera Association's Music Circus, Sacramento. (916) 557–1999. Almost fifty years of Broadway musicals for the whole family.

August. Sacramento Riverfest, Old Sacramento. (916) 264–7057.

August–September. California State Fair, Sacramento. (916) 924–2032.

October. Old Sacramento Boats on the Boardwalk. (916) 366–1146.

November. Indian Arts and Crafts Fair, Sacramento. (916) 324–0971.

December. Old Sacramento Holiday Festival. (916) 443–8653.

Other Recommended Restaurants and Lodgings

Isleton

Delta Daze Inn, 20 Main Street. (916) 777–7777. Bed-and-breakfast accommodations in a historic building, complimentary bikes, nice rooms over a soda fountain. Fireplace in main lounge with library, games. Only pet allowed is a blue-bellied, two-trunked orangutan, so bring it if you have it.

Viera's RV Resort, 15476 State Highway 160. (916) 777–6661. Between Rio Vista and Isleton on the Sacramento River; boat-launching headquarters.

Sacramento

Fountain Suites, 321 Bercut Drive. (916) 441–1444. Contemporary suites with separate living rooms, continental breakfast, some with microwaves and refrigerators. Jacuzzi, swimming pool, complimentary shuttle to airport, downtown, Old Town, and the Capital.

Abigail's Bed and Breakfast Inn, 2120 G Street. (916) 441–5007. A dream of a luxury bed-and-breakfast establishment, near the capitol. A 1912 Colonial Revival mansion on a street lined with old elms, antiques, brass beds, marble bathrooms, Jacuzzis, four-posters, canopy beds, gardens, full breakfasts.

Amber House Bed and Breakfast Inn, 1315 Twenty-second Street. (916) 444–8085. In two restored mansions, eight opulent, luxurious, romantic inn rooms, Jacuzzi tubs, gourmet breakfast in the dining room, on the veranda, or in guest rooms, evening refreshments, bikes available. One room has a heart-shaped Jacuzzi and a waterfall!

Old Sacramento

Fat City Bar and Cafe, 1001 Front. (916) 446–6768. Hundred-year-old bar, bistro-style cafe.

The Firehouse, 1112 Second Street. (916) 442–4772. In an 1853 firehouse, indoors in romantic surroundings and on the garden patio, continental cuisine voted "Best in Sacramento" and "Most Romantic."

For More Information

Sacramento Convention and Visitor's Bureau, 1421 K Street, Sacramento, CA 95814. (916) 264–7777.

Gold Rush North

Downtown Nevada City, a charming Gold Rush community.

Forty-Niner Towns in the Sierra Foothills

———————————— 2 NIGHTS ————————————

Gold mines and museums • River rambles • Victoriana
Antiques • Old West • Nuggets and gems

The foothills of the California Gold Country stretch more than 300 miles along the western slopes of the Sierra Nevadas all the way to the southern gate of Yosemite National Park. In several river corridors—the Yuba, the American, the Mokelumne, the Stanislaus, the Tuolumne, and the Merced—dozens of boomtowns exploded in population in the mid-1800s, when gold was discovered, only to be abandoned by the miners and adventure seekers when the lodes were exhausted.

Of the remaining communities still thriving today, Nevada City is the most completely original Gold Rush town in the state, having somehow escaped the devastating fires that plagued most of the rest of the Gold Country. More than a hundred Victorian mansions and Western falsefront saloons and hotels cluster cozily together here on a radiating wheel of tree-lined streets on small hills. At an elevation of about 3,000 feet, the whole place turns red and gold in the fall, when hundreds of maples, aspens, and oaks turn blazing bright.

Nearby, a historic gold-mining estate, the wild-and-woolly town of Grass Valley, and the pleasures of the South Yuba River add up to a busy weekend in the northern Gold Country.

Just a few miles to the east, 1.2 million acres of wilderness in the Tahoe National Forest afford endless hiking, camping, fishing, and cross-country skiing opportunities.

Day 1

Morning

From the Oakland Bay Bridge, drive north on Highway 80 beyond Sacramento to **Auburn**—about two and a half hours—and take the Maple Street exit, parking on or near Maple. On a ridge overlooking the north fork of the **American River,** where gold was discovered in 1848, Auburn has a compact, charming Old Town of antiques shops and restaurants, worth an hour or so of investigation. For breakfast or a snack on the deck above Old Town, go to **Awful Annie's,** on Sacramento Street. (916–888–9857).

Between Auburn and the town of Folsom, **Folsom Lake State Recreation Area** is one of the largest recreation areas in Northern California (916–988–0205). Behind Folsom Dam, on more than 75 shoreline miles, are marinas and fishing and boating resorts and campgrounds. There is a great bicycle trail that goes all the way to downtown Sacramento, and more than 80 miles of hiking and horseback-riding trails. Fishing for rainbow trout, catfish, bass, and Coho salmon keeps the lake busy with boaters all year-round.

Leaving Auburn, take Lincoln Way, off Maple, north past the 1894 courthouse, a domed dazzler still in use today; continue north on Highway 49 for about thirty minutes to **Nevada City.** Approaching the lower Sierras, the pines get taller, the dirt redder, and the rivers icier; in the winter a shallow blanket of snow may dust the ground, although it seldom snows enough to require tire chains.

Take the Sacramento Street exit into town, parking in the lot at Sacramento and Broad. Put on your walking shoes and head across the bridge into town on Broad, the main street. Take a right down to the stone-and-brick **Yuba Canal Building,** at 132 Main, built in 1850 on the banks of Wolfe Creek, where you can pick up tour maps at the **Chamber of Commerce.** Since early in this century, the downtown has remained lost in time, architecturally speaking, and there is much to discover within 3 or 4 blocks.

Next door, at 214 Main, the **Firehouse Museum** has two floors of Gold Rush and Indian artifacts.

Lunch: **Posh Nosh,** 318 Broad. (916) 265–6064. Eat on the tree-shaded patio. Sandwiches, pasta, salads, homemade desserts.

Afternoon

The National Hotel, 211 Broad (916–265–4551), is the oldest continuously operating hotel west of the Rockies; take a look at the long bar, shipped around the Horn more than a hundred years ago. Rooms here are small and sweet, with Victorian furnishings and gimcracks: some have balconies overlooking the street. The old **New York Hotel,** at 408 Broad, circa 1850, now houses several gift and antiques shops.

Tanglewood Forest, 217 Broad Street (916–478–1223), is a fantasyland of wizards, fairies, and strange dolls. **Four Winds,** 310 Broad (916–265–9021), is a gallery store featuring international folk art. Next to the **Nevada Theatre,** at 401 Broad, the oldest theater in California, is the **Fisher Glass Collection** (916–478–1007), a workshop of fantastic blown glass. **Utopian-Stone,** at 212 Main (916–265–6209), specializes in gold quartz jewelry.

Mountain Pastimes Fun and Games, 320 Spring Street (916–265–6692), has toys and games for grownups. Across the street you can taste Nevada County wines made right here at the **Nevada City Winery,** 321 Spring (916–265–9463). In the past couple of decades, vineyards and wineries have popped up all over the county; they celebrate in September with a Wine Fest and Grape Stomp at the Miners Foundry Cultural Center up the street.

Dinner: **Creekside Cafe,** 101 Broad Street. (916) 265–3445. Within sight and sound of rushing Deer Creek, the terrace is the place to be on summer nights; inside are candlelit tables before a fireplace. Fresh fish, poultry, and meats in exotic sauces, good wine list.

Lodging: **Kendall House,** 534 Spring Street 95959. (916) 265–0405. In a quiet neighborhood within walking distance of downtown; large, comfortable, very private rooms with baths; two-room cottage with living/dining room, fireplace, private deck, and kitchen; beautiful gardens and pool. Sensitive to your moods, Jan Kendall will regale you with stories or diplomatically leave you alone. Many of her guests rebook a year in advance. Be sure to save time for enjoying the pool and gardens, bright with color in the fall, cool and leafy on hot summer days.

Day 2

Morning

Breakfast: At the Kendall House. Eggs Benedict in the sunny solarium or on the garden terrace. Dr. Ted Kendall is an avid runner and will direct you to walking and running trails beginning right from his front door. One scenic 10-mile route starts at Factory Street in downtown and goes out Old Downieville Highway to Newtown Road.

Drive south on Highway 49 to the south end of Grass Valley to the Empire Mine exit, going east on Empire Street for five minutes to reach **Empire Mine State Park** (916–273–8522), a 784-acre mining estate. The largest, deepest, and richest hardrock gold mine in California operated here for more than a hundred years, producing $100 million in gold from 360 miles of underground channels, some 11,000 feet deep. On a tour or on your own, see an extensive complex of buildings and equipment, including part of the main shaft. A visitor's center recounts the history of the mine in photos, exhibits, and films.

Sweeping lawns beneath 100-foot sugar pines surround the mine owner's home, **Bourne Cottage,** an outstanding example of a Willis Polk–designed English country manor with lovely gardens and a fountain pool. An annual old-fashioned **Miners' Picnic** takes place in June in the park, with food, contests, gold panning, entertainment, and a foot race (916–273–4667).

Lunch: Drive back on Empire Street, across the freeway, to the first right, Mill Street, following Mill down and under the freeway to the **North Star Mining Museum** and powerhouse (916–273–4255), where a shady lawn over Wolf Creek makes a delightful picnic spot.

Marshall's Pasties is a good place to take out fresh Cornish pasties and English sausage rolls and other picnic fare. At 203 Mill Street in Grass Valley (916–272–2844), Marshall's is on the main street of town. five minutes from Wolf Creek.

Afternoon

Among the many pieces of antique equipment at the North Star Museum are a working stampmill and the largest Pelton wheel in the world, a waterwheel that produced power from the creek for the North Star Mine; a large collection of photos traces mining history.

Follow Mill Street north into downtown **Grass Valley,** parking near the center of town. Inhabited during the Gold Rush by thousands of English and Irish miners who worked five major gold mines in the area, the town is honeycombed with miles of underground tunnels and shafts.

Step into **The Holbrooke Hotel,** 212 West Main (916–273–1353), the grand dame of Grass Valley since 1862. A glance in the hotel register turns up such famous guests as Presidents Cleveland and Garfield. At 114 Mill are three antiques shops, and at 108 Mill, the **Little Silver Palace** (916–477–6009) has a huge inventory of Southwest and contemporary silver jewelry. At Church and Chapel streets, the **Grass Valley Museum** (916–272–4725) is a restored school and orphanage exhibiting Gold Rush artifacts, clothing, paintings, and domestic items. The **Nevada County Chamber of Commerce,** 248 Mill (916–273–4667), is in the reconstructed home of Lola Montez, a notorious dancehall entertainer of the 1800s. One block off Main take a stroll on Neal and Church streets to see several magnificent Victorian mansions and churches.

On the **Yuba River** a few miles southwest of Grass Valley in **Bridgeport** is one of only a dozen covered bridges still standing in the state. At 256 feet, the **Bridgeport Covered Bridge** is possibly the longest single-span covered bridge in the world. Mellowed sugar pine shingles and massive, old-growth Douglas fir beams are warm reminders that buggies and mule teams once clattered across the wooden floorboards. There are nice picnic spots near the bridge, walking trails along the river, and shallow wading pools among the rocks. During much of the year, docents and rangers teach gold panning and conduct interpretive tours of the bridge (916–432–2546).

Not far from Bridgeport, **Englebright Lake** on the Yuba River is a slender piece of water with nice camping and fishing spots accessible only by boat (916–639–2342). Pleasant boat-in campgrounds have sandy beaches and trees.

Take a predinner swim and enjoy wine and cheese with the Kendalls, who will recommend their favorite dinner houses.

Dinner: **Selaya's,** 320 Broad Street, Nevada City. (916) 265–5697. Superb continental and California cuisine menu, elegant presentation.

Lodging: **Kendall House** (see Day 1).

Day 3

Morning

Breakfast: Another extravaganza of a breakfast created by Jan at the Kendall House. (If you can squeeze in a piece of pie, stop in at the **Apple Fare,** 307 Broad Street, Nevada City, 916–265–5458, and sit at a big round table with the locals.)

For a fascinating trip along the south fork of the Yuba River, take Highway 49 north from Nevada City to Tyler Foote Crossing Road, turn right, and continue to where Tyler splits to the left to Alleghany; then turn right onto Cruzon Grade Road, proceeding to **Malakoff Diggins State Historic Park** (916–265–2740), the largest hydraulic mine site in the world, a rather shocking and strangely beautiful remnant of gold mining in the 1800s, when giant waterjets, called monitors, destroyed entire mountains. A mile of hillside here was washed away, the soil and rocks clogging rivers and streams until the practice was outlawed late in the nineteenth century. Weird and colorful pinnacles, domes, and spirals, as well as a milky lake, are fringed with second- and third-growth pines.

Swimming and fishing holes on the **South Yuba River** and a 21-mile river corridor park developed by the state are accessible near Malakoff Diggins and at other points in the area (see Tahoe National Forest, opposite). Near the arched bridge where Highway 49 drops down into the South Yuba canyon, **Independence Trail** is 7 miles of paved and boardwalk forest pathway that is wheelchair accessible and great for a run or a walk and for baby strollers. Some ramps lead to fishing holes.

Independence Trail was originally a canal built in 1856 to move water through the mountains for hydraulic gold mining. Chinese and Italian laborers constructed elevated wooden aqueducts over deep mountain ravines to connect miles of ditches. A unique attraction for today's visitor, the trail alternates between solid ground and wooden flumes, and you sometimes have the sensation of being suspended in mid-air. The most dramatic part, about a mile west of the trailhead, is a 500-foot-long trestle above a waterfall. You can get more information and a map: South Yuba Independence Trail, P.O. Box 1026, Nevada City 95959.

On your way back to the Bay Area, take Highway 174 south from Grass Valley to Colfax, on the oldest, the twistiest, and one of the prettiest roads in the county, past horse ranches and small farms. Another pie emporium is on this road—the **Happy Apple Kitchen** (916–273–2822).

There's More

Golf. Alta Sierra Golf and Country Club, 11897 Tammy Way, Grass Valley. (916) 273–2010. Eighteen holes, 4 miles south of Grass Valley on Highway 49.

Renaissance Vineyard and Winery, west of Grass Valley, by way of Highway 20, north on E21, east on E20. (916) 692–2425. At 2,300 feet with the northern Sierra Nevadas in the distance, the largest mountain vineyard estate in North America. Taste Cabernet or award-winning late-harvest Rieslings, and tour the fine arts museum of classical Chinese furniture. This winery has its own orchestra and chorus, opera, theater, and ballet companies that perform on the premises regularly!

Lake Spaulding, a half-hour east of Nevada City on Highway 20. Drive-in and walk-in campgrounds in pine groves, near a fishing and boating lake. Nearby **Fuller Lake** has just a handful of drive-in campsites but is quite a lovely, quiet, small lake for fishing and boating.

Hiking. The Tahoe National Forest is 5 miles west of Nevada City. Obtain maps and information on hiking and camping at the forest headquarters office at 631 Coyote Street in Nevada City. (916) 265–4531.

Special Events

February. Northern Mines Winetasting Exposition, Grass Valley. (916) 273–4667.

April. House and Garden Tour, Nevada City. (916) 265–2692.

May. Jewels to Junk Flea Market and Antique Fair, Auburn. (916) 823–3836.

June. Tour of Nevada City Bicycle Classic, Nevada City. (916) 265–2692.

June. Miners' Picnic, Empire Mine State Park. (916) 273–4667. Food, contests, gold panning, entertainment, marathon race.

July. Nevada County Airpark Fly-In, Nevada City. (916) 273–5273.

July. Summer Nights in Nevada City. (916) 265–2692. Everyone comes in costume, fine art, classic cars, food and drink, entertainment on four stages.

August. Nevada County Fair, Grass Valley. (916) 273–6217.

September. Nevada County Wine Fest and Grape Stomp, Nevada City. (916) 265–5040.

October. Golf Rush Jubilee Crafts Fair, Auburn. (916) 823–3836.

December. Cornish Christmas Celebration, Grass Valley. (916) 272–8315.

December. Victorian Christmas, Nevada City. (916) 265–2692.

Other Recommended Restaurants and Lodgings

Nevada City

Vlato's, 423 Broad. (916) 265–2831. Pretty garden patio setting, dinner only.

Red Castle Inn, 109 Prospect. (916) 265–5135. In a cedar forest, a spectacular four-story 1860 Victorian Gothic mansion overlooking the town, one of only two genuine Gothic Revival brick houses on the

West Coast. Seven romantically decorated rooms and suites with private verandas and sitting rooms, canopied beds, lace curtains. Expanded breakfast buffet and afternoon tea. A winding pathhway leads from the terraced hillside gardens to the town below. *San Francisco Focus* magazine calls it the best bed-and-breakfast inn in the state.

Northern Queen Inn, 400 Railroad Avenue. (916) 265–5824. On the south end of town; spacious, comfortable motel rooms, pool, cottages with kitchenettes and chalets on the creek, family-oriented restaurant, plus several restored train cars and a nineteenth-century narrow-gauge engine.

Historic Bed and Breakfast Inns of Grass Valley/Nevada City, P.O. Box 2060. (916) 477–6634.

Grass Valley

Empire House Restaurant, 535 Mill. (916) 273–8272. Swiss, German, and American cuisine; lunch and dinner.

Holbrooke Hotel, 212 West Main. (916) 273–1353. Twenty-eight restored rooms, beautiful dining room and saloon.

For More Information

Grass Valley/Nevada County Chamber of Commerce, 248 Mill Street, Grass Valley, CA 95945. (916) 273–4667.

Nevada City Chamber of Commerce, 132 Main, Nevada City, CA 95959. (916) 265–2692.

Heart of the Mother Lode

One of the many antiques shops in Sutter Creek.

Sutter Creek to Angels Camp

_____ 2 NIGHTS _____

Gold in them thar hills · Antiques shopping · Historic towns
Wineries · Mining museums · Caverns and cowboys

Amador County is rolling pastures, vineyards, and orchardlands, criss-crossed by rivers that produced more gold than any other county in the Mother Lode. Several still-alive-and-kicking Gold Rush towns and many abandoned settlements remain. The postcard-perfect settlement of Sutter Creek attracts weekenders who like to park for the day and enjoy shopping, sightseeing, cafe sitting, and resting in a country inn, all within a few blocks.

Jackson is the site of a major museum, more of the antiques shops that are liberally sprinkled throughout the area, and a historic hotel saloon still frequented by the rough-and-rowdy after all these years.

Housed in buildings from the mid-1800s that are museums in themselves, restaurants and inns in the Gold Country are surprisingly sophisticated, reflecting the fact that big-city visitors are discovering the quiet pleasures of Amador County.

In the northern foothills a cluster of Shenandoah Valley wineries are gaining attention for their hearty Zinfandels.

Day 1

Morning

From the Oakland Bay Bridge, take Highway 580 east to 205 east, connecting with Highway 99 north to Stockton. Drive east on Highway 88 to 49, the main highway through the Gold Country. Turn north on 49 and proceed for ten minutes to **Sutter Creek,** cradled in a valley surrounded by oak-dotted rolling hills, a picturesque little town with white frame houses giving it a New England look. Concentrated on and around Main Street is a rich cache of nineteenth-century architecture—elaborate Victorians, Western falsefronts with overhanging balconies, and even a Greek Revival church, the United Methodist, a circa-1860 beauty whose tall steeple anchors the south end of town.

Lunch: Walking into the **Chatter Box Cafe,** at 29 Main (209–267–5935), is walking back into the 1940s. It's an old-fashioned soda fountain made nostalgic with World War II posters, Big Band records, and a long counter where town regulars meet; burgers with homemade buns, grilled cheese sandwiches, world-class onion rings, and pies, floats, sodas, and shakes.

Afternoon

A dozen antiques shops on Main include several vendors at **Sutter Creek Antiques and Central Shops,** 28 Main (209–267–5574). **Creekside Shops,** 22 Main (209–267–5520), is another group of antiques and collectibles dealers. **Old Hotel Antiques,** at 68 Main (209–267–5901), specializes in estate jewelry and old advertising signs and paraphernalia. In the **Gold Miner Candy Shoppe,** 40 Main (209–267–1525), are barrels of penny candy that no longer costs a penny.

Gold and Gems, 67 Main (209–223–1308), is anything but country-style, a large store showing fine jewelry and precious stones. Across the street the **Fine Eye Gallery,** at 71 Main (209–267–0571), has contemporary jewelry, art, and ceramics.

Some of the best shopping is at the north end of Main. **Coming Attractions,** 79 Main (209–267–0665), sells handwoven clothing. Next door is museumlike **Cobweb Collection,** 813 Main (209–267–0690), with rustic willow furniture designed by the shop owner, plus Southwest furniture, art, and antiques. A step away, **Merchants Unlimited,** at 85 Main (209–267–0160), is in a garden cottage with several rooms of Victorian-motif imports, garden gifts, books, jewelry, artwork, antiques, and more.

In the **Eureka Street Courtyard** off Main is the **Glass Rush** (209–267–5097), with sand-carved and stained-glass art; **Ruby Tuesday Cafe** (209–267–0556), serving espresso, salads, and sandwiches; and the **Sutter Creek Wine and Cheese** shop (209–267–0945), where you can taste local wines, beers, and cheeses. Farther down Eureka Street, **Knight's Foundry** (209–267–5543), the only water-powered foundry still operating in the United States, is open for tours.

Duck behind a tall hedge at 75 Main for a peek at the **Sutter Creek Inn** (209–267–5606). In an overgrown country garden shaded by ancient oaks, the bed-and-breakfast inn has a long and lively history and has been completely restored to its former Greek Revival elegance, with nineteen rooms, some with fireplaces.

On **Spanish Street,** between Main and the creek that gives Sutter Creek its name, are rows of beautiful clapboard cottages and mansions.

If you're an antiques hound, make the 2-mile trip north to **Amador City** to browse in the tiny town, the state's smallest incorporated city.

North and east of here, the **Shenandoah Valley** is the heart of a grape-growing region where more than a dozen wineries are located in restored barns and stone cellars on sideroads branching off the Shenandoah Road; most are open for tasting and tours. Obtain a map from the first winery you encounter, or from the Amador Vintners Association, P.O. Box 667, Plymouth 95669.

Dinner: **Bellotti Inn,** 53 Main, Sutter Creek. (209) 267–5211. Satisfying family-style Italian dinners in a hundred-year-old hotel.

Lodging: **The Foxes,** 77 Main, Sutter Creek. (209) 267–5882. Next door to the Sutter Creek Inn. Another Greek Revival beauty, with fireplaces and clawfoot tubs in almost every room, canopy beds, air-conditioning, and *muchas* foxes.

Day 2

Morning

Breakfast: At The Foxes: full breakfast in bed on a silver tray in your room or in the gazebo.

Three miles south of Sutter Creek, **Jackson** looks like a toy town as you approach from above on Highway 49. From the **Amador County Chamber of Commerce,** at the corner of Highways 49 and 88, get a walking-tour map. Sightseeing is best accomplished by wandering the boardwalks and quiet lanes on foot; parking can be a problem on the narrow streets.

Dominating Old Town on Main Street is the **National Hotel** (209–223–0500), operating for well over a hundred years as a hotel and restaurant; simple hotel rooms with private baths are reasonable. Red velvet wallpaper and brass chandeliers intact, the hotel restaurant is popular and the saloon is a rollicking place to rub elbows with cowboys and Indians on a Saturday night.

Across the street the 1862 IOOF Hall, the tallest three-story building in the county, once housed Wells Fargo offices where more than $100 million in gold dust and bullion were weighed. Check out 22,000 square feet of pine furniture at **Water Street Antiques,** 19 Water Street off Main (209–223–3833).

Above Main on Church Street is a clutch of churches and homes from the mid-1800s and the **Amador County Museum,** 255 Church (209–223–6386), in one of the oldest houses in town, sheltering a huge collection of artifacts and antiques, perhaps the premier museum in the Gold Country. On the hottest day it's cool and quiet in the house. Hundreds of photos re-create the Gold Rush days, and there's a fine collection of Indian baskets, vintage fashions, furniture, and many domestic items from throughout Gold Rush homes. A working scale model shows the **Kennedy Mine,** whose 5,000-foot shaft was one of the world's deepest. Ask about the Kennedy Mine Tour, given weekends and some weekdays.

Lunch: **The Balcony Restaurant,** 164 Main, Jackson. (209) 223–2855. Quiche, sandwiches, salads, and pasta in a ferny, art-filled environment.

Afternoon

It's ten minutes south to **Mokelumne Hill,** through the wooded canyon of the Mokelumne River, which separates Amador and Calaveras counties. Drop down off the highway into little "Mok Hill," a ghost of its former rowdy self. Once the most lawless town in the Mother Lode, Mokelumne Hill is now a quiet burg of winding streets shaded by magnificent old locust and oak trees. The **Hotel Leger,** 8304 Main Street (209–286–1401), rocked and rolled in the 1860s, and it's still a good place to stop in and have a cold beer under the slow ceiling fans of the saloon. Rooms here are charming, with antiques, comforters, and fireplaces; there's a great veranda for Main Street watching, as well as gardens and a swimming pool. Ask about the murder mystery weekends. **Nonno's Cucina Italiana** (209–286–1331) in the hotel serves sumptuous Italian food family style at reasonable prices—rosemary garlic chicken, calamari, polenta, pasta.

Across the street from the hotel, the **Adams and Company Genuine Old West Saloon and Museum and Less** (209–286–1331) should not be missed.

Drive ten minutes south on the highway through farmlands and cattle ranches to **San Andreas,** following the signs to the Historic District.

In the **Calaveras County Museum and Archives,** 30 North Main (209–754–6513), take your time perusing the extensive displays of Indian and mining artifacts, interesting old documents and papers, re-created miner's cabins and stores, and a Miwok tepee. The jail out back is where Black Bart, the notorious stagecoach robber and poet, languished for a time.

Seek out the **Thorn Mansion,** at 87 East St. Charles (209–754–1027), the restored home of Sheriff Ben Thorn, who captured Black Bart. On three acres of gardens with ponds, creeks, waterfalls, and a putting green, it's now a bed-and-breakfast inn.

Eleven miles east of San Andreas, off Railroad Flat Road, is **California Caverns** (209–736–2708), where you can take a tour through narrow passageways and huge limestone chambers to see colorful stalactite and stalacmite formations.

It's fifteen minutes south to **Angels Camp,** the setting for Brett Harte's famous story, *The Luck of Roaring Camp.* On the way make a short stop at Altaville to see some colorful historic buildings and to prowl about three marvelous, circa-1850 cemeteries west of the highway.

Dinner: **La Hacienda,** 5 South Main, Angels Camp near the junction of Highway 4. (209) 736–6711. Best Mexican food in the county. Or, for a continental menu, try **Piaggi's,** 1262 South Main, Angels Camp (209–736–4862), serving fresh pasta, cioppino, steaks, and burgers.

Lodging: **Cooper House,** 1184 Church Street, off South Main, Angels Camp 95222. (209) 736–2145. A 1911 Craftsman-style beauty on a shady street; spacious suites with baths; air-conditioned.

Day 3

Morning

Breakfast: At Cooper House. Full breakfast in the elegant dining room or in the garden gazebo.

The Jumping Frog Jubilee brings thousands of spectators to Angels Camp every May to watch the jumpers do their thing. You can even rent a frog and try your own version of the wild gyrations necessary to make the frogs win the jumping contests. Jumping frogs have been part of Angels Camp lore since Mark Twain wrote "The Celebrated Jumping Frogs of Calaveras County."

On the north end of town, the **City of Angels Museum,** 753 Main (209–736–2181), is chock-full of displays relating to pioneer and Gold Rush days, with carriages, antique mining and farm equipment, and a steam locomotive on the grounds. On Main Street are a plethora of historic buildings, shops, hotels, and museums to fill your afternoon. In midtown a grassy park has remnants of five mines that pulled in more than $20 million in gold between 1886 and 1920.

Just south of Angels Camp, Highway 49 crosses the upper fingers of **New Melones Lake** (209–536–9094), created from the second largest earth-filled dam in the United States. On more than 100 miles of tree-lined shoreline are campgrounds and marinas, headquarters for fishing, sailing, waterskiing, and houseboating expeditions. The Melones Dam was constructed in a storm of protest as **Stanislaus River** gorges gradually flooded, destroying forever a dramatically scenic wilderness area in the state. The lake is now much loved by boaters and anglers. Large developed campgrounds called Glory Hole and Tuttletown (209–984–5248) are convenient to hiking trails and to good fishing for trout, bass, and catfish.

Take Highway 4 east to Stockton, then retrace your route to the Bay Area.

There's More

Volcano Sidetrip. A half-hour's drive east of Sutter Creek, a lovely route alongside a creek will yield a golden surprise between mid-March and the end of April. Wildflowers and 50,000 daffodils and tulips bloom in a farmer's field, an entire hillside exploding with color, called **Daffodil Hill**. From here, head on to **Volcano,** a little burg in a pine forest where a clutch of historic buildings remain, including the **St. George Hotel** where you can get lunch or dinner in a charming, rather eccentrically decorated dining room where the menu depends on the chef's whim of the day (209–296–4458). On a loop back to Highway 49, take the opportunity to stop at the **Indian Grinding Rock State Historic Park,** the only state park that is primarily a monument to Native American culture (916–296–7488). More than 1,000 grinding holes used by Miwoks are gouged out of a huge limestone surface, and you will see many petroglyphs, replicas of bark dwellings, and a museum. There are nature trails and a small campground. Once a month, Miwok elders spend time at the park, telling stories and recounting tribal history to park visitors.

Lake Amador, 33 miles east of Stockton off Highway 88. (209)

274–4739. Some 425 acres of warmwater fishing, boating, sailing, swimming, camping.

Pardee Lake, near Jackson. (209) 772–1472. About 2,200 acres of warmwater fishing, boating, sailing; pool; camping; no water skis, jet skis, or swimming in the lake.

Lake Camanche, near the junction of Highways 88 and 12, between Jackson and Stockton. (209) 772–1472. Some 7,700 acres of warmwater fishing, boating, sailing; camping.

Roaring Camp Mining Company, P.O. Box 278, Pine Grove 95665. (209) 296–4100. An old gold camp located on Highway 8 just east of Jackson in the Mokelumne Canyon on the Mokelumne River, wildlife museum, trading post, saloon, and snack bar. Daytrips and Saturday night cookout dinner in the canyon, with gold panning and steak barbecue, river swimming.

Special Events

February. A Taste of Amador Wines, Amador County wineries. (209) 245–4455. Barrel tastings, food, entertainment.

April. Antique Show and Sale, Sutter Creek. (209) 267–0773.

April. Mother Lode Dixieland Jazz, Jackson. (209) 223–0350.

May. Calaveras County Jumping Frog Jubilee, Angels Camp. (800) 225–3754.

May. Music at the Wineries, held at several Amador County wineries. (209) 267–0211. Jazz, classical, and global beat music; food, wine, art.

June. Amador County Wine Festival, Angels Camp. (209) 223–0350.

July. Christmas in July Jazz Festival, Sutter Creek. (209) 223–0350.

August. Gold Country Bluegrass Festival, Plymouth. (209) 223–0350.

September. Black Bart Day, San Andreas. (800) 225–3754.

December. Sutter Creek Courier and Ives Christmas Open House. (209) 223–0350. Tree lighting, food, carolers, Santa.

Other Recommended
Restaurants and Lodgings

Sutter Creek

Aparicio's Sutter Creek Hotel, 271 Hanford Street. (209) 267–9177. Two-room suites and rooms with two queen beds, plus handicapped-accessible units. Restaurant.

San Andreas

Black Bart Inn, 55 St. Charles. (209) 754–3808. A coffeeshop patronized by everyone in town.

Razzle Dazzle, Central Sierra Plaza. (209) 754–1108. Bagel sandwiches, quiche, gourmet burgers.

The Robin's Nest, 247 West St. Charles Avenue. (209) 754–1076. Bed-and-breakfast accommodations in an 1895 mansion; nine rooms with bath; full breakfast.

Jackson

The Court Street Inn, 215 Court Street. (209) 223–0416. An 1870 Victorian with six rooms and suites and a cottage, down comforters, fireplaces, four-posters, antiques, whirlpool tubs. Full breakfast, evening refreshments.

Wedgewood Inn, 11941 Narcissus Road. (209) 296–4300. Victorian replica in the woods, six elaborately decorated guest rooms with wood-burning stoves, antiques, balconies. Full gourmet breakfast and afternoon refreshments. Gardens, hammocks.

Broadway Hotel, 225 Broadway. (209) 223–3503. A white-with-blue-trim, three-story clapboard with verandas and beautiful gardens; rooms with private baths; large breakfast buffet.

Amador Inn, 200 Highway 49. (209) 223–0211. Nice motel, pool, coffeeshop.

Amador County Bed and Breakfast Referral. (209) 296–7778.

Plymouth

Forty-niner Trailer Village, P.O. Box 191, 95669. (209) 245–6981. Recreation halls, pool, playground, store, laundry, beauty shop.

For More Information

Amador County Chamber of Commerce, 125 Peak Street, corner of Highways 49 and 88, Jackson, CA 95642. (209) 223–0350.

Calaveras Lodging and Visitor's Association, 1301 South Main, Angels Camp, CA 95222. (209) 736–0049.

Stockton Visitor's Bureau, 46 West Fremont, Stockton, CA 95202. (209) 943–1987.

Sutter Creek Business and Professional Association, P.O. Box 600, Sutter Creek, CA 95685. (209) 267–5647. Tourism information.

Gold Country South

Bikes set out for a day trip from Bear Valley Lodge.

Columbia, Bear Valley, Jamestown

─────────────── 2 NIGHTS ───────────────

Big trees, big valley • Wineries • Rail town
Historic park • Caverns • Gold Rush village

From the charming village of Murphys to the wide-open meadows of
Bear Valley, then to old Columbia and rough-and-ready Jamestown,
you get a lot of Gold Country in this quick escape.

The most perfectly re-created Gold Rush town in the United States,
Columbia is a living museum, with costumed performers, horse-drawn

vehicles, and sights and sounds of the past that make you feel as if you've traveled back in time. Pines and maples shade the boardwalks in the hot summer months, when the place is packed with families; spring and fall are the best times to visit.

This brief warm weather introduction to Bear Valley may encourage a return visit when the snow flies. The ski resort appeals to Bay Area residents who prefer a casual country atmosphere for their cross-country and downhill skiing.

On the way home you'll spend a morning in the rowdy little burg of Jamestown, with perhaps a ride on a steam train.

Day 1

Morning

Drive from the Oakland Bay Bridge east on Highway 580, connecting with 99 north to Manteca, then 120 east to Highway 49, turning north to the Highway 4 junction, stopping in the town of **Murphys**— all told, about two and a half hours from the Bay Area.

Ulysses S. Grant and Mark Twain sat a spell on the veranda of the **Murphys Hotel,** before the locust trees became the tall umbrellas we see today. More than a dozen centuries-old buildings line the main drag, while narrow sidestreets are a kaleidoscope of wild country gardens, white picket fences, and ancient walnut trees shading turn-of-the-century cottages and mansions.

Murphys Creek runs cheerily through town, a small park on its banks, perfect for a picnic. "A Taste of Murphys" is a narrated horse-drawn wagon tour that you can take around town, on scenic backroads, and to nearby wineries (209–728–2602). The trip includes a gourmet picnic lunch creekside in Murphys Park.

Lunch: **The Peppermint Stick,** 454 Main, Murphys. (209) 728-3570. Soup, salad; Miner's Bread Bowl filled with soup, chili, or beef stew; espresso, ice cream sodas, sundaes.

Afternoon

Main Street strolling will turn up **L'Atelier** (209–728–2139), featuring the works of local artists, and **Murphys Cheap Cash Store** (209–728–2700), where you can get a Western outfit or a Victorian dress.

Bullet holes in the front door of Murphys Hotel, 457 Main (209–728–3444), remain from the good old days when Black Bart trod the floorboards; step in for a look at the great old long bar, where Saturday nights can be quite lively. Rooms and suites here are reasonable and include a substantial continental breakfast.

One mile north of Murphys, on Sheepranch Road, **Mercer Caverns** (209–728–2101) are irresistibly spooky, cool, and fascinating limestone chambers of crystalline formations. Seven small wineries are located within 5 miles of Murphys, including ivy-covered **Black Sheep Winery** (209–728–2157), on the west end of town. In an old carriage house on Main Street beside Murphys Creek, **Millaire Winery** (209–728–1658) is a tourist attraction in the fall, when crushing and pressing take place for all to see. Just off Sheepranch Road is the **Stevenot Winery** (209–728–3436), in a lovely valley at 1,900 feet. In the sod-roofed miner's cabin that is the tasting room, try medal-winning Zinfandel, Chardonnay, and Cabernet. A map and information on Calaveras wines are available by calling (800) 695–3737.

Take Highway 4 for about forty-five minutes through the Stanislaus National Forest to **Bear Valley,** in a spectacular, high mountain meadow at 7,200 feet, surrounded by dramatic granite peaks, snow-capped in wintertime and early spring. What can you do here? Just mountain-bike, walk in the pines, fish in seven nearby lakes, climb a rock, play tennis, or hike to scenic ridgetops in the **Calaveras National Forest** (209–795–1381). Camping and fishing are popular on the **Stanislaus River** and at alpine lakes sprinkled about the nearby **Ebbets Pass** area. Over 100 miles of off-road mountain-biking trails make this a prime area for bike nuts. On free Sunday Fun Rides in July and August, you can choose from beginner or intermediate guided trail rides. Maps, rentals, and tours are available at **Bear Valley Mountain Bike and Kayak Center** (209–753–2834).

Music from Bear Valley is a big annual summer festival that brings hundreds of people to hear big name classical, opera, jazz, and theatrical performers (209–753–BEAR).

Winter fun includes skiing on one of the most extensive networks of cross-country trails in the country, 65 miles of groomed trails and endless acres of unmarked meadows. Or you can ski downhill from 8,500 feet on **Mount Reba** or skate on an acre of ice. The **Bear Valley Ski Area,** on Highway 4, 28 miles east of Arnold, is one of the last family built and operated ski resorts in the west (P.O. Box 5038, Bear Valley 95223, 209–753–2301). With 450 inches of snow annually and an emphasis on beginner and intermediate skiing, this is a good place for families to learn to ski. Lift tickets and lodging costs are lower here than at Lake Tahoe ski resorts. Special programs are set up for little kids (Skiing Bears), nine to twelve year olds (Bear Scouts), and for teens and adults (age thirteen and up). There is all-day "Bear Care," too. The Grizzly Snowboard Den is a "boarder only" rental and lesson center.

Ice-skating is popular on a frozen lake near the lodge. On weekend nights, lights, music, and a bonfire make skating fun to try or to watch. You can take skating lessons here, too.

Except for the highway, most roads remain unplowed in the valley in wintertime, giving Bear Valley a unique Alpine atmosphere.

Between Calaveras Big Trees State Park and Bear Valley, **Cottage Springs** is a small resort offering a snow play area, a tubing hill, and downhill skiing for beginners and intermediates. This is a good, inexpensive place to take younger children for ski lessons (209–795–1401). Along Highway 4 are several snow play areas and cross-country ski trailheads, including Forest Service roads used by both skiers and snowmobilers. Two miles west of Bear Valley, **Tamarack Pines Lodge and Cross-Country Ski Center,** in the **Stanislaus National Forest** at 7,000 feet, grooms miles of trails (209–753–2080). You can rent equipment here, take lessons, and enjoy hearty meals in the lodge. Ski/lodging packages are available for simple lodge rooms.

Within walking and skiing distance of the village, **Bear Valley Cross-Country Ski Area** (209–753–2834) is the largest track system in the central Sierras, with three dozen trails dotted with warming huts.

A couple of miles from Bear Valley, **Lake Alpine Snow-Park** (916–322–8993) is where snowmobilers and cross-country skiers head into the backcountry on the road to **Mosquito Lake.** Snow-Park permits are necessary in order to park here and you can snow camp in this area (913–322–8993). A snow play area is just south of the parking lot. To make year-round campsite reservations at Lake Alpine and at other U.S. Forest Service sites, call (209) 795–1381.

Dinner and Lodging: **Bear Valley Lodge,** P.O. Box 5038, Bear Valley 95223. (209) 753–2327. Rooms in the five-story lodge are simple and comfortable, with a pool, tennis courts, and an inviting atrium lounge with a giant fireplace made of king-sized boulders. If you decide to stay more than a day or two, condominiums and cabin rentals may be the way to go (800–794–3866). Camping is also available.

Day 2

Morning

Breakfast: European breakfast buffet and cappuccinos at Bear Valley Lodge.

Heading back west on Highway 4, if you've a mind to see some *big* sequoias and take a walk or a hike, stop at **Calaveras Big Trees State Park** (209–795–2334). Short nature trails are accessible near the visitor's center, but the biggest trees—1,300 of them—are found in the South Grove, 1 mile from the parking lot up the **Big Trees Creek Trail.** One giant stands 320 feet high and another measures 27 feet around. Hike a network of trails leading to high ridgetops above the 4,800-foot elevation.

Winding throughout the park, the Stanislaus River has sandy and pebbly beaches for swimming and wading. Developed campsites are set up for RVs to 27 feet and there are environmental campsites for backpackers. The park is open all year and is a popular cross-country ski area. A 1-mile loop near the main parking area and an outer 3-mile loop are groomed; snowmobiles are not allowed.

Continue on Highway 4, connecting with 49 to **Columbia State Historic Park** (209–532–0150). When gold was discovered here in 1850, the population boomed within a month from fewer than 100 to 6,000 people, and 150 saloons, gambling halls, and stores opened up. Many Western falsefronts and two-story brick buildings with iron shutters remain, inhabited by costumed proprietors who contribute to the living history atmosphere. The state began accumulating artifacts and restoring the buildings in the 1940s. Musicians and performers are encountered on the street corners and in the restaurants and the theater; horse-drawn stages clip-clop up and down the streets; artisans demonstrate horseshoeing, woodcarving, and other vintage crafts; and you can pan for gold or take a horseback ride.

A few of the many shops and restaurants: **Fallon Ice Cream Parlor** (209–533–2355), for floats, shakes, and sodas at an authentic soda fountain counter; **Dreamwest Trading Company** (209–533–3300) has gold nuggets, rocks, guidebooks, and history books; **Columbia Candy Kitchen** (209–532–7886), where a four-generation family makes fresh taffy, brittles, fudge, and penny candy; **De Cosmos Daguerrean** (209–532–0815), to get your tintype taken; and **Bearcloud Gallery** (209–533–8660), specializing in American Indian art.

Columbia Candle and Soap Works in the old feed store sells freshly milled soaps in clove, oatmeal honey, rosemary, chocolate, and lavender scents, plus millions of beautiful handmade candles (209–536–9047). Next to the **Lickskillet Cafe, Sierra Madres** is the place for antiques and collectibles, with an astonishing array of unique greeting cards (209–532–6319).

Lunch: **Columbia House Restaurant,** Main Street. (209) 532–5134. Traditional American fare.

Afternoon

The Columbia experience is enriched by "talking buttons" outside several storefronts; push these buttons to hear about the museum displays in the windows. Trodding the creaky floorboards of the **William Cavalier Museum,** at Main and State streets, you'll see photos of the people who lived here during the Gold Rush, as well as huge chunks of ore, quartz, and semiprecious stones. More than $1.5 billion in gold was weighed on the Wells Fargo Express scales in this town.

On the north end of town, the **Columbia Grammar School,** in use from 1860 to 1937, is outfitted with an endearing collection of antique desks, inkwells, old books, and kids' stuff.

Snacks, sodas, and sarsaparillas are easy to find in one of the several saloons (kids OK). Take a ride through the woods nearby on the **Columbia Stage** (209–532–0663).

Farther along on Parrot's Ferry Road is **Natural Bridges,** where Coyote Creek has created a colorful limestone cave. Walk on the streamside nature trail and consider swimming or rafting through the cave—not as scary as it looks.

Dinner: **City Hotel,** Washington Street, Columbia. (209) 532–1479. Big-city cuisine in elegant Gold Rush–era surroundings; superb continental menu and good wine list; dinner daily, weekend lunch and brunch. You'll be surprised to find out who the chefs and waitpersons are, and you will love the marinated veal chops with roast garlic risotto and shiitake Marsala sauce, the rack of lamb with garlic pine nut crust, the mango tart with ginger cream!

The **What Cheer Saloon** in the hotel still has the original cherrywood bar shipped round the Horn from New England. Special vintner dinners hosted by renowned California winemakers are offered several times a year.

The hotel has ten charming, small rooms with many of the original antiques. They put on popular mystery weekends, with professional actors and hotel guests playing their parts all over town.

Lodging: **Fallon Hotel,** on Washington Street on the south end of town, next door to the City Hotel and the Fallon Theatre (209) 532–1470. A Victorian extravaganza of rococco wallpaper, antique furniture, and Oriental rugs.

Day 3

Morning

Breakfast: Expanded continental breakfast at the Fallon Hotel.

Continue on Highway 49 through Sonora to Jamestown. (**Sonora** is the county seat and a highway junction; traffic spoils somewhat the Old Town atmosphere here, although sidestreets, antiques shops, and historic buildings make this worth a stop if you have the time.)

Boomed and busted several times in the past 150 years, **Jamestown** retains an anything-can-happen, Wild West atmosphere, from the days when it was just a bawdy cluster of tents on a dusty road. When the gold began to rush, saloons and dancehalls were erected, then hotels and homes. Dozens of antiques and curio shops line the streets, and almost as many saloons and restaurants. If the town seems familiar to you, it may be because much of the movie *Butch Cassidy and the Sundance Kid* was filmed here.

Attractions include the **Railtown 1897 State Historic Park** on Fifth Avenue (209–984–3953), a twenty-six-acre exhibit of vintage steam locomotives and passenger cars, a roundhouse, and a grassy picnic area in an oak grove. You can take a one-hour train ride through the foothills or a two-hour "Twilight Limited," a sort of sunset cruise with refreshments, entertainment, and a barbecue dinner at the end.

A stroll up and down Main Street will turn up the **Saunders Gallery of Fine Art,** at 18190 Main, in the historic 1877 **Carboni House** (209–984–4421), showing carvings, photos, and paintings by local artists, and **Jamestown Mercantile I** and **II** (209–984–6550), two large antiques co-ops. Behind the Jamestown Hotel in the Marengo Courtyard, taste local wines at **Chestnut Wine and Gifts** (209–984–3366), and check out Native American art, jewelry, and baskets at the **Bear 'n Coyote Art Gallery** (209–984–4562).

The **Jamestown Hotel,** circa 1920, at 18153 Main (209–984–3902), is an old beauty restored to its former elegance, with a long bar and a restaurant famous throughout the region for prime rib, pepper steak, and seasonal specialites made with local fresh poultry and fresh produce. Eight rooms re-create the Gold Rush era, with antiques and Victorian baths. The Lotta Crabtree suite has a pink clawfoot tub, the Jenny Lind a king-sized brass and iron bed.

When you see people panning for gold in a wooden trough on the main street (18170 Main), you are at the headquarters for **Gold Prospecting Expeditions,** where you can find out about gold panning and prospecting day trips and rafting trips on nearby creeks and rivers (209–984–4653). One shady, gold-bearing creek is less than five-minutes away and fewer than 50 feet from the parking area. They also run a special one-day excursion to a re-created mining camp on Wood's Creek. You will get more gold on this trip than on others because of the use of a sluice box, and you can camp here, too.

Jamestown puts on an annual Gunfighter Rendezvous in April, with smokin' six guns and desperadoes swaggering up and down the sidewalks (209–984–4616).

Lunch: **Country Kitchen Gourmet Cafe,** 18231 Main. (209) 984–3326. Homemade American food in an old-fashioned ice cream parlor; save room for pie.

Afternoon

Retrace your route back to the Bay Area.

There's More

Bear Valley Sidetrips. A few miles east of Bear Valley off Highway 4, **Utica, Union, and Spicer Meadows Reservoirs** are undeveloped and great for launching your small boat and fishing for trout, bass, and catfish. Near here, the **Stanislaus River Campground** (916–440–2183) is an eight-site spot nicely located on the river, but with no running water. Up the highway on the way to **Ebbetts Pass, Highlands Lakes** has a small developed campground (209–795–1381).

From Ebbetts Pass, twisty, two-lane Highway 4 runs through some of the most dramatic alpine landscape you will ever see. It is a good idea to bring picnic fare along and take advantage of the many beautiful turnouts and rest stops along the way. You can connect to Highway 89, over **Monitor Pass,** to drop south to the east gate of Yosemite National Park or head north on 89 to Lake Tahoe or into Nevada. The Ebbetts Pass and Monitor Pass roads are closed in wintertime and are not recommended for larger RVs at any time of year.

Biking. Bear Valley Mountain Bike Center, Bear Valley. (209) 753–2834. Rentals, trail maps, guides.

Golf. Forest Meadows Golf Course, 14 miles east of Angels Camp on Highway 4, Murphys. (209) 728–3439. Eighteen holes in a pine forest.

Phoenix Lake Golf Course, 21448 Paseo De Los Portales, Sonora. (209) 532–0111. Ten minutes from Sonora; nine beautiful holes under oak trees beside a lake.

Rafting. Outdoor Adventure River Specialists, P.O. Box 67, Angels Camp 95222. (209) 736–4677. American, Stanislaus, Merced, Kern, and other rivers.

Special Events

April. Gunfighter Rendezvous, Jamestown. (209) 984–4616.

June. Dixieland Jamboree, Jamestown. (209) 984–4616.

July–August. Music from Bear Valley. (209) 753–BEAR. Big-name classical, opera, jazz, and theatrical performers.

July. Wine, Art and Beer Festival, Bear Valley. (209) 753–BEAR.

October. Harvest Festival, Columbia State Historic Park. (209) 532–0150.

October. Fiddle and Banjo Contest, Columbia State Historic Park. (209) 532–0150.

December. Christmas Lamplight Tour, Miner's Christmas, and Las Posadas, Columbia State Historic Park. (209) 532–0150.

Other Recommended
Restaurants and Lodgings

Jamestown

Lulu's Saloon and Grill, 18201 Main. (209) 984–3678. Fun and food in an antiquey atmosphere; dozens of vintage lamps and chandeliers.

Michelangelo's, 18228 Main. (209) 984–4830. Contemporary cafe and bar; nouvelle Italian menu, pizza, pasta.

Sonora

Serenity, 15305 Bear Cub Drive. (209) 533–1441. Five miles from Sonora off Highway 108 east. The Hoovers' big, beautiful country house is surrounded by porches and six acres of live oaks and pines, completely quiet; spacious, pretty rooms with private baths; sumptuous breakfasts.

Gold Country Inns of Tuolumne County, P.O. Box 462 95370. (209) 533–1845.

La Casa Inglesa B and B, 18047 Lime Kiln Road. (209) 532–5822. About 2.5 miles from town. English country elegance.

Columbia

Harlan House, 22890 School House. (209) 533–4862. Victorian mansion renovated in 1992; three rooms with baths; full breakfast.

Trails End RV Park, 21770 Parrotts Ferry Road. (209) 533–2395. Shady spots near the state park.

Bear Valley condominiums and cabin rentals, P.O. Box 5038. Bear Valley 95223. (800) 794–3866.

Murphys

Dunbar House, 271 Jones Street. (209) 728–2897. Luxurious, historic bed-and-breakfast inn near Main Street; private baths; gardens; bountiful breakfast and wine buffet.

Redbud Inn, 402 Main. (800) 827–8533. The first inn built in this town in more than a century. Eleven luxurious rooms, Jacuzzis, fireplaces, balconies, bay windows, big breakfasts.

Dorrington

Dorrington Hotel and Restaurant, P.O. Box 4307, Dorrington 95223. (209) 795–5800. Historic, small, cozy B and B, 20 miles south of Bear Valley on Highway 4, near Calaveras Big Trees.

Bear Valley

Red Dog Lodge, P.O. Box 5034, Bear Valley 95223. (209) 753–2344. Simple accommodations for those on a budget, fourteen rooms and dorm-style bathrooms, sauna. Ski out the door on cross-country trails, shuttle bus to chairlifts. Informal dining (burgers, ribs, steak), saloon.

San Andreas

Gold Strike Village, 1925 Gold Strike Road. (209) 754–3180. Mobile home and RV park; pool, clubhouse, laundry, hiking trails, camping.

Arnold

Lodge at Manuel Mill, White Pines Road. (209) 795–2622. Bed-and-breakfast inn, totally secluded on forty-three acres of woods; five rooms with private baths and wood stoves; full breakfast.

For More Information

Jamestown Visitor's Information Center, P.O. Box 699, Jamestown, CA 95327. (209) 984–4616.

Calaveras Lodging and Visitor's Association, 1301 South Main, Angels Camp, CA 95222. (209) 736–0049.

Bear Valley Ski Company, P.O. Box 5038, Bear Valley, CA 95223. (209) 753–2301; snow phone, (209) 753–2308.

Escapes Farther Afield

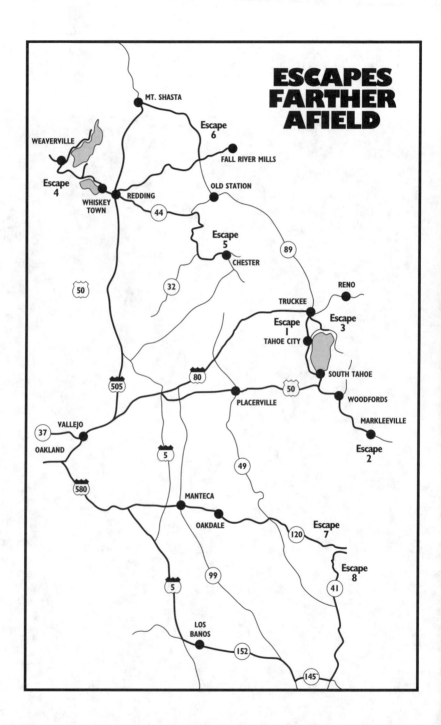

Old Tahoe on the West Shore

Emerald Bay is one of the most photographed spots in California.

Mansions in the Mountains

——————————— 2 NIGHTS ———————————
Vintage mansions · River rambling · Mountain hikes
Beaches, bikes, hikes · Boating on quiet bays · Winter fun

The 1920s were the halcyon days of Lake Tahoe's west shore, when wealthy nabobs from San Francisco built mansions and zipped about in sleek varnished speedboats, and when wooden steamers still cruised the lake, revelers aboard. Much of this area is still privately owned; restaurants and beaches are frequented by people who've spent their vacations here for decades. The pace is slow, except in the nightspots and shops of Tahoe City. Even in the high summer season, you can doze on a quiet beach, walk and bike on silent forest trails, and poke around contentedly in a rented boat. And the rowdy, rushing Truckee River is always there for fishing, rafting, and strolling along beside.

The sun shines an average of 274 days a year at Tahoe. Soft spring days are clear and wildflowery; fall is brisk, with aspen color glittering through the pines. Winter is lively at several small, inexpensive downhill and cross-country resorts, and positively posh at the big ski resorts: Squaw Valley, Northstar, and Alpine Meadows.

Day 1

Morning

To start your four-hour drive to Lake Tahoe from the Oakland Bay Bridge, drive north on Highway 80 for ninety minutes, to the Nut Tree Road exit, near Vacaville.

Breakfast: At an annex of the big **Nut Tree** complex across the freeway, the **Coffee Tree.** (707) 448–8435. Fresh and colorful, with big booths and a counter. The strawberry waffles and dollar-size pancakes are dynamite. Pick up some apricot nutbread and peanut brittle to keep you going on the road. (On one of your Highway 80 trips, you may wish to browse in the 100-plus discount store outlets located here.)

Now turn on the cruise control for your drive through the **Sacramento Valley** and up into the mountains. When you see Sacramento's skyline, watch for the Reno Highway 80 exit; you will skirt the city on the west side. Before long, the valley floor gives way to the foothills of the High Sierras and spreading oaks begin to share the hillsides with pines and firs. There's a highway rest stop at Donner Summit, at 7,227 feet, and a few miles farther you'll turn right onto Highway 89, driving 13 miles south to Tahoe City, past Squaw Valley, through the **Truckee River Canyon.** The paved **Truckee River Bike Path** starts at Alpine Meadows, winds along the Truckee 4 miles to Tahoe City, then takes a 9-mile route south along the lake. At some point during your west shore sojourn, you'll want to rent bikes at Tahoe City, or just walk, jog, or push a baby carriage on the path. In the low-water days of the late summer and fall, the river slides quietly along. In winter and spring it boils and crashes past ice-decorated trees and snowy islands.

Arriving in Tahoe City, turn right at the junction with Highway 89, which turns sharply south along the western lakeshore. Cross **Fanny Bridge**—where people are always lined up, leaning over to see the trout ladder where the Truckee joins the lake—and stop at the **Gate-keeper's Museum** and lakeside park, 130 West Lake Boulevard, Tahoe City (916–583–1762), to see an exceptional collection of Washoe and Paiute Indian baskets, artifacts, and historical memorabilia. Here you get a first view of Tahoe, North America's largest Alpine lake, 22 miles long and 12 miles wide.

Lunch: **Fire Sign Cafe,** 1785 West Lake Boulevard, Tahoe City. (916) 583–0871. Homestyle cooking, cozy country atmosphere.

Afternoon

Drive 9.5 miles south on Highway 89 to **Sugar Pine Point State Park** (916–525–7982) to visit one of the grand dames of Tahoe, a spectacular three-story, 12,000-square-foot Queen Anne–style summer home, the **Ehrman Mansion.** Built at the turn of the century by a San Francisco banker, the mansion still looks like the privately owned lakeside estate it once was, surrounded by sweeping lawns shaded by tall pines. Rangers give daily tours of the mansion and boathouse, imparting stories of old days on the lake. After the tour wander around the grounds, spread a blanket on the beach, or take a walk on trails along the lakeshore. A longer hike is accessible from the large campground across the road; rangers have maps for you.

In the late afternoon drive north on 89 to **Sunnyside Restaurant and Lodge,** 1850 West Lake Boulevard, 2 miles south of the Tahoe City Y (916–583–7200). Sunnyside has one of the best blue water and high mountain views on the lake. People-viewing is excellent here, too. Boats of every description come and go in the marina; French-fried zucchini and onion rings are tops; and once you get settled outside on the deck or inside by a lakeside window, you'll find it hard to move from the spot. Here you can rent jet skis, sail- and powerboats, and take a sailing lesson. Winter evenings are warm and friendly in the lounge in front of a giant river-rock fireplace. Old canoes are suspended from the high beamed ceiling; paintings of antique lake cruisers line the walls.

Dinner: **Chambers Landing,** 1 mile south of Homewood. (916) 525–7672. Overlooking the lake on a glass-enclosed and heated terrace. Try the Moroccan lamb or fresh fish, and you owe it to yourself to have a Chambers Punch. A small bar on the Chambers pier is popular with locals. On one side of the pier is a private beach for people staying in the Chambers Landing condos (see page 231), and on the other side is a public beach, one of the nicest on the west shore.

Lodging: **The Rockwood Lodge,** 5295 West Lake, P.O. Box 226, Homewood 96141. (916) 525–5273. A stone mansion, circa 1930, with a knotty-pine interior emboldened by hand-hewn beams, the Rockwood is only 100 feet from the lake but seems a million miles away. The four rooms are cozy and comfortable, with European-style down beds, in-suite basins, robes, and views of the trees or the lake. The main lounge has a huge stone fireplace and a bottle of wine waiting for you.

Day 2

Morning

Breakfast: Here at the Rockwood Lodge. Belgian waffles and fruit crepes are part of a robust selection of goodies. The dining room looks onto a grassy meadow shaded by tall pines. An expert on local wildlife, proprietor Connie Stevens runs a wildlife reserve on the property, taking in injured animals and birds until they are well enough to be returned to the wild.

Go out the back door of the inn and stroll or bike up the road to the **Homewood Ski Area** (916–525–2922); Connie can suggest an easy or a challenging route. (Adjacent to the lodge, the ski area is small and friendly, less expensive and less intimidating than the big glitzy resorts.)

With Rockwood beach chairs and towels, step across the road to the public beach at **Obexer's Marina** (916–525–7962) and swim, if you dare; at 6,229 feet, the miraculous sapphire-blue, clear water of the lake is always chilly. Surface temperatures in August allegedly reach the low seventies. Get a few rays on the beach, or rent a boat here and motor along the shoreline.

Now pick up picnic supplies in Homewood and head south toward Emerald Bay. On the way check out **Meeks Bay Resort and Marina** (916–525–7242), owned by the U.S. Forest Service, a popular jet- and water-ski beach with an unparalleled view of the lake. This is a good place for beachy activities like rowing, canoeing, and paddleboating (all rentable) or just hanging out in the sun, though all the motors create plenty of noise during the summer. A little cafe serves snacks and burgers, and there are a few cottages and a 150-unit campground.

About 5.5 miles from Meeks Bay, **Emerald Bay** appears in its glittering blue-green glory far below. One of the most photographed pieces of scenery in California, the bay can be seen from several vista points along Highway 89, but you must trundle down a steep 1-mile trail (or take a tour boat) to reach the real treasure of the bay—the Scandinavian castle of **Vikingsholm** (916–525–7232), built in 1928. A cross between an eleventh-century castle and an ancient church, the mansion is considered the finest example of Scandinavian architecture in North America. Take a ranger's tour to see the extensively decorated and furnished estate home.

Lunch: Have your picnic here at Vikingsholm.

Afternoon

From Highway 89 at Emerald Bay, there is an easy 2-mile loop hike to **Eagle Falls** and beautiful **Eagle Lake,** surrounded by the sheer walls of Desolation Wilderness, where many trailheads lead into the southern Tahoe National forestlands.

One of the most accessible but least known wilderness areas at Tahoe is **Blackwood Canyon,** off Highway 89 just north of Tahoe Pines. Perfect for easy walks, roller-blading, and biking, the paved road is the only development and has almost no traffic; this road is a good add-on to the shoreline bike path. Forests, meadows, and the banks of Blackwood Creek make good picnic spots. You can hike on the flat valley floor or drive up the road to the steep trails of 8,000-foot **Barker Pass,** hooking up with the **Pacific Crest Trail.** An off-road-vehicle camp and a trails area are also here in the canyon.

Dinner: **Gar Woods Grill and Pier,** 5000 North Lake Boulevard, Carnelian Bay. (916) 546–3366. About fifteen minutes north of Tahoe City, on the lake, with a zinger of a view. The glassed-in deck with heaters is a place to take your time enjoying pasta, fresh seafood, or the restaurant's famous "Hot Rock" specialties, wherein you grill your own dinner. The bar is popular and lively, a good place to have an appetizer and people-watch. Sunday brunches are legendary. Try the White Chocolate Snickers Cheesecake. Uh-huh.

Lodging: Rockwood Lodge.

Day 3

Morning

Breakfast: Rockwood's.

Explore the small town of **Tahoe City,** the action and shopping headquarters of the west shore. Boutiques are found in the **Cobblestone, Boatworks,** and **Roundhouse** malls; pine-scented breezes and lake views make shopping at the Boatworks particularly pleasant. The **Heritage Gallery** (916–581–2208) features vintage Tahoe photos and original paintings of the area. **Sports Tahoe** (916–583–1990) is jammed with fabulous clothes for every season at the lake.

Just north of Tahoe City is the **Watson Cabin Living Museum,** 560 North Lake Boulevard (916–583–8717), one of the oldest structures on the lake. Docent guides in period costumes will point out the interesting original furnishings.

Lunch: **River Ranch,** Highway 89 and Alpine Meadows Road. (916) 583–4264. On your way out of Tahoe City to head home, stop here for lunch and a last look at the Truckee. A small, charming hotel on the river, River Ranch offers a popular indoor/outdoor restaurant and bar, located at the south end of the Truckee bike path. Highway 89 takes you to Highway 80 south and the Bay Area.

A secret: At Bowman, 5 miles north of Auburn, is **Ikeda's,** 13500 Lincoln Avenue (916–885–4243), visible from the freeway. Only you and I know that this is a terrific little place for burgers and fresh veggies and fruit to take home. For another good place to purchase fresh valley produce, nuts, olives, and juices, take the Pedrick Road just north of the Nut Tree, stopping at the Quonset hut building on the west side of the highway.

There's More

Squaw Valley USA, P.O. Box 2007, Olympic Valley 96146. (800) 545–4350. The 1960 Winter Olympics were held in this huge resort area, one of the world's largest and best ski mountains, actually five peaks with three dozen lifts and more than 8,300 acres of skiable terrain. Here, you will see the best skiers, the most skiers, the fashion-conscious skiers, the coolest skiers. The ski school is the best, too, for all ages, from toddlers on up, with lessons, supervised skiing, and snow play. The Fun in the Sun program introduces those thirteen and up, including adults, to skiing for the first time, including a free cable car ride, free rentals, and demonstrations.

The Squaw Valley Nordic Center consists of 20 miles of groomed track and wilderness trails, plus a telemark downhill area accessed by lifts. The valley is spectacular in every season. You can stay here in a luxury hotel, a reasonable lodge, a bed-and-breakfast inn, a rented condo, or a house. A 150-passenger aerial cable car accesses the High Camp complex, where you can ice-skate, hike, mountain-bike, swim, picnic, play volleyball and tennis, bungee-jump, or just blink in amazement at the mountain surroundings.

Alpine Meadows Ski Area, P.O. Box 5279, Tahoe City 96145. (916) 583–6914. A major ski area for all abilities, priding itself on having the longest season and a casual, family-oriented atmosphere. And, Alpine is snowboard-free! Ski runs have scary names like Chute That Seldom Slides, Promised Land, and Our Father. Kids are VIPs at Children's Snow School and Kids Ski Camp. The rental shop here offers what may be the largest variety of equipment in the Sierras. Free shuttle busses connect skiers with most resorts on the west and north shores.

Tour boat. Departing from Round House Mall in Tahoe City, the only tour boat on this side of the lake is the *Sunrunner* (916–583–0141), a 65-foot motorized catamaran that goes to Emerald Bay and along the shoreline past Fleur du Lac and other magnificent old Tahoe estates.

B. L. Bliss State Park, 3.6 miles south of Meeks Bay. MISTIX reservations: (800) 444–7275. 168 campground sites, beautiful white sand beach, picnics, good swimming, and a lovely 4-mile trail leading to Emerald Bay.

Granlibakken Ski Area, P.O. Box 165, Tahoe City 96141. (916) 583–9896. Nordic skiing.

Homewood Ski Area, Highway 89, 6 miles south of Tahoe City at Homewood. (916) 525–2992. Nine lifts on a small mountain with big views of Lake Tahoe. A good choice for kids and beginners, day-care, moderate lesson and lift rates. Easy, close-by parking.

Public beaches. Chambers Landing, Obexer's, Sugar Pine Point, Meeks Bay, Homewood.

Just north of Tahoe City is the uncrowded beach and pier at Lake Forest; boats can be launched and camping is available.

Note: It's legal and perfectly acceptable to access any beach from the water, even if adjacent to private property.

Hiking. Mount Tallac. (916) 573–2600. A four-hour loop to the 9,700-foot summit; trailheads at Baldwin Beach and Fallen Leaf Lake.

Donner Lake to the Pacific Crest Trail. Drive 4 miles west on Old Highway 40 from the lake's west end; watch for the trailhead on the left. A 15-mile, strenuous hike along the ridge of the Sierra crest, descending down Squaw Valley's Shirley Canyon. You'll need to park your car at Squaw Valley's Olympic Village Inn.

Camp Richardson Pack Station, P.O. Box 8335, South Lake Tahoe 96158. (916) 541–3113. Horseback riding and packing into Desolation Wilderness.

Shirley Lakes trail starts behind the Olympic Village Inn. A nice 4-mile hike from the Squaw Valley; do all or part of a four-hour round-trip, stopping to wade or swim in the creek or the lake, gambol in wildflower-strewn meadows, and nap under the pines.

Tahoe Rim Trail. Maps and information, call (916) 577–0676. From Fairway Drive in Tahoe City, you can connect with the 150-mile hiking and equestrian path that follows the ridge tops of the Lake Tahoe Basin, passing through six counties in Nevada and California and incorporating about 50 miles of the Pacific Crest National Scenic Trail. The Tahoe Rim Trail is also accessible from several other trailheads around the lake.

Golf. Tahoe City Golf Course. (916) 583–1516. Nine holes.

Resort at Squaw Creek, Squaw Valley. (916) 581–6637. Eighteen-hole, Robert Trent Jones course, surrounded by the glory of the valley.

Northstar, Basque Drive, Truckee. (916) 562–2490. Eighteen holes; one of the prettiest and most challenging courses at Tahoe.

River rafting. Truckee River Rafting Center, 205 River Road, Tahoe City 96145. (916) 583–RAFT.

Fanny Bridge Raft Rentals, Tahoe City. (916) 583–3021.

Ballooning. Mountain High Balloons. (916) 587–6922.

Tahoe Paddle and Oar, in King's Beach. (916) 581–3029. Tours to Brockway Point, kayak and small boat rentals.

Special Events

March. Snowfest, Tahoe City and at several ski resorts. (916) 583–7625. Largest winter carnival in the western United States.

July. Squaw Valley Community of Writers Poetry Session. (916) 583–6985.

August. Tahoe Yacht Club Concours D'Elegance, Boatworks Mall, Tahoe City. (916) 583–8022. Classic wooden boats.

August. Squaw Valley Community of Writers Fiction and Screen Session. (916) 583–6985.

August. Squaw Valley Festival of Fine Arts and Crafts. (916) 583–6985.

August. Truckee Championship Rodeo. (916) 587–6462.

September. Splendor of the Sierra Fine Art Show, Northstar-at-Tahoe. (916) 587–0288.

September. Antique and Classic Car Show, Tahoe City. (916) 525–4429.

October. Octoberfest, Alpine Meadows Ski Resort. (916) 583–2371. Dining, dancing, and Bavarian festivities.

Other Recommended Restaurants and Lodgings

Tahoe City

Wolfdale's, 640 North Lake Boulevard. (916) 583-5700. California cuisine with a unique Japanese flair; reservations essential.

Jake's on the Lake, 780 North Lake Boulevard, Boatworks Mall. (916) 583–0188. Groovy, popular, lots of fun, right on the lake. Seafood bar and backgammon in the lounge; continental cuisine and hearty mountain food.

Sunnyside Restaurant and Lodge, 1850 West Lake Boulevard. (916) 583–7200. Casually elegant lakefront rooms and suites, each with tiny balcony, some with fireplaces, wetbars, sundecks. Tahoe mountain-style decor, down comforters, pine armoires. Ask for a quiet room, away from the dining room and the road. Breakfast buffet and afternoon tea are served in a cozy lounge.

Cottage Inn, 1690 West Lake Boulevard. (916) 581–4073. Two miles south of Tahoe City on Highway 89. Fifteen mountain-style cottages with Scandinavian decor, fireplaces, hearty breakfasts, sauna, private beach. Ask for a unit away from the road.
Tahoe Taverns, 300 West Lake Boulevard. (916) 583–3704. Near Fanny Bridge. Large complex of casual condos in a pine grove, right on the water; pool, lawns; quiet, pretty location on the edge of town.

Tahoe Vista

Captain Jon's, 7220 North Lake Boulevard. (916) 546–4819. French country cuisine, fresh seafood, casual elegance, one of the best restaurants at Tahoe. Cocktail lounge and lunch cafe on the lake; the dinner house has a partial view.

Homewood

West Shore Cafe, 5180 West Lake Boulevard. (916) 525–5200. A terrace on the beach, heaters, umbrellas, nouvelle cuisine, fresh fish, grilled meats, excellent wines, lunch, dinner; accessible by boat.
Chambers Landing, P.O. Box 537, Homewood on West Lake Boulevard near Sugar Pine Point 95718. (916) 525–7202. Some forty-three privately owned condos; a quiet, private hideaway in an aspen grove; lawns, views; private beach and pool. One of the nicest condo complexes at Tahoe, offering three- and four-bedroom luxury.

Tahoma

Alpenhaus Country Inn, 6941 West Lake Boulevard. (916) 525–5000. Swiss Alpine lodge run by a retired navy captain and his kids; across from the lake, on the bike route. Several upstairs rooms have old-fashioned, rather feminine decor, with rocking chairs and quilts, private baths; ask for a room at the back. Rustic, remodeled cottages have two bedrooms and kitchens. Pretty pool area and hot tub. Rates include hefty breakfasts of mountain omelettes and home fries. Hearty lunches and dinners: bratwurst, fresh fish, steak, pasta. Family-style Basque dinners one day a week are popular and noisy, with live music and sing-alongs; the kids will love this.

Soda Springs

Rainbow Tavern Lodge, P.O. Box 1100, 677 Highway 80 at Rainbow Road exit 95728. (916) 426–3871. Old Tahoe–style lodge, circa 1925; small, comfortable hotel rooms; good restaurant and bar. On the Yuba River near cross-country and downhill skiing, hiking, fishing.

Sugar Pine Point State Park Campground, Meeks Bay. MISTIX reservations: (800) 444–7275. Offers 175 sites.

Olympic Valley

Resort at Squaw Creek, 400 Squaw Creek Road. (800) 3CREEK3. A 400-room luxury destination resort with a championship Robert Trent Jones golf course, shops, a tennis complex, and a chair lift to ski runs and to High Camp. The terraces of three outdoor pools (and a 120-foot waterslide) overlook waves of wildflowers in the summer and snowy meadows in the winter. Mountain Buddies is the daytime camp for ages three to thirteen, and there are special excursions for teens. Golf and ski packages. Cross-country ski from the hotel.

Squaw Valley Lodge, 201 Squaw Peak Road. (800) 922–9970. All suites with kitchens, Nautilus room, steam, sauna, large heated pool, and tennis courts.

Olympic Village Inn, 1909 Chamonix Place. (916) 581–6000. Suites with kitchenettes, pool and five Jacuzzis.

Tavern Inn, 203 Squaw Valley Road. (800) 435–9467. Luxury condos sleep four to ten, all with fireplaces. All of the Squaw Valley inns and condos are convenient to a ski shuttle and hiking and biking trails.

Squaw Valley Inn, 1920 Squaw Valley Road. (800) 323–7666. Charming shingle-and-stone complex near the ski tram; hotel rooms, swimming pools, neato lounge with big stone fireplace.

For More Information

Tahoe North Visitors and Convention Bureau, P.O. Box 5578, Tahoe City, CA 96145. (800) TAHOE–4–U.

Cal Trans Road Conditions. San Francisco: (415) 557–3755. Sacramento: (916) 653–7623.

Nevada Road Conditions. (702) 793–1313.

Advice: In the summer and on snowy weekends, avoid driving to Tahoe on Friday afternoons or returning on Sunday afternoons, unless you've got hours to waste. Every month of the year, check the weather and road conditions. Snow can fall even in June.

Tahoe South and the Hope Valley

A winter scene at Lake Tahoe.

Aspens and Silver Dollars

_____ 2 NIGHTS _____

Peaceful valley · Cozy cabins · Apple pie · Hot springs
Casino night · Old Tahoe estates · Beachtime

A triple-header: quiet hours in the aspen meadows and along the trout streams of Hope Valley; historical sights and lakeside fun; and casino-hopping under the neon lights of South Lake Tahoe. You'll get your first glimpse of Lake Tahoe, the largest alpine lake on the continent, at Echo Summit on Highway 50.

Day 1

Morning

Take Highway 80 to Sacramento, then Highway 50 to Kyburz, a three-and-one-half-hour trip from San Francisco or the East Bay.
Lunch: **Strawberry Lodge,** Highway 50, Kyburz. (916) 659–7200. Good American food and soda fountain specialties in a restored 1940s lodge; walking trails nearby.

Afternoon

Continue a half hour to Meyers, just south of South Lake Tahoe, and turn right onto Highway 89 for the half-hour drive over Luther Pass, sliding down into the aspen-studded, stream-freshened high mountain meadows of **Hope Valley,** at 7,180 feet. Sparsely developed, green, and gorgeous, the 1-mile-wide valley is crisscrossed by the **Carson River,** a trout angler's dream. Cross-country skiing is superb on dozens of flat meadows; downhill skiing can be had at Kirkwood, at the southwest end of the valley, over Carson Pass.

Turn left at the Highways 89 and 88 intersection, then immediately right into **Sorensen's Resort,** 14255 Highway 88, Hope Valley (800–423–9949), where you will spend the night. About Hope Valley, John Muir said, "You wade out into the grassy sun-lake, feeling yourself contained in one of nature's most sacred chambers, withdrawn from the sterner influences of the mountains."

A clutch of log cabins in a pine and aspen grove, Sorensen's is romantic and family-oriented at the same time. Some old and some new rustic cabins have homespun country decor, brass beds, wood stoves, and some kitchens, all in forested, creekside settings. Cozy with a wood-burning stove, **Sorensen's Country Cafe** serves hearty breakfasts, lunches, and dinners, indoors and outside under the trees. Buy guidebooks and fishing licenses here. The west fork of the Carson is just across the road.

Owners John and Patty Brissenden will direct you to fishing holes and wildflower walks and will arrange river-rafting or cross-country skiing expeditions. Located in the **Toiyabe National Forest,** Sorensen's provides flyfishing and cross-country-skiing instruction and rentals.

Ask about the guided hike on the Emigrant Trail. Worn smooth by pioneers on their way west, it's a fascinating route, with evidence of how wagons and animals were winched and hauled up and down steep grades and cliffsides.

Once a rest stop for emigrants of the 1800s, Sorensen's idyllic piece of the High Sierras is thick with wildflowers until the snow flies; in the fall the aspens look like streams of fire across the valley floor. At night lights twinkle around the cabin doors, wood smoke is in the air, and if you've a cabin away from the road, all you can hear is the sound of a rushing stream.

Dinner: Here in Sorenson's Country Cafe. Sit at a big wooden table with other guests, and tuck into beef stew or fresh fish, homemade bread, and fruit cobbler. Everyone seems to turn in early to enjoy the cabins and rest up for early-morning outings. But if you can't stand the quiet, make the forty-five-minute drive into the **Carson Valley** and pay your dues at the **Carson Valley Inn Casino,** 1627 Highway 395, Minden (702–782–9711).

Day 2

Morning

Breakfast: At Sorensen's. Fall out from under your comforter into the cafe for all-you-can-eat waffles with fruit or an old-fashioned bacon-and-eggs breakfast. There are a little stocked trout pond and a small play area to keep kids busy.

An old logging road adjacent to the resort leads up a pine forest, past huge boulders and views of the rugged mountains. It's 7 moderately strenuous miles to the top of the mountain, an 11-mile loop. Looking out over the valley, you'll see that it's greener than the bark beetle–stricken Tahoe Basin. Say a silent thank-you to the tireless Friends of Hope Valley, who continue valiantly to hold off developers.

In the late morning drive ten minutes east on Highway 89, to the **Woodford Stage Stop,** 92 Old Pony Express Road (916–694–2930). There are many roadside pullouts where you can stop and fish in the Carson or play along the banks.

A hundred-year-old stop on the Pony Express route, Woodford's is now a great old general store with groceries and fishing gear. The famous "Snowshoe" Thompson stopped here regularly on his Placerville-to-Genoa mail crossing in the mid-1800s.

Lunch: At the Woodford Stage Shop. Eat at the counter, have a sandwich or some chili, followed by the sour cream apple pie that people drive hours to get.

Afternoon

Proceed 6 miles southeast on Highway 89 to **Markleeville,** population one hundred, circa 1875, the seat of Alpine County. A stroll around town will turn up the **Cutthroat Saloon** (916–694–2150), **Gunslinger's Pizza** (916–694–2483), and the **Alpine County Historical Museum Complex** (916–694–2317). Bikers in leathers and tourists hobnob in the gloom of the saloon, shooting pool, playing pinball, pretending to be regulars. Some 10,000 rough-and-tumble silver miners once lived here, but now this is a sleepy 2-block-long burg of clapboard buildings, where travelers alight briefly on their way to campgrounds and fishing.

In the middle of Markleeville, you'll see the sign for **Grover's Hot Springs** (916–694–2248), a state park 4 miles west of town. Here 148-degree water flows out of underground springs into swimming and soaking pools—wonderful any day of the year, and delightfully steamy when snow is on the ground. There are campgrounds here and walking trails, although the hot pools are the main attraction.

Between Grover's and Markleeville, trout fishing and cool wading are good in **Markleeville Creek.** Several nearby creeks, lakes, and the upper **East Carson River** are planted with rainbows; information can be obtained at **Monty Wolf's Trading Post,** in Markleeville (916–694–2201).

(*Note:* The route from here to Bear Valley on Highway 4 is 39 miles over 8,700-foot Ebbets Pass on a treacherous two-lane road. If you've got extra vacation days and you're not driving a large RV, consider taking this route. The scenery is incredible, and there are many lakes, streams, trails, and campgrounds.)

It's about an hour from Markleeville back to Meyers. Turn right (north) onto Highway 50, then right again onto the **Pioneer Trail,** proceeding 5.5 miles to make a left onto Tahoe Boulevard and drive into the town of South Lake Tahoe.

Check in at **Lakeland Village,** Highway 50 near the base of Ski Run Boulevard, in **South Lake Tahoe** (916–541–7711). Here are 260 condo and lodge units on the lake, set back from the road in nineteen acres of pines and featuring a private sandy beach, two swimming pools, tennis courts, saunas, and some fireplaces and kitchens.

This is your night to hit the casinos, so get into your sequins and silver-tipped cowboy boots. Several multistory casinos are within a hop of one another, some connected by an underground walkway. Big names put on big shows at **Harrah's** (702–588–6611), **Caesars** (702–588–3515), **Harvey's** (702–588–2411), and the **Horizon** (702–588–6211). Up-and-coming stars play in the lounges and smaller clubs. Casino restaurants are a bargain; views are dizzying from rooftop restaurants. South Lake Tahoe is 8 miles of hotels, motels, restaurants, tourist traps, and neon lights. A blazing tunnel of excitement at night, the town's charm wears a bit thin in the light of day, especially if your wallet is lighter than when you blew into town.

Dinner: **The Summit,** on top of the world at Harrah's at the north end of South Lake Tahoe, P.O. Box 8, Stateline, NV. (702) 588–6611. Continental dining, tables on terraced levels, breathtaking views.

Do it.

Day 3

Morning

Breakfast: **Ernie's,** near the Y, 1146 Emerald Bay Road, Stateline, NV. (916) 541–2161. Down-home American breakfasts; only Tahoe locals and you know about Ernie's.

Toss your last few quarters away and head south, following Highway 89, also called **Emerald Bay Road,** out of town to the south end of the lake. At 9,735 feet **Mount Tallac** towers over a plethora of sights and things to do on the south shore. Relive the 1920s heydey of the rich and famous at the **Tallac Historic Site** (916–573–2600). Restored and open to tour are several formerly private estates, an old casino, and a hotel. Many musical and art events are held at Tallac, from jazz to bluegrass, from craft demonstrations to photo exhibits. In August the **Great Gatsby Festival** looks like the good old days, with antique boats and merrymakers in period costume. The 5-mile, 3,500-foot hike to the top of Mount Tallac rewards the hiker with magnificent views; trailheads are across the road from Baldwin Beach.

Also at Baldwin Beach is the **U.S. Forest Service Lake Tahoe Visitor's Center** (916–573–2600), offering exhibits of geology, natural environment, and history; nature trails; and interpretive programs.

Baldwin, Pope, and **Kiva beaches** are accessible by bus (916–573–2080) from South Lake Tahoe; a network of hiking trails connects the beaches, the visitor's center, and the Tallac Historic Site. Near Baldwin Beach is the only virgin forest remaining in the entire Tahoe Basin, which was logged out completely in the 1800s. The beautiful, green forests you see around the lake are second- and third-growth. The ancient sugar pines and Douglas fir of the primary forests were cut for railroad construction and for the building of San Francisco and other boomtowns. Shorter in height, sparser and lacking in the rich biodiversity that sustained earlier timberlands, today's trees are vulnerable to erosion, disease, and the vagaries of weather; a long-term drought and a bark beetle infestation in the 1980s and early 1990s devastated much of what remains of Tahoe's precious woods.

Lunch: **Fresh Ketch Lakeside Restaurant,** 2433 Venice Drive (watch for the left turn, just north of the Highway 50/89 Y at the south end of town). (916) 541–5683. Indoor or outdoor dining, overlooking busy Tahoe Keys Marina; salads, sandwiches, fresh fish; bar.

Afternoon

Head home on Highway 50, or head for the beach, the Heavenly Valley aerial tram, a golf course, or out on the lake on a paddlewheeling cruise boat.

There's More

Beaches. Three public beaches in South Lake Tahoe, each with extensive recreational facilities, including pools: El Dorado Beach, Regan Beach, and Connelly Beach (behind Timber Cove Lodge, between El Dorado Beach and Ski Run Boulevard).

Beaches not as overrun in the summertime are Nevada Beach, 1.5 miles north of town at Elk Point Road, and Zephyr Cove, 4 miles north of the stateline on Highway 50.

Tours on the lake. *Tahoe Queen,* South Lake Tahoe. (916) 541-3364. A huge paddlewheeler, day and evening trips to Emerald Bay, departs from Ski Run Marina.

The MS *Dixie.* (702) 588-3508. A smaller paddlewheeler, departing from Zephyr Cove. A cotton barge on the Mississippi in 1927, the *Dixie* was a floating casino at Tahoe; then it sank and was raised and converted to a tour boat.

Heavenly Valley Ski Area, P.O. Box 2180, Stateline, NV 89449. (916) 541-SKII. One of the biggest ski resorts in the world with one of the highest skiable summits in the United States. Nearly eighty runs get an average of 250 inches of the white stuff a year. On the Nevada side hundreds of miles of high desert stretch out into the distance, and on the California side you have the phenomenal experience of feeling like you are skiing right into the lake. If your legs can take it, start from the top of Sky Express and ski nonstop 5 miles. Super-high-speed express lifts and snow-making capability. Learn to ski programs—downhill and snowboard— for all ages, as well as special features such as senior programs, complete child care, special presentations by the ski patrol, demos by grooming vehicles, appearances by the avalanche dogs, and even cooking lessons.

Heavenly's Aerial Tram, at the east end of Ski Run Boulevard, South Lake Tahoe. (916) 541-1330. Open all summer for a five-minute, 1-mile ride up into the sky overlooking the lake and mountains. An easy 2-mile trail loops the mountaintop; a restaurant serves pretty good lunches, brunches, and dinners—romantic, with lights twinkling below.

Kirkwood Meadows, P.O. Box 1, Kirkwood, CA 95646. (209) 258-7000. Thirty-five miles east of South Lake Tahoe; at 7,800 feet, highest base elevation in the Tahoe area. Extraordinarily long ski season and dependably top snow conditions. Tyrolean-style, laid-back village atmosphere, less commercial, more like ski mountains used to be, where you can ski in your jeans and dare to be seen with equipment more than five years old. Complete child care, lessons, and a kids-only lift. On hundreds of acres of alpine meadows, Nordic skiing is perfection. Condos, lodge rooms, and rental houses make Kirkwood a major vacation destination in the summertime when the meadows turn to rippling waves of wildflowers. Biking and hiking trails and lake and stream fishing are popular, from the day school closes until the snow flies. Nearby at the summit of **Carson Pass, Caples Lake** attracts trout fishermen, canoers, windsurfers, and swimmers. Trails lead into the **Mokelumne Wilderness.**

Golf. Edgewood Tahoe Golf Course, Highway 50 at Stateline. (702) 588–3566. Eighteen holes; the site of major tournaments; the most challenging course at the lake. Located behind the Horizon Casino.

Glenbrook Golf Course, Highway 50 at Glenbrook. (702) 749–5201. Nine holes; no reservations taken.

Tahoe Paradise Golf Course, on Highway 50 in Meyers. (916) 577–2121. Eighteen-hole course.

Hiking. Desolation Wilderness. Hundreds of lakes, thousands of acres of outback, many trails. Easy accessibility makes it extremely popular; best off-season. For an 11.4-mile loop day trip, take the Glen Alpine trailhead at the end of Fallen Leaf Lake Road, hiking to Lake Aloha. (At Glen Alpine Springs is a covey of Bernard Maybeck–designed cabins at streamside.)

Round Lake, 6.4-mile loop to a neato swimming hole. Take Highway 89 south out of Meyers; 3.6 miles before Luther Pass is roadside parking on the north, trailhead on the south.

Showers Lake, 10.2-mile easy loop to the highest lake in the Upper Truckee River basin. From the intersection of Highways 88 and 89 in Hope Valley, take 88 to Carson Pass; continue to a bend with a parking area.

Silver Lake, Highway 88, 40 miles from South Lake Tahoe, at 7,200 feet in the Eldorado National Forest. A very beautiful lake where you can still see the tree markers cut for the Emigrant Trail by Kit Carson. There is a ninety-seven-site U.S. Forest Service campground (916–622–5061) here as well as a private campground and cabins operated by the descendants of Raymond Plasse, who built a trading post here in the 1850s (209–258–8814). Trout fishing is terrific, as are hiking and horseback riding.

Tahoe Rim Trail. Trailhead information: (916) 577–0676. A 150-mile trail.

Kayaking. Kayak Tahoe at Camp Richardson, P.O. Box 11129, Tahoe Paradise, CA 96155. (916) 544–2011. Day tours, camping, lessons, rentals.

Lake Tahoe Historical Society Museum, 3458 Lake Tahoe Boulevard, South Lake Tahoe. (916) 541–4975.

Shopping. Factory stores at the Y of Highways 50 and 89.

Tahoe Factory Stores, 2501 Highway 50.

Round Hill Mall, north of South Lake Tahoe at Zephyr Cove. Unique, nontouristy shops and a good Mexican restaurant.

Boating. Tahoe Keys Marina, South Lake Tahoe. (916) 541–2155. Boat launch, sail- and powerboat rentals, *Tahoe Paradise* tour boat, restaurant.

Woodwind Sailing Cruises. (702) 588–3000. Thirty-passenger, 41-foot trimaran with a glass bottom; peaceful way to cruise the lake; departs from Zephyr Cove.

Special Events

March. Echo to Kirkwood Cross Country Race, Kirkwood. (209) 258–7248.

June. Reno Rodeo, Reno. (702) 329–3877.

June. Wagon Train, South Lake Tahoe. (702) 883–4551. Annual mile-long historic wagon train rolls through town bringing the Old West to life. Hundreds of people dressed in period costume in wagons, stage coaches, or on horseback, mountain men, scouts tracing the original route of the Pony Express.

June–July. Lake Tahoe Sailweek, Tahoe Keys Marina. (800) AT–TAHOE. Sailboats from across the country converge for a week-long series of races.

June–September. Valhalla Summer Festival of Art and Music, South Lake Tahoe. (916) 542–4166. Concerts and exhibits in and around historical mansions.

July. Glenn Amundson Memorial Air Fest, Lake Tahoe Airport. (916) 541–4082. Military fly-bys, aerobatics, skydivers, vintage aircraft, hot-air balloons, food.

July–August. Music and Shakespeare at Sand Harbor. (916) 583–9048.

August. Hot August Nights in Reno. (702) 829–1955. Fifties and sixties cars, rock-and-roll.

August. Great Gatsby Festival, Tahoe Keys Marina, Tallac Historic Site. (916) 546–2768. Antique and classic wooden boat show, Roaring Twenties living history.

September. Reno National Championship Air Races, Reno. (702) 972–6663.

Other Recommended Restaurants and Lodgings

Kyburz

Strawberry Lodge, Highway 50. (916) 659–7200. Twenty miles west of the town of South Lake Tahoe. Quiet, comfortable, restored 1940s lodge surrounded by the pines of a National Forest. Good restaurant, ice cream parlor; cross-country skiing, mountain-biking, tennis, swimming; nearby fishing, hiking, downhill skiing.

Hope Valley

Hope Valley Resort, 14655 Highway 88. (916) 694–2292. Store, restaurant, RV park.

South Lake Tahoe

Christiania Inn, P.O. Box 18298. (916) 544–7337. Eclectic Swiss chalet design; five rooms with private baths upstairs; restaurant downstairs; five-minute walk to ski.

Camp Richardson, P.O. Box 9028. (916) 541–1801. Just east of Emerald Bay on Highway 89. A big resort with marina, beach, riding stables, lodge, restaurant, cottages, 230-unit campground, and a general store. A favorite family summer-vacation venue for decades. Rooms in the cavernous main lodge are small and simple. Convenient headquarters from which to set off on horseback or on foot into Desolation Wilderness. Rent kayaks here and/or take a guided tour with Kayak Tahoe, (916) 544–2011.

Accommodation Station, 2520 Lake Tahoe Boulevard, #3. (916) 542–5850. Rental of homes, condos, and cabins.

Cantina los Tres Hombres, Highway 89, .25 mile north of Highway 50. (916) 544–1233. Good Mexican food in a lively cantina atmosphere.

Hot Gossip, Highway 50 at Ski Run Boulevard. (916) 541–4823. Espresso, pastries, light breakfast, lunch, magazines and books, a locals' spot.

Embassy Suites Resort, 4130 Lake Tahoe Boulevard. (800) 362–2779. Luxury suites; Old Tahoe–style architecture; full breakfast and cocktail hour free. Indoor pool and spa, sun deck, workout room, seasonal packages, shuttle to airport, Heavenly ski area, and casinos.

Tahoe Keys Resort, 599 Tahoe Keys Boulevard, Lake Tahoe 96150. (916) 544–5397. Homes and condos for rent. You can fly into the international airport and be there in ten minutes. Some of the amenities: indoor and outdoor swimming pools, a health club, bicycles, outdoor games, a playground, a private beach, ski shuttles, power boat rentals, parasailing, jet skis, boat launching—in other words, vacation central. Sailboats from across the country converge at Tahoe Keys for a week-long series of races in June, the Lake Tahoe Sailweek.

Forest Inn Suites, 1101 Park Avenue. (800) 822–5950. One- and two-bedroom suites with equipped kitchens on five acres of forest with pools, spas, and health club, shuttle to Heavenly ski area.

Emerald Bay

State park campgrounds at Emerald Bay. MISTIX reservations: (800) 444–7275. Drive-in and boat-in sites.

Kirkwood

Caples Lake Resort in the Hope Valley, P.O. Box 88 (209) 258–8888. Launch and rent powerboats, canoes, sailboats, paddleboats. Lodge and cabins, restaurant, store.

For More Information

Lake Tahoe Visitor's Authority, 1156 Ski Run Boulevard, South Lake Tahoe, CA 96151. (800) AT–TAHOE. Use this number to book reservations, get tickets to events and casino shows, airline tickets, and hear about weather and road conditions.

Alpine County Chamber of Commerce, P.O. Box 265, Markleeville, CA 96120. (916) 694–2475.

Cal Trans Road Conditions. South Lake Tahoe: (916) 577–3550. San Francisco: (415) 557–3755. Sacramento: (916) 653–7623.

Nevada Road Conditions. (702) 793–1313.

Advice: In the summer and on snowy weekends, avoid driving to Tahoe on Friday afternoons or returning on Sunday afternoons, unless you've got hours to waste. Every month of the year, check the weather and road conditions. Snow can fall even in June.

The drought: Water levels have dropped steadily in the lake for years, and many boat-launching locations are out of commission. Check before you arrive with your boat.

Tahoe North

Hiking near Incline Village, Lake Tahoe.

Peaceful Pines and a Western Town

_____ 2 NIGHTS _____

Mountain meadows · Lakeside walks
Old railroad town · Beachtime · Winter resorts

The Washoe Indians called it _Tahoe_, or "Big Water." Twenty-six miles long and 12 miles wide, Lake Tahoe is 1,600 feet deep and "clear enough to see the scales on a cutthroat trout at 80 feet," according to Mark Twain. Surrounded by snow-frosted mountains and dense evergreen forests, the translucent blue water is hypnotic and cold, very cold. Legends tell of Indian chiefs in full regalia and women in Victorian garb floating motionless and frozen at the bottom of the lake.

On the north shore are little traffic, no neon, and few people. Fewer beaches and restaurants, too, but some of the best. A handful of small casinos add spice. The high life at south Tahoe and the action in Tahoe City are both within a half-hour or so, but on this short trip you'll want to stay put.

The old miners' and loggers' town of Truckee, still rough-and-tumble after all these years, makes a fun stop on your way to the lake.

Day 1

Morning

From the Golden Gate Bridge, drive north on Highway 101, turning east onto Highway 37 to Vallejo, where you'll catch Highway 80 north to Sacramento; it's a four-hour drive to the north shore.

Breakfast: At Sacramento take the J Street/Old Sacramento exit, stopping for breakfast at the **Whistle Stop Cafe,** on Front Street between K and L, in Old Town (916–446–4445). Open at 6:30 A.M. for Belgian waffles, homemade cinnamon rolls, and steak and eggs.

From here it's an uphill pull, two hours from the valley floor to Donner Summit, at 7,135 feet. Just past Baxter stop at the **Emigrant Gap Viewpoint,** on the west side of the road. Looking out over hundreds of miles of high country, you see the tremendous tilted block of the Sierras, sloping shallowly toward the west. Glacial canyons are gouged out of the granite, and the Yuba and Bear rivers have cut their own valleys. Pioneers winched their wagons down into the Bear Valley from here at 4,000 feet, then dragged themselves back up to Washington Ridge on the opposite side of the valley, the most difficult section of their journey to a new life in the West. In the Tahoe area you can find worn pioneer trails and grooves cut into cliffs and tree trunks by the winching ropes.

Beyond the summit of Donner Pass, take a reststop at **Donner Memorial State Park** (916–587–3841), a camping and picnic area at 5,950 feet, with a short, pleasant walking trail. The **Emigrant Trail Museum,** located within the park, depicts stories of the Donner party tragedy and the building of the railroad through the Sierras in the 1800s. You'll see train tracks, mostly covered with snow buildings, running along rugged mountainsides above Donner Lake. Taking the Amtrak train from Oakland to Truckee is a relaxing way to get to Tahoe; parties of skiers have fun doing this in the wintertime, and the scenery—wow!

Donner Lake, 3 miles long with a shoreline of 7.5 miles, is a smaller, quieter, less developed version of Tahoe, and many vacationers prefer it. You can camp, launch a boat, rent a cabin, fish, hike, ski, and enjoy the crystal blue waters. **Donner Lake Village Resort** rents lodgettes, studios, and one- and two-bedroom condos (916–587–6081). On the west end of Donner Lake is a trailhead for the **Pacific Crest Trail.** From here, you can take a 15-mile strenuous hike along the ridge of the Sierra crest, descending down into Squaw Valley's **Shirley Canyon.**

Continuing on Highway 80, take the Central Truckee exit into **Truckee,** where 2 blocks of restored brick-and-stone falsefront buildings face the railroad tracks. It looks and feels like the rollicking old railroading and logging town it's been since the mid-1800s. In 1873 at least one prisoner a day was hauled out of a Truckee saloon to the Nevada County jail. The jail is now a charming museum of the old days. Amtrak blasts into town a couple of times a day.

There's good shopping on Truckee's Commercial Row, a string of boutique, western wear, and ski equipment stores. Here you can purchase a sheepskin coat, moccasins, a fringed vest, or a stocking cap. *Lunch:* **O.B.'s Pub and Restaurant,** on the main street of Truckee. (916) 587–4164. In a hundred-year-old building; a cacophony of antiques, stained glass, wooden booths, Old Town ambiance. California cuisine; soup, chili, salads, sandwiches; Watney's on tap.

Afternoon

Proceed east out of Truckee on Highway 267 through the **Martis Valley,** passing **Northstar** (see page 251) as you climb up Brockway Summit—a short but icy ascent in the winter—on your way to the stoplight at Kings Beach. Stop here and jump in the lake, then take a left onto Highway 89, crossing into Nevada at Crystal Bay; it's five minutes to **Incline Village.**

If there is a secret hideaway at Tahoe, it's Incline Village, a small community of gorgeous homes and condos sprinkled on the shores of the lake and across steep mountainsides, with breathtaking views. Quiet and traffic-free, Incline has many virtues, such as the small, excellent ski resort of Diamond Peak; two Robert Trent Jones golf courses; two of Tahoe's loveliest beaches; and one elegant casino hotel.

Some people spend their entire vacation at Incline, using only their feet or bikes for transportation. A small, exquisite beach park, **Burnt Cedar Beach,** is available only to those who rent or own (renting a condo or house is the way to go here); the park has a big heated pool, a lifeguard, a snack bar, a kids' playground, shady lawns for lounging, picnic tables, barbecues, shallow water for wading, deep water for swimming, and a killer view. **Ski Beach,** in front of the

Hyatt Regency Lake Tahoe, has all of that except the pool, and it's long enough for a morning walk.

Park at the east end of Lakeshore Drive at the Hyatt and walk back along the lake on the paved walking/biking/jogging path, stopping to snap photos, take in the view, fill your lungs, and pick up pinecones.

Have a sundown cocktail at the **Lone Eagle Grill** (702–832–1234), a stunning wood and granite bar with a massive river rock fireplace, a floor-to-ceiling view of the lake, and an elegant restaurant. You may find it difficult to leave here.

Dinner: **Azzara's,** 930 Tahoe Boulevard, in the Raley's Center. (702) 831–0346. Comfortable, very popular place serving Italian everything. Especially good are the Sicilian artichokes, turkey with mozzarella and tomatoes, saltimbocca, and pizza; reservations necessary.

Lodging: **Coeur du Lac Condominiums,** c/o Brat Realty, P.O. Box 7197, Incline Village, NV 89452. (800) 869–8308. Contemporary mountain-style condos tucked into a pine forest, with walking paths, a heated pool, saunas, fireplaces, one to four bedrooms, lots of privacy; within walking distance to shopping, beaches, and ski shuttles.

This evening lurk around the **Hyatt Regency Lake Tahoe,** even if you're not a gambler. The "Fantasy Forest" in the casino is something to see: full-size pine trees studded with a zillion tiny lights and huge chandeliers reflected in a mirrored ceiling—even lights in the carpet. You can lounge in front of the big fireplace and people-watch, or you can plunge in and throw some money away. *Tip:* Play the slot machines at the ends of the aisles, near the center of the room; payoffs occur on the most visible machines.

Day 2

Morning

Breakfast: **Wildflower Cafe,** 769 Tahoe Boulevard. (702) 831–8072. Rubbing shoulders with skiers (snow or water) and construction workers at the counter or at a wooden table, have a Paul Bunyan–size breakfast of waffles or eggs and potatoes.

If tennis is your game, you will be glad to know that Incline has the largest concentration of top quality tennis facilities at the lake, with twelve professional courts at the **Lakeside Tennis Club,** Highway 28 at Ski Run Boulevard (702–832–4860), and seven courts at the **Incline Village Recreation Center,** 980 Incline Way (702–832–1310). At the rec center, you can come in for the day and use the indoor Olympic pool and fitness facilities, as well as the child care.

You can launch a boat at Incline Beach (702–831–1310) or at Sand Harbor (702–831–0494). Rentals of ski boats, paddleboats, canoes, and kayaks are available at **Action Water Sports** on the beach in Incline (702–831–4386).

You'll find every kind of clothing and equipment for outdoor recreation at the **Outdoorsman** (702–831–0446); pick up picnic supplies at **Raley's** (702–831–3400); both stores are near Azzara's. Now head east on Tahoe Boulevard to Country Club Drive and turn left, then right at the top of the hill onto Highway 431, also known as the Mount Rose Highway.

Dominating the mountain skyline on the north shore is **Mount Rose,** above Incline. From the scenic overlook on 431, almost the entire 22-mile-long lake gleams below, rimmed by the Sierras on the west and the Carson Range on the east. Seven miles beyond the lookout point is **Tahoe Meadows,** at 8,600 feet, a series of huge meadows where you can enjoy miles of cross-country skiing and summertime hiking, easy or strenuous. Sometimes a little soggy, the meadows are crisscrossed with small streams and crowded with wildflowers most of the year—buttercups, purple penstemons, marsh marigolds, Alpine shooting stars. Chickadees and jays flit through the willows and the pines.

The 12-mile-loop hike to the summit of Mount Rose, at 10,776 feet, is a half-day trip that starts on an old jeep road near the cinderblock building. Even if you can't make it to the top for the view that awaits, you may wish to start up this trail; there are a pond with a frog chorus in residence and wildflowers galore. At the top you'll see the whole lake basin and the Carson Valley sweeping away into the distance, and even Lassen Peak on a very clear day.

Lunch: Have your picnic here or take it back down the mountain to Tahoe Boulevard, going east out of Incline—actually Highway 28—a few miles to **Sand Harbor State Park** (702–831–0494), picturesque, with two white sand beaches, tree-shaded picnic spots, and lake and mountain views—the most beautiful beach park at the lake.

Afternoon

The annual **Music and Shakespeare Festivals** (916–583–9048) are held here at Sand Harbor on July and August evenings. On a clear summer night, you'll watch the sun go down over the lake while you sit on a blanket sipping wine and the kids play on the sand nearby. The lights go down, the stars come out, and magic begins on stage. Many people come back every year.

After an afternoon dip in the lake or a dip in the Burnt Cedar pool, or perhaps a nap, drive to **Crystal Bay,** at Stateline (five minutes west of Incline on Highway 89), and go into **Cal-Neva Lodge** (800–225–6382), the high-rise hotel casino at Stateline. It's one of the oldest casinos on the lake, made famous by a former owner, Frank

Sinatra. Off the lobby the Indian Room is a vast, beam-ceilinged lounge with a big boulder fireplace and a fascinating collection of early Tahoe artifacts, bearskins, and bobcats. If you're in the mood to tie the knot, step into one of three wedding chapels on the grounds.

Just down the road at **Kings Beach,** if it's a summer weekend, there's probably an arts and crafts fair going on.

As the sun starts to set, continue on Highway 89 to **Gar Woods,** 5000 North Lake Boulevard, Carnelian Bay (916–546–3366), for cocktails or tea; this is one of a handful of restaurants located right on the lake.

Dinner: **Colonel Clair's,** 6873 North Lake Boulevard, Carnelian Bay. (916) 546–7358. Cajun specialties and fresh fish; knotty-pine booths; noisy, popular, elbow-to-elbow friendliness; amazing food.

Lodging: Coeur du Lac Condominiums.

Day 3

Morning

Breakfast: **The Original Old Post Office,** 5245 North Lake Boulevard, Carnelian Bay. (916) 546–3205. Only the locals knew about this place, until now. Down-home cooking, monster-size breakfasts starting at 6:00 A.M. every day. You may wait on weekends, but not long.

Before heading back to the Bay Area, play a round of golf on one of Incline's falling-off-the-mountain golf courses; play tennis on one of the town's twenty-six courts; or take the kids to the Ponderosa Ranch (see below).

On Highway 89, within a few minutes drive of Incline, are a string of small villages attuned to the tourist trade, including **Crystal Bay, Kings Beach, Tahoe Vista,** and **Carnelian Bay.** At Crystal Bay are clustered a few casinos. Kings Beach has huge arts and crafts fairs on summer weekends near the beach and a golf course that turns into a snowmobile park when the snow flies. At Tahoe Vista, the **North Tahoe Regional Park** has a great snow hill for toboggans, saucers, and inner tubes, with equipment rentals (916–546–7248).

Heading back toward Truckee, you may wish to stop at **Northstar** (see page 249) and take the chairlift—anytime of year—to walking trails on the mountaintop.

There's More

Ponderosa Ranch, on the east end of Incline Village on Highway 28. (702) 831–0691. The original set used to film the TV show *Bonanza.* An elaborate Western town and theme park, haywagon breakfasts, shooting gallery, museum, gold panning, Hossburgers, ice cream parlor. If the kids are under twelve or so, this is a must.

Golf. Incline Championship and Executive Courses, Incline Village. (702) 832-1144. Two beautiful mountainside courses; also good cross-country skiing on the lower course. The lower course doubles as a cross-country ski area used primarily by residents, but you can rent skis in town and ski here, too.

Old Brockway Golf Course, North Lake Boulevard at Kings Beach. (916) 546-9909. Nine holes; inexpensive and easy.

Tahoe Donner Golf Course, Truckee. (916) 587-9440. Eighteen holes.

Skiing. Diamond Peak at Ski Incline, 1210 Ski Way, Incline Village. (702) 832-1177. Dazzling views, best for intermediates and beginners. Diamond Peak was the first U.S. resort to install a "launch pad" lift loading system, similar to the moving walkways at airports.

Mount Rose Ski Area, 2222 Mount Rose Highway, 5 minutes north of Diamond Peak on Highway 431. (702) 849-0706. Two sides of a big mountain; plenty of runs for all abilities; check wind conditions before purchasing a lift ticket.

Tahoe Donner Ski Area. (916) 587-9494. For beginners and families.

Royal Gorge, near Donner Summit. (916) 426-3871. Largest Nordic ski area in the nation, voted the best in North America. Spend the day on the trails, or ski to the lodge and stay overnight. Wrapped in fur robes, you can also be ferried in a horse-drawn sleigh to the European-style wilderness lodge, built in the 1930s. Bunk rooms, hearty meals. Warming huts with snacks available are scattered generously throughout the trail network.

Northstar-at-Tahoe, between Truckee and the lake on Highway 267. (916) 587-0248. One of the largest ski resorts at the lake and one of the best for intermediate and beginning skiers and for families, dozens of downhill, cross-country and snowboarding runs. One of the many annual events at Northstar is the exciting Inverted Aerial Freestyle Ski Competition in February.

Boreal Ski Area, near Donner Summit on Highway 80. (916) 426-3666. Reasonably priced, nonintimidating choice for new skiers. The Nugget chairlift is free and there is a snow-play area with rental saucers. Night skiing is popular at Boreal. You can also explore ski history from the 1850s to the present at Boreal's **Western America Ski Sport Museum** (916) 587-3841.

Hiking. Marlette Lake. Trailhead at Spooner Lake, near the junction of Highways 28 and 50. A 10-mile, moderately strenuous loop with a lake and killer views at the top; aspens make this a stunner in the fall.

Also at Spooner Lake (702-831-0494): trout fishing, hiking, picnicking, mountain-biking, equestrian trails, cross-country skiing, rentals.

Tahoe Meadows Whole Access Trail. From Incline Village, take Highway 431 uphill 7.5 miles to the paved parking lot at the trailhead. The wide, 1.3-mile loop is for those in wheelchairs and others, through meadows and lodgepole pine forests. Wildflowers are positively spectacular much of the year.

Mountain-biking. The famous Flume Trail starts at Spooner Lake, rides up to Marlette Lake, across the mountainside, then downhill at a 60 percent slope to Incline Village, 14 miles. For information on biking on Brockway Summit and other areas, call the Tahoe Area Mountain Bicyling Association at (916) 541–7505.

Fishing. Giant Kokanee salmon, released into the lake by accident in 1940, lurk below rocky ledges on the north shore, along with several species of trout. Crystal Bay is the best spot to catch them.

Casinos. Cal-Neva Lodge, the Tahoe Biltmore, and the Crystal Bay Club at Crystal Bay Stateline, five minutes west of Incline Village on Highway 28.

Tennis. Twenty-six courts in Incline Village, at the Lakeside Tennis Resort (702–831–5300), and at public courts.

Special Events

June. Gigantic Arts and Crafts Fair at Kings Beach. (916) 546–2935.

June. Truckee Tahoe Air Show. (916) 587–1119. You can fly your small plane into this airport and be picked up by the nearby resort, Northstar-at-Tahoe, for a day on the ski slopes.

July–August. Music and Shakespeare at Sand Harbor. (916) 583–9048. Beautiful outdoor amphitheater.

July. North Lake Tahoe Symphony Association Summer Music Series. (702) 832–1606. Sunday-afternoon concerts.

October. Pray for Snow Party (Tahoe Biltmore) and Native American Snow Dance (Incline Village). (800) GO–TAHOE. One hundred performances by four tribes of traditional, jingle, and snowshoe dances, drums, food, crafts. Two days after the 1994 Pray for Snow Party, the snow began to fall and scarcely stopped until spring, making for the fourth biggest snowfall in history, ending a severe decade-long drought with more than 60 feet of the white stuff.

Other Recommended Restaurants and Lodgings

Incline Village

Spatz, 341 Ski Way. (702) 831–8999. Dramatic lake view from 7,000 feet, nouvelle cuisine, bar, lunch on the deck, elegant ambience.

Vacation Station, P.O. Box 7180. (702) 831–3664. Homes and condos to rent.

Hacienda de la Sierra, 931 Tahoe Boulevard, across from Raley's. (702) 831–8300. Tops for Mexican food and margaritas.

Hyatt Regency Lake Tahoe, 111 Country Club Drive at Lakeshore. (702) 832–1234. A 460-unit, full-service hotel and casino with several restaurants: Lone Eagle Grill, on the beach, upscale, fresh seafood, steaks, lunch, dinner, and elaborate Sunday brunch; Ciao Mein, classy Italian/Oriental cafe, great name; Sierra Cafe, open twenty-four hours, a fancy coffeeshop with good food and keno. Shuttle service to major ski resorts. European-mountain-lodge interior; hotel rooms and lakeside cottages; state-of-the-art health club; outdoor pool; tennis.

Tahoe Vista

Le Petit Pier, 7238 North Lake Boulevard. (916) 546–4464. In the French country tradition, a small, elegant place with a world-class wine list and a nouvelle cuisine menu; on the lake, pricey, for *very* special occasions. Sundown cocktails in the lakeside bar.

Soda Springs

Rainbow Lodge, P.O. Box 1100, off Highway 80 at Rainbow Road exit 95728. (916) 426–3661. Historic thirty-room hotel, restaurant, bar. Like an old chalet in the alps, beside a rushing bend in the Truckee River. Comfy sitting room with fireplace. Fresh fish, cioppino, chicken Caesar salad, zowie desserts. Small, country-style inn rooms are fresh with comforters and brass beds. Cross-country ski from here right onto Royal Gorge trails.

Truckee

Northstar-at-Tahoe, between Truckee and the lake on Highway 267. (916) 587–0248. A complete resort village, with lodge rooms, condos, and houses to rent; a major ski resort; golf course; equestrian trails; shops, cafes, and restaurants. In the summer chairlifts take hikers and mountain-bikers up to wonderful mountain trails.

For More Information

Tahoe North Visitor's and Convention Bureau, P.O. Box 5578, Tahoe City, CA 96145. (916) 583–3494.

Truckee Donner Visitor's Center, P.O. Box 2757, Truckee, CA 96160. (800) 548–8388.

Incline Village Visitor's Bureau, 969 Tahoe Boulevard, Incline Village, NV 89451. (702) 832–1606.

Cal Trans Road Conditions. San Francisco: (415) 557–3755. Sacramento: (916) 653–7623.

Nevada Road Conditions. (702) 793–1313.

Advice: In the summer and on snowy weekends, avoid driving to Tahoe on Friday afternoons or returning on Sunday afternoons, unless you've got hours to waste. Every month of the year, check the weather and road conditions. Snow can fall even in June.

Trinity Loop

Discover the wonders of nature at Eagle Creek Falls.

The Lakes, the Alps, Weaverville

_____ 2 NIGHTS _____

Gold Rush towns · Lakes, rivers, forests · Historical sites
Trout fishing · Exploring the alps · Antiques and junque

Freshened with fifty-five sparkling alpine lakes, the dark, brooding
forests of the Trinity Alps loom 9,000 feet above Trinity Lake, which
snakes several miles through a rugged valley. This is one of the
wildest regions of the United States, sparsely populated and little
known, even to Californians. You'll see no stoplights and no parking

meters in Trinity County. Black bears, mountain lions, Roosevelt elk, mink, river otters, eagles, and spotted owls still inhabit the 500,000 acres of the Shasta-Trinity National Forest, one of the least visited national forests in the country.

The Trinity River leaps with salmon and steelhead, yielding fish of ten pounds or more. In the many lakes and streams, trout and bass keep fisherpersons happy in every season. The Trinity can be a stretch of calm water or rapids raging in a gorge. Wildflowers run riot in the spring and fall foliage is brilliant all along the river. The South Fork Trinity River National Recreation Trail follows the South Fork Trinity River for 21 miles, from Scott Flat Campground near Forest Glen to Wildwood Road, and for 4 miles from a trailhead near Hyampom to Forest Glen.

When you tire of the lakes, rivers, and forests of the Trinity outback, explore the charming little towns once inhabited by Gold Rush forty-niners, pioneers, and Chinese immigrants from a hundred years ago.

The 130-mile Trinity Scenic Byway between Old Shasta and Blue Lake on Highway 99 traces the path of the Trinity River and passes through two Gold Rush–era towns, two national forests, and a National Recreation Area, by museums, a bird sanctuary, and more sights.

Day 1

Morning

Drive north from the Golden Gate Bridge on Highway 101, connecting with Highway 5 north to Redding, 246 miles all told. Drive through Redding on Highway 299 (see Escapes Farther Afield Six).

Lunch: **Westside Deli Redding French Bakery,** 1561 West Cypress, downtown Redding, (916) 222–0787. Luscious deli sandwiches, pastries.

Afternoon

Drive west out of Redding on Highway 299 for 8 miles, to Whiskeytown Lake. It's a winding two-lane mountain road, but passing lanes and pullovers make it comfortable. Turn left to **Whiskeytown Lake Visitor Information Center** and overlook, at Highway 299 and Kennedy Memorial Drive. (916) 241–6584. **Whiskeytown Lake** is a cool blue jewel with 36 miles of primarily undeveloped shoreline. About 3 miles from the visitor's center, park at **Brandy Creek** and take a walk along the lake's edge on **Davis Gulch Trail,** about 2 miles long. This is a great family lake, where kids catch catfish, bluegill, and crappie. Their moms and dads go for the bass, trout, and kokanee—up to five-pounders. There are three boat ramps, and the Oak Bottom and Brandy Creek resorts rent boats. The **Whiskeytown General Store** (916-246-3444) started supplying groceries and fishing tackle over fifty years ago and never stopped. At the **Oak Bottom Marina** (916-359-2269), you can camp in a tent or an RV and can rent a canoe, fishing boat, or small sailboat and have a picnic; this is the best swimming spot.

Turning back onto Highway 299 at the north end of the lake, drive forty minutes to **Weaverville,** a nineteenth-century town beneath a dramatic **Trinity Alps** backdrop. Most of the town's original structures were destroyed by fire and replaced in the mid-1800s by brick buildings with wooden overhangs and spiral wooden staircases. A circa-1900 bandstand and the second oldest courthouse in California contribute to an Old West atmosphere.

A must-see here in the center of town is the **Joss House State Historic Park** (916-623-5284), where the "Temple amongst the Forest beneath the Clouds" has been restored to its ornate glory. In the 1850s thousands of Chinese sought gold along the Trinity, and this Chinese temple, with its carved altars, tapestries, and colorful artifacts, was built for their Taoist worship. Continuously used as a temple since then, the Joss House is now part of a state park, shady and cool with a creek running through.

Next door, the Gold Rush and pioneer days are alive and kicking at the **Jake Jackson Museum and Trinity County Historical Park** on Main Street (916-623-5211); stampmill, miner's cabin, blacksmith shop, and other displays are here. Across the street in a hundred-year-old building is the **Highland Art Center** (916-623-5111), where local artists show their works.

At the **Western Shop,** 226 Main Street in Old Town (916-623-6494), outfit yourself with cowboy boots or moccasins and a Western shirt. Go to **Brady's Sport Shop,** 201 Main (916-623-3121), for hunting and fishing equipment and information. Brady's is on the ground floor of the **Weaverville Hotel,** 201 Main (916-623-3121), which has been operating continuously since 1861; rooms upstairs are inexpensive and comfortable.

Dinner: **Pacific Brewery,** 401 South Main, across from the Joss House. (916) 623-3000. Hearty American food in a circa-1850 brick building. Large variety of microbrewery beers, indoors or in the streetside cafe.

Lodging: **Weaverville Victorian Inn,** 1709 Main Street, Weaverville 96093. (916) 623-4432. Sixty nice rooms, contemporary Victorian decor; some rooms with spas and views of a woodsy setting. Ask about the inn's meals-and-lodging specials.

Day 2

Morning

Breakfast: **The Mustard Seed,** 210 Main Street, Weaverville. (916) 623–2922. In Old Town, surrounded by wonderful elm trees; sit indoors or out. Belgian waffles, quiche, bacon-and-eggs; try the homemade apple pie—yes, for breakfast!

Head northeast out of town on Highway 3, beginning your exploration of the **Trinity Lake** area and the **Shasta-Trinity National Forest.** The jagged teeth of **Trinity Alps** loom to the west over the entire lake basin, covered on lower slopes with dense forestlands. Long and skinny, Trinity Lake has 157 miles of rugged shoreline and hundreds of coves that seem to absorb and hide houseboats, water-skiers, jet skis, and fishing boats; the lake always seems quiet and uncrowded, even in the summertime. The west side of the lake is dotted with campgrounds, resorts, and boat launches, while the east side, with somewhat restricted auto access, is largely undeveloped; campers and backpackers love it. Try your luck at fishing for trophy-size largemouth bass, trout, kokanee salmon, and catfish.

About 20 miles out of Weaverville, there is an interesting sidetrip on Rainier Road (a dirt road across the highway from the Mule Creek Guard Station). If you've an interest in forest management, this is an opportunity to see areas of clear-cutting, replantings, and selective cutting, as well as one of the tallest sugar pines alive, the 247-foot-tall **Sandam Tree.**

Three miles farther is another sidetrip—a 2-mile round-trip on a paved road to **Bowerman Barn.** On the National Register of Historic Places, it's one of the last of its unique type of structure. Docents will point out the stone foundation, whipsawn siding, and hand-forged square nails.

Lunch: **The Trinity Alps Resort,** at Stuart Fork Road. (916) 286–2205. The ninety-acre resort has one of the area's best restaurants, with a deck overlooking a stream. The forty private, rustic housekeeping cabins with sleeping verandas are right on **Stuart's Fork River,** which rushes clear and cold down from the alps. There are also a bar, general store, trail horses, and sports equipment. Not much changed since the 1920s, this is a great place for families. Weekly actitvities are scheduled (square dancing, trail rides, bonfires, movies, and more) and there are a million things to do: tennis, horseshoes, ping-pong, tubing, badminton, basketball. The resort is within 2 miles of trailheads into the Trinity Alps Wilderness Area. Running through the property, Stuart Fork is filled with rainbow and brown trout.

Afternoon

Proceed 6 miles to **Trinity Center,** a small town that was entirely relocated to this spot when the giant **Trinity Dam,** one of the highest earth-filled dams in the world, was constructed in 1961. At the **Scott Museum,** on Airport Road (916–266–3367), you can see Indian artifacts, covered wagons, stagecoaches, and tons of artifacts reminiscent of old pioneer and Gold Rush days.

Highway 3 continues north along the shore of Trinity Lake to the **North Shore Vista;** stop to wade and play in the lake and take a walk. Arrive at your lodging destination early enough to stroll about and enjoy the farm animals and peace and quiet of the ranch.

About 10 miles above Trinity Center is **Coffee Creek,** where several resorts are located. Turn left onto Coffee Creek Road and meander along to see zowie views of the alps and access traiheads into the Trinity Alps wilderness.

Dinner: **Ycatapom Inn Restaurant,** in a historic building on Mary Road in Trinity Center. (916) 266–3321. Steak, fish, world-class salad bar, casual.

Lodging: **Carrville Bed and Breakfast Inn,** P.O. Box 3536, Trinity Center 96091. (916) 266–3511. Six miles north of Trinity Center. A turn-of-the-century stage stop, now a country-ranch resort, circa 1920, with spreading lawns, pool, llamas, and miniature horses. Gracefully decorated Victorian-era bedrooms open to long verandas; a massive rock fireplace warms the main lounge.

Day 3

Morning

Breakfast: At the Carrville Inn. Big breakfasts of homegrown fruit and farm eggs, plus homemade sausage and muffins.

Drive south on Highway 3 to the junction with Highway 105, turning east toward the **Trinity Vista;** from here you get a spectacular view of mountain peaks and a number of managed forest units in various states of harvest. Some 25 million board feet of timber are removed annually from this section of the national forest; new timber crops are scheduled for harvest in 80 to 120 years.

It's another 8 miles or so to **Lewiston,** a flower-bedecked burg dating from the 1860s. The town is so tiny that you can see all of it in one glance, strung out prettily along the rushing **Trinity River.** A 1903 landmark is the **Old Lewiston Bridge,** one of the last one-lane bridges still in use. Below the bridge and in nearby **Lewiston Lake,** anglers flycast for rainbows, brooks, and browns. A 10-mile-per-hour speed limit on the lake makes it attractive to float tubers and canoeists. The wildlife viewing is excellent: bald eagle, osprey, otter, deer.

The Country Peddler, TNT Antiques, and the **Old Lewiston Mercantile,** all on Main Street, sell antique bottles, folk art, and collectibles of every description—literally thousands of square feet of good browsing, something to think about if your companion is fishing and you're not. Also on Main Street, **The Hitchin' Post** (916–778–3486) is a general store and deli.

Lunch: **Lewiston Hotel,** on Deadwood Road. (916) 778–3823. Built in the 1860s as a stagecoach stop, authentically funky historic ambience; burgers, sandwiches, salads, bar. Grizzle-bearded denizens of Lewiston sit on the hotel porch—or are they stockbrokers from the city who vowed not to shave or change clothes while on a fishing trip?

Afternoon

Between Lewiston and the Trinity Dam, you can picnic by the river, wade, swim, and fish in calm waters from the side of the road or from a small boat. Across from **Pine Cove Trailer Park,** P.O. Box 255, Lewiston (916–778–3838), are a fishing pier, swimming beach, boat ramp, and marina, a nice place for an evening swim.

It's 36 miles from Lewiston back to Redding and the Highway 299 junction with Highway 5, where you turn south to the Bay Area.

There's More

The Laag's Place and Big Ben's Doll Museum, P.O. Box 783, Weaverville 96093. (916) 623–6383. Across from the Victorian Inn on Main Street; 3,000 dolls from 1840 to the present; old bottles; gift shop (in midwinter, call first).

Trinity River Gorge/Burnt Ranch Falls, Highway 299 West. One mile past Burnt Ranch, turn right into the U.S. Forest Service campground. Take the trail at the end of the campground road to the most spectacular and scariest part of the Trinity River, where kayakers and rafters shoot the rapids. A fifteen-minute hike down the sheer walls of Burnt Ranch Gorge. Do it.

Scott Museum on Airport Road, Trinity Center 96091. (916) 266–3367. Indian artifacts, covered wagons, stage coaches, artifacts from old pioneer and Gold Rush days.

Cutting Edge Adventures. (916) 926–4647. Guided raft trips on the Klamath, Sacramento, and Salmon rivers.

Turtle River Rafting Company. (916) 926–3223. Guided raft trips on the Klamath, Rogue, Trinity, and Sacramento rivers.

Trinity Canyon Fly Fishing, P.O. Box 51, Helena, CA 96048. (916) 623–6318. Flyfishing instruction and guide service for the Trinity watershed, alpine lakes, streams, and the Trinity River. Accommodation packages available.

Trinity River Rafting, P.O. Box 572, Big Bar, CA 96010. (916) 623–3033. White-water rafting on the Trinity River, guided and self-guided. Raft and kayak rentals.

Bigfoot Rafting Company, P.O. Box 729, Willow Creek, CA 95573. (800) 722–2223. One- to three-day white-water trips on the Trinity, also scenic floats for beginners.

Special Events

May. Whiskeytown Lake Regatta. (916) 628–5223. Held Memorial Day.

June. Peddlers' Fair, Lewiston. (916) 778–3486. Antiques, art, and crafts dealers from all over California display and sell; music; food.

July–August. Ruth Rodeo, in Ruth. (800) 421–7259.

August. Trinity County Fair, Hayfork. (916) 628–5223.

Other Recommended Restaurants and Lodgings

Trinity Center

Wyntoon Resort, P.O. Box 70 96091. (916) 266–3337. Just north of Trinity Center, on Highway 3; ninety wooded acres; RV, trailer, and tent camping; marina; store; boat, jet-ski, and bike rentals; picnic and barbecue areas.

Ripple Creek Cabins, Star Route 2, Box 3899. (916) 266–3505. Four miles north of Coffee Creek, on Trinity Lake. Several nicely decorated housekeeping cabins located in a pine grove on Coffee Creek; wonderful views.

Weaverville

Granny House Bed and Breakfast, 313 Taylor. (916) 623–2756. Two-story Queen Anne–Victorian; *mucho* breakfast.

Indian Creek Bar and Grill, 7 miles west of Weaverville on Highway 299. (916) 623–4775. Built early in this century and still chock-full of strange old memorabilia. Mexican food, steaks, ribs, great pies.

Lewiston

Old Lewiston Bed and Breakfast Inn, on Deadwood Road, P.O.

Box 688 96052. (916) 778–3385. Small, comfortable rooms; back porch overlooking the Trinity River. Separate entrances and individual decks, breakfast.

Trinity River Lodge, P.O. Box 137. (916) 778–3791. Camper, trailer, and fishing resort; trees, lawns, boat launch, store.

Old Lewiston Bridge RV Resort, near Lewiston Bridge on Rush Creek Road, P.O. Box 148. (916) 778–3894. Twenty-six acres on the river; shady and green; tent sites.

For More Information

Trinity County Chamber of Commerce, P.O. Box 517, Weaverville, CA 96093. (800) 421–7259.

Lewiston Chamber of Commerce, P.O. Box 105, Lewiston, CA 96052. (916) 778–3730.

MISTIX, state park camping and RV site reservations. (800) 444–7275.

Backpacking permits: Trinity Alps Wilderness, P.O. Box 1190, Weaverville, CA 96093. (916) 623–2121.

Mount Lassen, Lake Almanor

Majestic Mount Lassen rises above Lake Helen.

Mountain Magic, Lake Country

_____ 2 NIGHTS _____

Volcano vibrations · Lakeside walks · Fishing · Forest trails
Picnic on top of the world · Summer and winter sports

The largest "plug dome" volcano in the world, 10,457-foot Lassen
Peak last blew its top in 1921. Hot springs, boiling mudpots, and sul-
fury steam vents remind us that sometime in the next few hundred
years, a drive through Lassen Volcanic National Park may not be a
good idea. For now, though, it's one of the wonders of the world, and

a great deal of the giant park can be seen on a 35-mile drive up and over the 8,000-foot summit and on 150 miles of interconnecting wilderness trails. Beneath a dramatic skyline of craggy volcanic peaks lie fifty mountain lakes surrounded by cedar, fir, pine, and aspen forests. And this is one of the only parts of the world where peregrine falcons and bald eagles can be seen.

Anglers from all over the world come to the Lassen area for wild-trout fishing in the cold, clear waters of Hat Creek and the Fall and McCloud rivers on the north side of the National Park. In the winter-time cross-country skiers, snowshoers, and snow campers take off into the spectacular backcountry; snow may fly as early as September and as late as May. South of Lassen, 13-mile-long Lake Almanor is a laid-back fishing and camping destination.

Day 1

Morning

From the East Bay take Highway 80 to Highway 505 near Vacaville, connecting with Highway 5 to Red Bluff, a four-hour drive.

Lunch: **Golden Corral,** 250 Antelope Boulevard, Red Bluff. (916) 527-3950. Bountiful buffet and salad bar, Philly steak, burgers.

Afternoon

Continue on Highway 5 for a half-hour to Redding, then take High-way 44 east through Shingletown, passing grassy meadows and llama and horse farms on the way to **Lassen Volcanic National Park,** P.O. Box 100, Mineral, CA 96063 (916–595–4444). At the north park en-trance, stop at the visitor's center (916–335–7575) for the *Lassen Park Road Guide* and a schedule of naturalist-led tours, interpretive pro-grams, and kids' story hours that may fit in with your plans. (You'll be spending most of the day there tomorrow.)

Very near the entrance is **Manzanita Lake,** a postcard-perfect, evergreen-surrounded lake with dazzling views of the mountain. Take the easy one-hour-long, 1.5-mile hike around the lake by your-self or on a ranger's tour. Nonmotorized boating and camping are per-mitted at Manzanita, a lake favored by trout anglers; camping sites are pretty and private. In the fall Canada geese and wood duck can be seen in great numbers, resting on their way south.

Leaving the park, continue on Highway 44 about 14 miles to **Old Station,** where you will spend the night. A stagecoach stop in the 1850s, it was abandoned due to Indian troubles, then became an army outpost and a rest stop for loggers. Now Old Station is a tiny, rustic community at the headwaters of upper **Hat Creek,** one of the most challenging and most rewarding wild-trout streams in the United States. The water is easy to access here in the village and from several campgrounds on Highways 44 and 89, which meet at Old Station. Nonfishing members of the family will enjoy wildlife viewing in the Hat Creek area, where osprey, bald eagles, elk, bats, and a variety of waterfowl are commonly seen.

The Fall River is a true spring creek, one of the few in the state. Averaging 3,000 fish per mile, many exceeding 20 inches in length and eight pounds in weight, the Fall is a "catch and release only" river, a gently flowing ribbon of water meandering through lush green farmland meadows in the wide Fall River Valley.

About half a mile west of Old Station, across from Hat Creek Campground, is the **Spattercone Crest Trail,** a 2-mile self-guided trail winding past volcanic spattercones, lava tubes, domes, and blowholes, a two-hour walk, best in early morning.

Dinner and Lodging: **Mount Lassen Inn,** at Highways 44 and 89, P.O. Box 86, Old Station 96071. (916) 335–7006. Hat Creek rushes right by the back door of this circa-1930 clapboard bed-and-breakfast inn. Suites with private baths have brass beds and dormer windows. Innkeeper Gene Nixon will serve a memorable dinner to you in an antiques-filled dining room—game hens with fruit and nut dressing, perhaps. Or try **Uncle Runt's Place,** across the road (916–335–7177), for plainer fare.

Day 2

Morning

Breakfast: At Mount Lassen Inn. Smoked salmon and cream cheese omelets or heart-shaped waffles, either in a little dining area in your room or downstairs with other guests.

Ask Gene to put together a picnic lunch for you to take on your trek through Lassen National Park. Or pick up supplies at the little store at Manzanita Lake.

Head back to the National Park for your day-long explorations by car and on foot. **Lassen Park Road** winds for 35 miles around three sides of the park, past woodlands, meadows, and clear streams and lakes. Miles of trails, including 17 miles of the **Pacific Crest Trail,** twist through aromatic conifer forests, magnificent stands of aspens and cottonwoods, and wildflower-strewn meadows. You'll see old lava flows, natural sulfurworks, hot steam, and boiling mud. Several lakes allow fishing, canoeing, and nonpowered boating. In the *Lassen Park Road Guide,* more than sixty points of interest and trails are specified, numbered to correspond with road signs. Lassen can get snow any day of the year, and you may wish to carry chains from October through April.

Lily Pond Nature Trail, starting at the **Loomis Museum** parking lot near Manzanita Lake, is a 1-mile, hour-long, easy walk around a small lake and through a shady forest to **Chaos Jumbles,** an interesting avalanche area.

The **Bumpass Hell Trail** is a 3-mile, easy walk into the park's most active thermal area, where you'll walk on boardwalks over hot springs, steam vents, mudpots, and other eerie manifestations of the earth's hot insides. An easy 3-mile walk on the **Trail to Paradise** brings you to a beautiful glacier-carved meadow for spectacular displays of wildflowers most of the year.

The .25-mile **Devastated Area Interpretive Trail,** at road marker #44, is one of several trails that are handicapped accessible. Lodgepole pines and aspens are particularly lush here, breathtaking in the fall.

It's a 700-foot descent, 1.5 miles one way, to **Kings Creek Falls,** a 30-foot cascade, with streams, meadows, and lots of trees along the way.

Lunch: A picnic in a mountain meadow.

Afternoon

In the 8,000-foot summit area, views of mountains 1,000 feet above and plunging valleys and canyons below are distracting, to say the least. Crystal-clear, blue-green **Emerald Lake** and **Lake Helen** lie beside the road. A less-than-delicate scent of rotten eggs from the misty **Sulfur Works** vents gradually becomes a memory on the last 6 miles in the park, a downhill drop of 1,400 feet.

Near the southwest entrance of the park is the **Lassen Park Ski Area** (916–595–3376). Equipment can be rented for sledding, snowshoeing, snowboarding, and cross-country and downhill skiing; the downhill skiing is challenging only for beginners. The entire main road through the park is available for cross-country skiing, with unending views of snowbound mountains, valleys, and lakes. Off Highway 89 near the park, the **Spencer Meadows National Recreation Trail** is 12 beautiful miles of aspen groves, cedar forests, meadows, and bubbling springs (916–257–2151)

(East of Lassen is high desert Wild West country of guest ranches and hunting lands. Fragrant with pine and sage woods, **Eagle Lake,** near **Susanville,** is famous for trophy trout averaging three to five pounds. Once a lumber town, **Westwood** is the home of a huge carving of Paul Bunyan and the Paul Bunyan Mountain Festival. The **Honey Lake Wildlife Area** northwest of Susanville contains hundeds of acres of wetlands attracting clouds of migrating waterfowl. A great way to see the scenic **Susan River Canyon** between Westwood and Susanville is on the 26-mile **Bizz Johnson Rail Trail.**)

Dinner: Continue out of the park on Highway 89 to the **Black Forest Lodge,** 10 miles west of Chester at Mill Creek. (916) 258–2941. German and American food; fresh trout; bar; friendly and fun.

Lodging: **Stover's St. Bernard Lodge,** P.O. Box 5000, Mill Creek 96061. (916) 258–3382. Next door to the Black Forest. A 1912 hotel with knotty-pine walls and country-fresh decor, shared baths; good restaurant and fabulous bar with stained-glass and antiques. Cross-country ski out the back door.

Day 3

Morning

Breakfast: At St. Bernard Lodge. Blueberry pancakes; steak and eggs.

Drive 10 miles to the resort town of **Chester,** at **Lake Almanor,** a pine-fringed lake at 4,500 feet, the snowy peak of Lassen and surrounding mountains mirrored in its clear, calm waters. Almanor is popular for trout, bass, catfish, and perch fishing, plus king salmon, not usually found in landlocked lakes. Swimmers, boaters, and water-skiers like the sandy beaches, small lodges, and campgrounds on the western shore.

Lunch: **Timber House Lodge,** Highway 89 at First Street, Chester. (916) 258–2729. This place you've got to see. Massive stone-and-tree-trunk construction, including the furniture; good basic American food, bar.

Afternoon

From the south end of the lake, take Highway 89 south, connecting with Highway 70 west though the **Plumas National Forest,** along the north fork of the Feather River. Turn south onto Highway 99 to Highway 80 south to Sacramento, for a three-hour drive back to the Bay Area.

There's More

Ahjumawi Lava Springs State Park, 3.5 miles north of Highway 299E, near the town of McArthur. (916) 335–2777. Accessible only by boat. Launch into Big Lake, 6,000 acres of wetlands and wilderness encompassing Big Lake, Ja-She Creek, and portions of the Tule, Fall, and Pit rivers, a sanctuary for thousands of birds, including bald eagles.

Fishing. Boat-launching access on the Fall River and Hat Creek is limited; it's best to get advice at local fishing shops like The Fly Shop, 4140 Churn Creek Road, Redding. (916) 222–3555. Take the Churn Creek Drive exit off Highway 5; go east over the highway to Bechelli Lane to a weathered gray building with a big fish on the side, visible from the highway. Advice on what's biting and where to catch 'em; top-quality equipment and clothing; guides, tours, and maps—a fisher-person's mecca. Call ahead for fishing conditions.

Fishing tours. Clearwater Trout Tours, 274 Star Route, Muir Beach, 94965. (415) 381–1173. Flyfishing schools, public and private outings, guides, lodge on the Fall River.

W.O.A. Float Tours, Horse Creek 96045. (916) 496–3652. Scenic float trips on 6 miles of the Klamath River, oar-powered drift boat, quiet, dry, and safe for all ages, even babies. Streamside picnic, gold panning, birdwatching.

Sidetrip. For the intrepid backpacker, RVer, or four-wheel driver, 11 miles from Old Station on Highway 44 East is the 7-mile rough road to Butte Lake, at 6,000 feet. A beautiful campground sits at lakeside, surrounded by ponderosa pines and rugged volcanic outcroppings. Motorized boats are not allowed, and the fishing is phenomenal. Interesting cindercones and other volcanic formations, plus two more lakes and backcountry trails, make this a great way to go.

Golf. Fall River Valley Golf Course, west of Fall River Mills on Highway 299. (916) 336–5555. Eighteen holes; clubhouse, restaurant, pro shop.

Fort Crook Museum, in Fall River Mills. (916) 336–5110. Open May–October. Pioneer history, Indian artifacts; pioneer cabin, schoolhouse, jailhouse, blacksmith shop, and more.

Bizz Johnson Rail Trail, between Susanville and Westwood. (916) 257–0456. A 26-mile BLM-maintained gravel trail winding through the Susan River Canyon, following the old Fernley and Lassen rail line built in 1914 to serve the world's largest pine mill. Flat, great for bikes, walking, cross-country skiing, horseback riding. Several trailheads, camping, eleven massive bridges, and two tunnels. Best cross-country skiing conditions are found on the upper 18.5-mile segment west of the Devil's Corral Trailhead, with elevations between 4,760 feet and 5,500 feet.

Special Events

May. Airport Day at Fall River Airport. (916) 243–2643. Air show, jet fly-bys, parachute jumping.

July. Burney Basin Days. (916) 336–5840. Parade, barbecue, dances, fireworks, entertainment.

July. CCA Rodeo, McArthur. (916) 243–2643.
July. Paul Bunyan Mountain Festival, Westwood. (916) 256–2456.
July. Basco Fiasco, Susanville. (916) 257–4323. Traditional Basque festival with costumes, athletic events, outdoor dinner and dance.
August. Main Cruise, Susanville. (916) 257–4323. Car show, outdoor bands, dances, Lassen County Fair.
September. Street Rod Extravaganza, Chester. 1950s nostalgia experience. (916) 258–2426.
September. Intermountain Fair of Shasta County. (916) 243–2643.

Other Recommended Restaurants and Lodgings

Lassen National Park

Drakesbad Guest Ranch, booking office is at 2150 Main Street, Dept K, Red Bluff, CA 96080. (916) 529–1512. Secluded within the national park, a century-old hot springs resort and ranch to which families return year after year. Trail rides, kids' program with hikes, crafts, swimming. Lodge rooms, cabins, or bungalows. Old-fashioned Western ranch experience in spectacular surroundings.

Ravendale

Spanish Springs Guest Ranch, P.O. Box 70, Ravendale, CA 96123. (800) 272–8282. Family ranch vacations, cattle drives, buckaroo camp, horseback rides.

Shingletown

Wild Horse Sanctuary, P.O. Box 30, Shingletown 96088. (916) 474–5770. Frontier-style cabins at a ranch that shelters wild horses. Campfires, hearty meals, daily safaris by horseback into ruggedly beautiful tree-studded foothills to observe and photograph wild horses and burros, and sometimes wild turkey, deer, and bobcat, in their protected habitat. A little advance riding experience makes this more enjoyable, although it is not required.

Eagle Lake

Eagle Lake R.V. Park, on the east side of Eagle Lake. (916) 825–3133. Full hook-ups, motel and cabins rental, store.

Lake Almanor

Lassen View Resort, 7457 Highway 147. (916) 596–3437. Cottages, RV and tent sites, boat rental, grocery.
P. G. and E. Campgrounds. (800) 624–8087.
U.S. Forest Service Campgrounds. (916) 258–2141.

Chester

Bidwell House Bed and Breakfast, 1 Main Street. (916) 258–3338. Victorian farmhouse with fourteen lovely rooms, some with Jacuzzi tubs and wood stoves. Full breakfast.

Cassel

Clearwater House on Hat Creek. 274 Star Route. (415) 381–1173. Located between Lassen and Shasta (Clearwater Trout Tours). Flyfishers' delight. A turn-of-the-century farmhouse, seven rooms with baths, all meals.

Fall River Mills

Rick's Lodge, Glenburn Star Route. (916) 336–5300. Restaurant/bar, three meals, pool, boat and motor rentals, guide service, flyfishing school. Beautiful location on the Fall River; store selling flyfishing gear, snacks; free airport service from Fall River Mills.

Paynes Creek

Oasis Springs Ranch, P.O. Box 454 96075. (800) 339–9887. A first-class flyfishing lodge; horseback riding available as well. The crystal-clear, rushing waters of Battle Creek run by the door. Situated 25 miles east of Red Bluff off Highway 36; guests are transported from Payne's Creek by jeep.

Old Station

Hat Creek Resort, P.O. Box 15 96040. (916) 335–7121. Motel, cabins, RV park.

For More Information

Fall River Valley Chamber of Commerce, P.O. Box 475, Fall River Mills, CA 96056. (916) 336–5840.

Shasta Cascade Wonderland Association, 14250 Holiday Road, Redding, CA 96003. (916) 275–5555. Tourist information.

Chester–Lake Almanor Chamber of Commerce, P.O. Box 1198, Chester, CA 95020. (916) 258–2426.

Lassen Volcanic National Park, P.O. Box 100, Mineral, CA 96963. (916) 595–4444.

MISTIX, state park camping and RV site reservations. (800) 444–7275.

Lassen County Chamber of Commerce, P.O. Box 338, Susanville, CA 96130. (916) 257–4323.

Snowfone ski reports. (916) 595–4464.

Road conditions. (916) 244–1500.

Shasta Cascade

White rivers of ice cap beautiful Mount Shasta.

Mountain Majesty, Rivers, Lakes, Timberlands

_____ 2 NIGHTS _____

Lakeside walks · High country views · Waterfowl, waterfalls, wilderness
Houseboating and fishing · Cavernous pursuits

One in a chain of Cascade Range volcanoes stretching from Northern California to southwestern Canada, Mount Shasta is a frosty, 14,162-foot presence that seems to take up half the sky in Siskiyou County.

Mist-shrouded glacial peaks and white rivers of ice are visible for hundreds of miles.

Mount Shasta presides over vast timberlands and wilderness areas freshened with lakes, rivers, and streams, offering a paradise for hikers, anglers, summer- and winter-sports enthusiasts, and just plain lovers of high country scenery.

On a weekend in the Shasta area, you may fall under the magic spell of the mountain and return again to see it streaked with lightning in a summer thunderstorm or transformed into a frozen white wave in winter.

Your route along Highway 5 follows the mighty Sacramento River—wide, cool, and green; fringed with overhanging trees; plied by fishing boats and water-skiers; and nourishing a valley that feeds the world.

Day 1

Morning

From the Oakland Bay Bridge, it's 325 miles to Redding. Take Highway 80, connecting with Highway 505 above Vacaville; then take Highway 5 north to Redding through miles of farmlands, lush and green in the winter and spring, golden dry in summer. Bordering the valley are the crumpled eastern foothills of the Coast Range and the distant peaks of the Sierra Nevada. Defunct volcanoes called the **Sutter Buttes** rise dramatically above the valley floor.

Two hours from the Bay Area, it's fun to make a pit stop at Corning, the "Olive City." Right off the freeway at the Central Corning exit, on Main Street, is the **Olive Pit** (916–824–4667), since 1967 the place to taste and buy dozens of kinds of olives, plus almonds and nut butters. The cafe serves olive burgers, sandwiches, and frozen yogurt. Back on the highway just beyond the Olive Pit is a pretty, shaded rest stop with lawns and trees.

Between **Redding** and **Red Bluff** is most of the mature riparian woodland left in the state, home to an incredible concentration of wildlife, including 20 species of fish and 200 species of birds. Overhanging the banks of the salmon-spawning riffles are sycamores, cottonwoods, oaks, and willows. (See page 275 for information on fishing and boating access.)

Near Redding the valley begins to roll, and the peaks of the Klamath Mountains and the Cascades emerge in the distant north and east. The Sierra Nevada ends; the Cascades begin.

Lunch: Take the Central Redding/Highway 99 exit into town, turning left on Market for ½ block to **Cheesecakes Unlimited,** 1334 Market Street, Redding (916–244–6670). Super sandwiches, pita bread concoctions, and that *cheesecake.*

Afternoon

Go to the **Shasta Cascade Wonderland Association,** at 14250 Holiday Road (916–275–5555) for maps, brochures, and guidebooks.

It's 23 miles beyond Redding on Highway 5 north to **Lake Shasta,** one of the best fishing lakes in California, fed by the Sacramento, McCloud, Pit, and Squaw rivers. At an elevation of 1,000 feet, surface water reaches eighty degrees in the summer, perfect for houseboating and waterskiing.

Take the Shasta Caverns Road exit, driving 2 miles to **Lake Shasta Caverns** (916–238–2341), a dramatic natural wonder. The tour includes a fifteen-minute boat ride across the lake to a wooded island, where a bus takes you 800 feet up a steep road through aromatic bay, oak, and manzanita, past exciting dropoffs and views of the lake that you'll see from no other spot. Groups of about twenty people are guided into a series of giant chambers, up and down hundreds of stone steps. The atmosphere is delightfully spooky, damp, and drippy—a constant fifty-eight degrees, refreshing in the summer when outside temperatures can reach over a hundred degrees. Multicolored columns, 20-foot-high stone draperies, stalactites and stalagmites, brilliant crystals, and unusual limestone and marble formations are subtly lighted and fascinating. After the cavern tour you can explore the walking paths, have a picnic overlooking the lake, or try panning for gold.

It's 38 miles from the caverns to the town of **Mount Shasta,** in the shadow of the mountain and almost completely surrounded by the **Shasta National Forest.** Motels line the road into the town, a flower-bedecked overnight stopping point for travelers on their way to the Northwest.

Dinner: **Avalanche,** at the south end of town, 412 South Mount Shasta Boulevard. (916) 926–5496. A small, friendly cafe and fish market; mountain views; giant shrimp cocktail, chowder, a wide variety of fresh fish every day.

Lodging: **Ward's Big Foot Ranch,** 1530 Hill Road, Mount Shasta. (916) 926–5170. A country estate located 2 miles northwest of downtown. Spectacular mountain views; redwoods, pines, lawns, and gardens; llamas; a rushing stream; walking and biking trails. Two bedrooms in the house; a cottage with fireplace sleeps six.

Day 2

Morning

Breakfast: At Ward's Big Foot Ranch. On the deck or in the family dining room; Barbara Ward's Scandinavian *abelskivers* and hearty egg dishes.

Just up the road from Ward's are the **Sisson Museum** and **Mount Shasta Fish Hatchery,** 1 North Old Stage Road (916–926–5508), with displays of the history, geology, and climate of the mountain. Walk around to see the hatching and rearing ponds. Trail maps and guidebooks of the area are sold here.

Drive 3 miles south on Stage Road to **Lake Siskiyou,** surrounded by dazzling mountainscapes and a tree-lined shore. Fresh, clean, pine-scented **Lake Siskiyou Camp-Resort,** 4239 West Barr Road, Mount Shasta (916–926–2618), is one of the prettiest multi-use camping and RV facilities in California. You can even rent a fully equipped trailer for use on-site. Walk around the 430-acre lake, lounge on the beach and swim, launch a boat, or rent water toys, kayaks, canoes, pedal-boats, sailboats, and fishing equipment. A store, snack bar, outdoor movies, and playground are also found here.

For a more challenging hike, take the **Sisson-Callahan National Recreation Trail.** Start by driving southwest out of Mount Shasta along West Barr Road to North Shore Road to the north fork of the Sacramento River. You wade through a shallow stream, then go .5 mile on an old logging road alongside the river to hook up with the trail. The route has spectacular views of the Trinity Alps, Mount Eddy, Castle Crags, and Mount Shasta. At the 9-mile point you'll meet up with the **Pacific Crest Trail.** For maps and information on area trails and hiking Mount Shasta, go to **Fifth Season,** North Mount Shasta Boulevard (916–926–3606), or **Shasta Mountain Guides,** 1938 Hill Road (916–926–3117).

Lunch: **Michael's,** 313 North Mount Shasta Boulevard, Mount Shasta. (916) 926–5288. Homemade pasta, soup, burgers.

Afternoon

From Mount Shasta take Highway 89 east around the base of the mountain into the **Shasta National Forest** and **McCloud River Valley.** Two miles south at the first exit is **Mount Shasta Ski Park** (916–926–8600), with ski runs at 5,000 feet. Here you'll find downhill and cross-country skiing; two triple chairlifts; a day lodge, restaurant, and ski school; and equipment rental and night skiing. In the summer try the excellent mountain-bike trails, and ride up the chairlift for the view of a lifetime, a forty-minute round-trip. For more cross-country ski trails, watch for **Bunny Flat, Sand Flat,** and **Panther Meadows** off Highway 89.

Ten miles farther is the logging town of **McCloud.** To reach the Nature Conservancy's **McCloud River Preserve,** go 9.2 miles south on Squaw Valley Road in McCloud; at the McCloud Reservoir bear right, go 2.2 miles, then turn right onto a dirt road to the preserve. Rushing down from the mountain, the river has cut a steep, narrow canyon teeming with wildlife and densely forested with old-growth Douglas fir and ponderosa pine. The Nature Conservancy's precious piece of wilderness includes several miles of protected wild trout waters, open to the public on a restricted basis. Beautiful nature trails are yours for the walking. For complete information and maps, call the conservancy at (415) 777–0487.

Seven miles from McCloud on Highway 89, at Fowlers Campground, the **McCloud River Falls** are a sidetrip well worth taking. Accessible by car, the three falls on a 2-mile stretch of river plunge into deep pools perfect for swimming. The third cascade has picnic tables above and a ladder that divers use to jump into the pool.

Along Highway 89 the bare spaces on the forested hillsides are examples of clear-cut logging.

It's about an hour's drive, over 4,000-foot Dead Horse Summit, to **McArthur-Burney Falls State Park** and **Lake Britton** (916–335–2777). The big attraction here is two million gallons of water a day tumbling over a misty, fern-draped 129-foot cliff. Take the 1.5-mile hike down into a forest fairyland gorge where wild tiger lilies, maples, dogwood, black oak, and pines decorate the streamside; the loud rush of the falls and the stream intensifies the experience. It takes about a half-hour for the fit and fast, an hour for amblers and photographers, and two hours for waders, fisherpersons, and walkers who take offshoot trails. Good trout fishing can be had in the deep pool at the foot of the falls and in the 2-mile stream above and below.

Hikes in and near the park include a 1.5-mile flat route to **Lake Britton Dam,** then 3 miles farther to **Rock Creek,** and an 8-mile route to **Baum Lake** and the **Crystal Lake Hatchery.**

Around 9-mile-long Lake Britton are camping and RV sites, not too private. Accessible by boat (rentals here), with a terrific swimming hole at its foot, **Clark Creek Falls** is a jet of frigid water crashing into the lake. Crappie, bass, and catfish bite all season; some of the best fishing is downstream from the lake at the outlet of Pit River #3 Powerhouse, a piece of water designated as a wild-trout stream where only artificial lures with barbless hooks can be used.

It's fifteen minutes from here to Highway 299, where you turn north to Fall River Mills.

Dinner: **Rick's Lodge,** Glenburn Star Route, Fall River Mills. (916)

336–5300. Have a steak and listen to anglers spinning tales of big trout on the Fall River and Hat Creek, believed to be the finest flyfishing waters in the state; the Fall averages 3,000 fish per mile, rainbows up to 24 inches long. Restaurant/bar; three meals.

Lodging: Simple rooms at Rick's Lodge. Beautiful location on the Fall River. Pool; boat and motor rental; guide service; flyfishing school; store selling flyfishing gear and snacks.

Day 3

Morning

Breakfast: At Rick's Lodge. All-American bacon-and-eggs, biscuits and gravy.

Fall River Mills is headquarters for fishing and hiking in the northern Lassen river valleys. There is golf to be had at the **Fall River Valley Golf Course,** west of town on Highway 299 (916–336–5555). Open May through October, the **Fort Crook Museum,** in town (916–336–5110), has exhibits of pioneer history, Indian artifacts, and several historical buildings.

Take Highway 299 west at Redding (or proceed on to Mount Lassen; see Escapes Farther Afield Five). Children will enjoy **Waterworks Park,** 151 North Boulder Drive, Redding (916–246–9550), where three giant waterslides and a 400-foot "Raging River" are great summer coolers. Take a walk in Redding: there's a 6-mile round-trip on the banks of the Sacramento. Drive north on Market Street and take a left onto Riverside. You'll see a sign for parking near the trail.

Lunch: **Westside Deli French Bakery,** 1600 California Street. (916) 222–0787. Sandwiches for here or for the road.

Afternoon

On the way south on Highway 5, 400-acre **Anderson River Park,** on the Sacramento River, has hiking, biking, and jogging trails. This is the destination for rafters floating down from Redding; raft rental companies pick you up here and shuttle back to Redding.

Just north of Red Bluff is a lovely spot on the river, **Ide Adobe State Park,** 3040 Adobe Road (916–527–5927), cool and shady, with giant oaks, lawns, picnic tables, and historical displays. You can fish here, but swimming in the fast current is not advisable.

Head south to the Bay Area.

There's More

Castle Crags State Park, 6 miles south of Dunsmuir off I–5. (916) 235–2684. A 6,000-foot granite fortress of giant pillars and monster boulders; good trout fishing in several streams; 2 miles of the Sacramento River; swimming, hiking, rock climbing. Get maps at the park office and amble up the sun-dappled Indian Creek Nature Trail, a 1-mile loop. The Vista Point loop is 5 view-filled miles. The Crags Trail to Castle Dome is 5.5 strenuous miles up and into the Castle Crags Wilderness; the Pacific Crest Trail is accessible from here. People often stop here just to fill up jugs with natural soda water.

Shasta Dam, fifteen minutes off Highway 5 above Redding (a thirty-minute trip in the summer, longer on the weekends). Walk out on the dam; see old photos and a film.

Houseboats. With a shoreline of 365 miles, Shasta is very popular for houseboating. Boats range from 15 to 56 feet long, sleeping four to twelve people; they're easy to navigate and may include air-conditioning, TV, and washers and dryers. Rentals at twelve houseboat marinas cost $1,000 per week and up.

Jones Valley Resort, 22300 Jones Valley Marina Drive, on the Pit River arm of Lake Shasta. (916) 275–7950. Specializes in luxury houseboats with gourmet galleys, fancy entertainment systems, and flying bridges.

Bridge Bay Resort, at the south end of the lake under a bridge that spans the water. (916) 275–3021. A full-service marina with houseboat rentals, cabins, ski boats, patio boats, and a motel with a swimming pool.

Antlers Resort and Marina, P.O. Box 140, Lakehead, 96051. (916) 238–2553. Houseboat rentals, cabins, and water-sports equipment.

Wilderness Adventures, 19504 Statton Acres Road, Lakehead. (916) 238–8121. White-water rafting expeditions on the upper Klamath, Salmon, and upper Sacramento rivers.

Fishing. Best in fall, not in August when it's hot.

Ice fishing at Castle Lake; road plowed all winter.

River fishing on the McCloud, Sacramento, Klamath, Salmon, and Scott.

One of the state's best-kept trout fishery secrets is the 12 miles of the lower Sacramento River between Redding and Anderson, fishable every month of the year. You'll need a driftboat and a guide, at least the first time; call Bob's Guide Service at (916) 222–8058. For more fishing information, see Escapes Farther Afield Five.

Golf. Lake Shastina Golf Resort, 5925 Country Club Drive, Weed. (916) 938–3201.

Railroading. The Blue Goose, P.O. Box 660, Yreka 96097. (916) 842–4146. A circa-1910 train hauling lumber and freight daily between Yreka and Montague, a 7-mile trip. Climbing on board the steamer at 10:00 A.M., you'll cruise past cattle ranches, sawmills, and lovely landscape. The train may be attacked by bandits as it approaches the historic town of Montague. There's an hour or so to picnic on the village green or take a horse-drawn tour; then it's back to Yreka.

Wild Horse Sanctuary, P.O. Box 30, Shingletown 96088. (916) 474–5770. Stay in frontier-style cabins at the base camp; track wild horses through the foothills of Mount Lassen; observe and photograph wild horses and burros in their protected habitat. Wild West adventure, campfires, hearty meals.

Llama packing. Rainbow Ridge Range Llama Backpacking of Mount Shasta, P.O. Box 1079, Mount Shasta. (916) 926–5794. Marble Mountains, Trinity Alps, Scott and Salmon river areas.

Box Canyon Dam, W. A. Barr Road, 2.5 miles southwest of the town of Mount Shasta. Stunning views of the rugged 200-foot-deep Sacramento River canyon and Lake Siskiyou. You can proceed across the dam and turn left onto paved Castle Lake Road to Castle Lake, a clear alpine lake in a granite bowl surroundeed by pine forests, where you can enjoy swimming, fishing, picnics, ice-skating, walk-in campsites.

Backpacking. The Shasta-Trinity National Forest offers exceptional backpacking. The Pacific Crest Trail can be accessed west of Mt. Shasta at Parks Creek, South Fork Road, Whalen Road, and at Castle Crags State Park. Trailheads up the east side of Mt. Shasta offer challenging hikes. Wilderness permits and maps are available at Mt. Shasta Ranger District, 204 West Alma Street, Mount Shasta. (916) 926–3606.

Clikapudi Trail, from Highway 5, 6 miles north of Redding, take the Mountain Gate exit to the visitor's center. (916) 275–1589. An easy 7-mile loop along the upper Pit River arm of Shasta Lake through woods and meadows, good fishing and wildlife watching for otter, deer, osprey, eagles.

Hiking around Lake Shasta can be a hot, dry experience in the summertime, but trails are green and gorgeous at all other times of year. From Packer's Bay Road, take Waters Gulch Trail through an oak forest, about 3 miles, up to great views of the Sacramento arm of the lake. Eastside Trail, also at Packer's Bay, is a half-mile, easy walk to swimming and fishing spots. From the Bailey Cove parking lot, a trail runs for almost 3 miles through a pretty, wooded area with lake views and you can swim at several places along the way.

Bidwell Park, off Highway 99 at Highway 32, northeast on Eighth Street in Chico, an hour south of Redding. (916) 891-4671. A pleasant place to picnic and take a walk in an old 2,500-acre park with magnificent big valley oaks and sweeping lawns, Chico Creek, swimming, a nature center, biking trails.

Special Events

May. Old Time Fiddler's Jamboree and Art Fair, Mount Shasta. (800) 874–7582.

June. Heritage Days at McArthur Burney Falls State Park. (916) 335–2777. Large crowds turn out for Native American dancers, musicians, pioneer crafts, square dancing, fiddlers.

June. Dunsmuir Railroad Days. (916) 235–2177. Since 1940, a celebration of historic railroad days, parade, barbecue, jazz festival.

June. Sacramento River Jazz Festival, Dunsmuir. (916) 235–2721. Great day on the green in Dunsmuir City Park.

July. McCloud Lumberjack Fiesta. (916) 964–2520. Fishing tournaments, parade, barbecue, entertainment, lumberjack show.

July. Redding Air Show. (916) 222–1610.

Other Recommended Restaurants and Lodgings

Fairfield

Fusilli Ristorante, 620 Jackson. (707) 428–4211. A favorite upscale dinner spot for skiers and vacationers on their way south to the Bay Area. Take the Travis Boulevard exit, going east on West Texas to Jackson in downtown Fairfield.

Tail of the Whale restaurant and bar at Bridge Bay Resort, Redding, under the bridge at the south end of Lake Shasta. (916) 275–3021. Views of the lake, dependable American food, bar.

Mount Shasta

Mount Shasta KOA Campground, 900 North Mount Shasta Boulevard. (916) 926–4029. A grassy, gardeny place for RVs and tents; animal corrals, camping cabins, store; on-site recreation; area tours; pool, playground.

Mount Shasta Ranch, 1008 W. A. Barr Road. (916) 926–3870. Bed-and-breakfast inn in a circa-1920s ranchhouse. Spacious rooms, suites, and cottages, gigantic common living room and game room, full breakfast, five minutes from Lake Siskiyou, children welcome.

Edson House, 203 Birch Street. (916) 926–1754. On a secluded knoll with panoramas of the mountain and Castle Crags, a large 1904 farm home. Some rooms have fireplaces, Jacuzzis, kitchenettes, sitting areas.

Dunsmuir

Railroad Park Resort, 100 Railroad Park Road. (916) 235–4440. Restaurant and motel in antique railroad cars; pool; spa. Good jumping-off point for exploring and hiking in Castle Crags. Also, RV park, campground, cabins.

Redding

Tiffany House Bed and Breakfast, 1510 Barbara Road. (916) 244–3225. Pretty rooms with bath; huge, beautiful yard; pool and spa.

River Inn, 1835 Park Marina Drive. (916) 241–9500. Edge of town on a small lake with mountain views, nice motel rooms, pool, barbecue, boat launch into Sacramento River.

Lakehead

Lakeshore Villa RV Park, 20672 Lakeshore Drive. (916) 238–8688. Twenty-five miles north of Redding; boat launch; waterskiing, swimming, fishing.

O'Brien

Holiday Harbor, P.O. Box 112, 96070. (800) 776–BOAT. Eighteen miles north of Redding on Shasta Caverns Road. RV hookups, boat launch, houseboats, waterskiing, fishing, boat rental, restaurant.

McCloud

McCloud Guest House, 606 West Colombero Drive. (916) 964–3160. Circa-1907 mansion, fine woodwork, antiques, claw-foot tubs, parlor with billiards, lawns and oaks, continental breakfast.

McCloud Hotel, 408 Main Street. (800) 964–2823. Fourteen spacious rooms and suites, Jacuzzi tubs, four-poster beds, big, comfy lounge with fireplace, expanded continental breakfast.

For More Information

Shasta Cascade Wonderland Association, 14250 Holiday Road, Redding, CA 96003. (916) 275–5555.

Mount Shasta Visitor Pavilion, 2 blocks east of the Highway 5 central exit at Lake and Pine streets. (800) 926–4865.

Mount Shasta, U.S. Forest Service, 204 West Alma, Mount Shasta, CA 96057. (916) 926–4511.

McArthur–Burney Falls State Park, Route 1, Box 1260, Burney, CA 96013. (916) 335–2777.

MISTIX, state park camping and RV site reservations. (800) 444–7275.

Yosemite

A view of Bridalveil Fall from Wawona Tunnel.

The Big Valley

_____ 2 NIGHTS _____

Waterfalls and wildflowers · Historic hotels · Hetch Hetchy
Trailside picnics · Mountaintops, monoliths · Sequoia groves

The Indians called it *Ahwahnee,* or "Deep, Grassy Valley." John Muir
saw it as a "great temple lit from above." You'll wax poetic in
Yosemite Valley when a setting sun paints a shining 4,000-foot curtain
across the face of Half Dome and glitters like a crown on snowcapped
peaks high above the lush river valley where you stand.

Americans have camped and hiked below the granite monoliths of Yosemite Valley since before Abraham Lincoln dedicated the valley and the Mariposa Big Trees to the state in 1864; sixteen years later the national park was created. Automobiles were officially admitted in 1913, and in the 1930s victims of the Great Depression lived here in their cars, eating fish from the streams.

Today Yosemite Valley is an international tourist attraction, jam-packed with visitors in the summertime, when miles of cars line up at dawn, each heading for one of 2,700 campsites. It's the most *re*visited national park in the country. A million people come in July and August, 80 percent of them staying in the valley, where most of the public facilities and the best-known postcard views are found; nevertheless, it's just 1 percent of the park.

Fall is a good time to come. Kids are back in school and the Merced River becomes a stream of molten gold, bright maples reflecting in its chilly waters. Crunchy carpets of rust-colored pine needles are rimmed with fernrows turned yellow. Crisp breezes rustle hauntingly through the aspen groves. In spring the wildflowers are a riot of color, and the valley's famous waterfalls are at their booming best. Nowhere in the world are so many high falls concentrated in so small an area as the seven square miles of Yosemite Valley. And a winter weekend at Yosemite can be unforgettable, whether you cross-country ski on silent forest trails or view a white wonderland through the tall windows of the old Ahwahnee Hotel.

Bay Area residents are lucky to be close enough to visit Yosemite in every season.

Day 1

Morning

Drive from the Oakland Bay Bridge east on Highway 580, connecting with 99 north to Manteca, then 120 east to the Big Oak Flat entrance to **Yosemite National Park,** a four-hour drive. The highway narrows here, ducking under huge overhanging boulders before emerging above the boiling Merced River into the valley, at an elevation of 4,000 feet. At the **visitor's center** in the Yosemite Village Mall at midvalley (209–372–0299), outfit yourself with a map and a guidebook. Depending on the weather and the season, plan explorations on foot and by shuttle.

If you plan to take an extensive hike or backpack trip now or in the future, stop at the new **Wilderness Center** (209–372–0740) next to the post office. Here you will find pre-trip planning stations for hikes and backpacks and a wilderness skills trail to test your knowledge of the wilderness and camping techniques. You can also obtain wilderness permits and purchase maps and guidebooks specifically for wilderness travel and education.

Sightseeing in the valley is best done on foot, on 9 miles of bike trails, on a tour bus, or on free shuttle buses—in other words, without your car.

Lunch: **Degnan's Deli,** in Yosemite Village, near the visitor's center. Sandwiches and salads for a picnic. Or, for a sit-down lunch, **The Loft,** in the same building: steak, chicken, sandwiches, homemade soups.

Afternoon

Jump on the shuttle bus and tour the valley. At stop #7, walk a short path to the base of **Yosemite Falls,** three cascades dropping 2,425 feet, the third highest waterfall in the world. (At stop #8 is the trailhead for a six-hour, strenuous hike to the top of the falls.)

For an hour's easy walk in the meadows around **Mirror Lake,** with wonderful views of Half Dome and Mount Watkins, get off at stop #17. The **Tenaya Zig Zags/Snow Creek Trail** is a little-used, 3.5-mile route to the rim of the valley, beginning east of Mirror Lake—not an easy hike but views are eye-popping.

You can leave children at **Happy Isles** at shuttle stop #16 for free one-hour walks and talks on nature, birds, and forest lore. Happy Isles is the start of several trails, including the 1.5 mile (one-way) **Mist Trail** to **Vernal Falls,** an exciting route but too strenuous and slippery for kids under age seven or eight. This is the most popular hike in the valley because the rewards are a breathtaking close-up view of the falls dropping over a 317-foot cliff plus knockout vistas of many peaks, domes, and water cascades.

Now that you're warmed up to Yosemite, go into the **Ansel Adams Gallery** (209–372–4413), near the visitor's center; since 1902 the place has been a camera store and gallery of signed Adams photos, prints, and posters of the valley in its seasonal raiments. Free two-hour photography workshops with professional teachers are conducted here. Visitors have enjoyed the workshops since the beginning of the century, and some were lucky enough to meet Ansel Adams himself, who taught these classes for over fifty years. To prepare for the photo workshop, attend the free documentary film about Adams's career and his lifelong love affair with Yosemite, screened on Sundays at the gallery.

Dinner: **Ahwahnee Hotel Dining Room,** Mid Valley. (209) 372–1489. Twenty-four-foot trestle-beamed ceiling and two-story windows with views of **Royal Arches,** spectacular when frosted with snow and ice. Continental cuisine in a restaurant that's been called America's most beautiful. Dress is casual at breakfast and lunch. At dinner men must wear coats and ties; women, dresses or nice slacks. *Lodging:* **Ahwahnee Hotel.** (209) 252–4848.

Standing gloriously aloof in a woodland setting, with granite cliffs rising up startlingly all around, the art deco hotel is in perfect shape, with painted beams, decorated floors, and stained-glass windows faded into subtle Indian colors. Sofas, armchairs, and fabulous old Oriental rugs are arranged by a huge fireplace in the Great Lounge. Built in 1927, the place still has a halcyon-days atmosphere and is museumlike, enriched with paintings, photos, and priceless Native American baskets. When fall leaves blow along the footpaths and wood smoke curls silently into a twilight glow, the spirit of summers past comes alive at the Ahwahnee. Reservations must be made well in advance; see page 287.

Day 2

Morning

Breakfast: An American breakfast in the Ahwahnee Hotel Dining Room.

Purchase picnic goodies and set off on the 32-mile drive on Glacier Point Road to **Glacier Point,** atop the sheer southern wall of the valley. Several waterfalls, as well as **Half Dome, El Capitan,** and other famous pinnacles, surround the valley. Looking 3,200 feet down, you can spot the river snaking along, and you're likely to see climbers making a several days' ascent to the dizzying 2,850-foot summit of El Capitan. A vertical wall of granite four times as large as Gibraltar, "El Cap" is a memento of glaciers that tore off and ground into little pieces great sections of mountain. The Ice Age created Yosemite's domes, spires, stacks, and split mountain faces. Rivers and streams deepened the canyons and ravines, watering a natural garden on the flat valley floor and filling the Merced River. Mesmerizing, the view from Glacier Point puts hundreds of millions of years of geologic history on display. The faint thundering sound you hear in the springtime is **Nevada Falls,** 2 miles away.

In the summer it's possible to take a hikers' bus to Glacier Point and walk all the way down to the valley, 4.8 miles, a three- to four-hour hike. This time of year, robust climbers trek to the top of Half Dome by hiking the John Muir Trail or Mist Trail to Little Yosemite Valley, where they camp overnight. The next day, the climb is made with the aid of cables strung along the shoulder of the dome. This is a strenuous walk and a challenging climb, but many physically fit people do it.

Along Glacier Point Road are several memorable stops to make. **Dewey Point,** at 7,385 feet and overlooking **Bridalveil Fall** and El Capitan, is accessible by a beautiful 7-mile round-trip trail just west of Bridalveil Campground. According to the time of year, the path may be bordered with sky-blue lupine, Indian paintbrush, or 6-foot-tall rose-colored fireweed. Crossing a footbridge over a creek, bear left around **McGurk Meadow,** where mule deer graze in grasses sprinkled with shooting stars and goldenrod.

To reach **Mono Meadow** and **Mount Starr King View,** park 2.5 miles beyond Bridalveil Campground and take the trail east, dropping for .5 mile to the meadow, continuing to a spectacular view 1 mile farther on: 3 miles round-trip.

Six miles past Bridalveil Campground, park on the left, the starting point for an easy 2-mile ranger-led interpretive hike called "A Short Walk to Canada" that takes place every day, June through September. You will walk in a red fir and lodgepole pine Canadian life zone past deep rock fissures to **Taft Point,** overhanging the valley.

Lunch: Have a picnic on top of the world at Glacier Point or on a nearby nature trail.

Afternoon

Explore some of the 800 miles of hiking trails in the Yosemite backcountry or amble along the banks of the Merced River, trying your luck at trout fishing. Lie about on a sunny beach or take a swim in the river or at the Ahwahnee. If you've become fascinated by the history and geologic wonders of the park, you may wish to get in on one of the many seminars, lectures, theater presentations, and tours offered throughout the year.

Dinner and Lodging: At the Ahwahnee Hotel.

Day 3

Morning

Breakfast: At the Ahwahnee Hotel Dining Room.

Take Big Oak Flat Road to the **Merced Grove** of giant sequoias. It's a 2-mile walk into the grove from the road; few people take this hike, thus giving you the opportunity to be alone with the big beauties.

If you'd rather drive, take the 6-mile steep, narrow road to **Tuolumne Grove,** a magnificent stand of sequoias that includes the famous "Dead Giant" drive-through tree.

Lunch: A picnic amid the sequoia groves.

Afternoon

Proceed to the Big Oak Flat entrance to Yosemite (trail maps here), then north on Evergreen Road to the **Hetch Hetchy Valley and Reservoir,** where there is much to see. The drowning of the spectacular valley in the 1930s was vigorously opposed by John Muir and the Sierra Club, but the dam was built; today the reservoir continues to supply San Francisco with water and power.

A sun catcher, the valley is quite hot in the summer, but delightful for hiking October through May. Hetch Hetchy Reservoir is 8 miles long, ringed with granite domes and dramatic cliff faces, a habitat for a great variety of wildlife; fishing is good, although swimming and boating are not allowed. From the top of the dam, take the flat trail through the tunnel and along the north edge of the reservoir; about 2 miles beyond, **Tueeulala Fall** and **Wapama Falls** thunder down, the latter so enthusiastic that it sometimes washes out the trail. And at 6.5 miles out, **Rancheria Falls** are misty and refreshing.

Return to the Big Oak Flat entrance and take Highway 120 east through Oakdale to 99, crossing Highway 5 to 205, connecting with 580 to the East Bay.

There's More

Winter fun in Yosemite. Yosemite is open all year. Avoid the crowds and enjoy the supercolossal winter beauty of the park, as well as off-season room rates. Although frosty white on the clifftops and often in the valley, winter weather is usually mild. The valley accumulates about 29 inches of snow, Badger Pass Ski Area about 180 inches. Wildlife is spotted in the open much more often at this time of year: coyotes, mule deer, raccoons, bears. Ice-skating at Curry Village, with spectacular views of Half Dome. Downhill skiing at Badger Pass, with six lifts to the 8,000-foot summit. Nordic skiing on 350 miles of trails and roads; 23 miles of machine-groomed track and skating lanes. Snowcat and snowshoe tours. Guided snowshoe walks, motor coach guided winter tours, winter nature walks, Junior Snow Ranger program, winter field trips for photographers and artists. Snowplay areas at Crane Flat on state Route 120, and just outside the southern entrance on state Route 412 near Fish Camp. For more information call (209) 372–1244.

Rafting. Ahwahnee Whitewater Expeditions, P.O. Box 1161, Columbia 95310. (209) 533–1401. Rafting on the Merced, Tuolumne, Stanislaus, and Carson rivers.

Hershey Chocolate Company, 1400 South Yosemite Avenue, Oakdale. (209) 848–8126. Free tours of the chocolate factory during the week; located 20 miles east of Manteca on Highway 120.

Complimentary shuttle bus service is provided year-round to points in the eastern end of Yosemite Valley. In summer, it also runs from Wawona to the Mariposa Grove and between Tenaya Lake and Tuolumne Meadows Lodge. In winter, buses run from valley hotels to the Badger Pass Ski Area. The shuttle serves most of the valley trailheads and all of the major buildings and attractions in the valley. New in the national park shuttle fleet are two quiet, zero-emission electric buses.

Tuolumne Meadows, at 8,600 feet, is the largest open meadow in the Sierras at the subalpine level, bordered by the snow-fed Tuolumne River and surrounded by peaks and glacier-polished domes. The nearest access is by Tioga Road near the town of Lee Vining, on the northeasern side of the park, a road that is closed for about half the year, due to snow. You can also take the beautiful drive up from the valley (also closed during the wintertime).

A hub for backpacking trails, 2.5-mile-long Tuolumne Meadows may sparkle with frost or be awash in purple nightshade, golden monkeyflowers, and riots of magenta lady-slipper orchids. You can drive to the rustic Tuoloumne Meadows Lodge (209–252–4848) and the Tuolumne Meadows Campground (800–365–2297), the largest in the park, with 325 sites; the most desirable sites are on the east side near the river. Campfire programs are held most nights. Within walking distance of the campground are a grocery store, stables, and a restaurant in a tent beside the river, serving substantial American fare. Tent cabins with wood stoves are located in a picturesque setting near the river.

A variety of guided walks begin at Tuolumne Meadows. The "Night Prowl," an after-dark caravan around the meadow, turns up great gray owls, spotted bats, and other nocturnal denizens of the High Sierras.

Between Tuolumne and the valley off the Tioga Road, **White Wolf**, a summertime-only headquarters for backcountry trails, has rustic tent cabins, a "first-come" campground, store, stables, and a lovely old clapboard dining hall that serves simple meals all day; dinner reservations are recommended (209–372–1316). The campground here is a favorite of those who like the cooler daytime temperatures at 8,000 feet and easy access to lakes nearby.

Overnights in the Tuolumne backcountry require a wilderness permit, free of charge. Trailheads have quotas that are occasionally "sold out" in the high season, so permits may be requested by mail in advance from the Wilderness Office, P.O. Box 577, Yosemite 95389 (209–372–0310). A hiker's bus from the valley will drop you off near Tioga Road trailheads.

Dog Lake is the closest lake to Tuolumne and the warmest of the chilly lakes at this altitude. It's a 1.5-mile one-way trek, a little steep at first but easy enough for all ages and there's good swimming and fishing at the end. Two hundred thirty species of birds and eighty species of mammals have been sighted here, including bobcats, bears, eagles, and endangered peregrine falcons. **Yosemite High Sierra Camps Saddle Trips.** (209) 372–1445. Four- and six-day saddle trips to camps between 7,150 and 10,300 feet. Camps are 8 miles apart, and each provides tents, beds, linens, and blankets. Breakfast and dinner are served in a heated dining tent. Groups are limited to ten people and are accompanied by an experienced guide. Personal belongings are carried on a pack mule. A trip of a lifetime.

"Sunrise Camera Walk" begins at Yosemite Lodge at 6:00 A.M. from June through September. (209) 372–0299. Two-hour guided expedition on flat trails to the best sites on the valley floor for taking pictures of the natural landmarks.

Kayaking, canoeing, inner tubing on the **Merced River,** which winds through the valley. Rent rafts and life jackets at Curry Village. It's best to call ahead (209–372–0299) before you arrive with water sports in mind. Sometimes access is limited or banned due to water conditions or habitat restoration.

"Stars Over Yosemite," a special moonlit experience after dark at Glacier Point, most Friday and Saturday nights at 8:00 P.M. if the skies are clear. Peer through an astronomer's telescope to see the vast river of the Milky Way, a lively parade of satellites and constellations that probably are not visible in your sky at home. As the moon washes over silvery granite domes and peaks, the lunar-like landscape seems lost in time. The Sierra "Range of Light," as Ansel Adams called it, takes on a new mystery.

Special Events

January–February. Chef's Holidays, Ahwahnee Hotel and Yosemite Lodge. (209) 454–0555. Demonstrations, seminars with prominent chefs, gala banquets.

February. Yosemite Renaissance, Yosemite Valley Visitor Center. (209) 372–0299. National juried art show with Yosemite as the theme; paintings, photography, sculpture, lithography.

November. Ski Season Opening Day, November 23, Badger Pass. (209) 372–1244.

November–December. Yosemite Vintners' Holidays. (209) 454–2020. Banquets and seminars with prominent vintners.

December. Christmas Bird Count, in Yosemite Valley. (209) 372–0291. Experienced and novice birdwatchers invited.

December–January. The Bracebridge Dinners, in the Ahwahnee Hotel Dining Room. (209) 372–1489. The Renaissance is re-created at elaborate performances and monumental banquets; reservations by lottery.

Other Recommended Restaurants and Lodgings

Accommodations in the National Park at the Ahwahnee Hotel, Yosemite Lodge, Wawona Hotel, White Wolf Lodge, Curry Village, and in tent cabins and cabins without baths can be arranged by calling (209) 252–4848 or writing to P.O. Box 577, Yosemite 95389. The **Curry Village** area of the valley offers a variety of accommodations, from tent cabins to hotel rooms and loft rooms sleeping six or more; all are clean and quite basic, some can be noisy. Nearby, Yosemite Lodge has 484 simple rooms in a compound that includes a cafeteria, restaurants, a post office, gift shops, a swimming pool, an outdoor theater, bike rentals, and a tour desk.

Reservations are hard to get. Call at 7:00 A.M. Pacific time (8:00 A.M. on weekends), 366 days before your intended arrival. Visit off-season in midweek. Tent cabins are in the least demand, and there is always the possibility that you can upgrade to a room upon arrival. If you want to make a reservation on short notice, call thirty days, fifteen days, or seven days in advance. These are dates when rooms held by reservation may be cancelled without penalty. If all else fails, join a package tour through a travel agent.

Camping: Large, usually crowded, valley campgrounds—Lower and Upper River, and North, Upper, and Lower Pines—can be noisy with road traffic and RV generators, but they're convenient for walking and biking to most public places and trailheads. If you are interested in the wide variety of classes, interpretive hikes, and performances scheduled throughout the high season, a valley campground may be your best choice (800–365–2267).

A compromise between accessibility to the valley and a quieter, prettier place to camp is found at **Bridalveil Creek Campground,** 25 miles from the valley on the Glacier Point Road at an elevation of 7,200 feet. Each of the one hundred tent and RV sites here and at other higher elevation camps are provided with "bear lockers," secure boxes where your food can be kept safe from black bears. Reservations.

Yosemite Cedar Lodge, 8 miles from Yosemite, El Portal. (800) 321–5261. Featuring 200 deluxe and moderate rooms, some family units and suites, a restaurant, swimming pools, access to the Merced River.

Coulterville

Hotel Jeffery, 1 Main Street. (209) 878–3471. Gloriously restored, circa-1850 twenty-room hotel; garden patio, saloon, restaurant.

For More Information

Yosemite National Park, P.O. Box 577, Yosemite, CA 95389. General information: (209) 372–0200. Reservations: (209) 252–4848.
Yosemite Deaf Services Coordinator. (209) 372–4726.
Badger Pass Snow Conditions. (209) 372–1000.
MISTIX, campground reservations. (800) 365–2267.
Tuolumne County Visitor's Bureau, P.O. Box 4020, Sonora, CA 95370. (209) 533–4420.

Advice: Hikers and campers should keep in mind that sudden storms are not uncommon in Yosemite, any month of the year. Weather changes rapidly in the Sierras, and snow can fall as early as September.

Southern Sierras

Clark's Cabin is dwarfed by a giant sequoia tree.

Wawona and the Lake Country

_____ 2 NIGHTS _____

Walks in the woods · Sequoia giants · Fireside chats
Yosemite history · Railroad ride · Lunch at the lake

The southern part of Yosemite National Park, called Wawona, is the place to go in midsummer, when Yosemite Valley is crowded with cars and people. Wilderness trails are silent, except for the crunch of your own footsteps and the prattle of squirrels and Stellar's jays.

The historical heart of the park, Wawona is anchored by the gracious old Wawona Hotel, riding the edge of magnificent Wawona Meadow like an aging but still glistening white oceanliner.

Between Yosemite and Kings Canyon National Park, the lake country of the central Sierras remains relatively undiscovered by Californians. Some 700 miles of trout streams and numerous lakes, reservoirs, and campgrounds make this an area you'll want to explore on many weekends. Just off Highway 41, at an elevation of 3,400 feet and situated on the 1,000-acre blue sparkler of Bass Lake, are a luxury resort; cabins, condos, and campgrounds; marinas for sailing, fishing, and waterskiing boats; and endless hiking trails in the surrounding Sierra National Forest.

Day 1

Morning

It's 200 miles from the Bay Area to Yosemite. From the East Bay take Highway 580 east to I–5 south. Then take Highway 152 through Los Banos to 99 south and 145 east in Madera to 41 north to **Oakhurst,** an antiques center and busy gateway to Yosemite and the recreational lakes country. Take Highway 41 north from Oakhurst for twenty minutes, to the right turn onto Highway 222; it's now 4 miles to **Bass Lake.**

A warm-water lake reaching seventy-eight degrees in the summer, Bass Lake is good for fishing in the spring and fall for trout, bass, catfish, and bluegill; it's also popular for all types of water sports and camping. You can rent windsurfers and boats for canoeing, sailing, rowing and waterskiing. For a short, easy walk at the lake, take the half-mile **Way of the Mono Trail,** along Road 222. You'll learn some American Indian history and see some great views. Once a day in the summer, the *Bass Lake Queen* takes fifty passengers on an open-air tour of the lake (209–642–3121).

Lunch: **Ducey's on the Lake,** at Pine Lake. (209) 642-3131. Dine on a sunny deck overlooking Bass Lake. Grilled chicken, salads, burgers, fresh fish, pasta.

Afternoon

It's 14 miles on Highway 41 to **Marriott's Tenaya Lodge at Yosemite,** 1122 Highway 41, Fish Camp (800–635–5807)—a destination resort overlooking forested mountains and valleys and located five minutes from Yosemite Park. The two-story atrium lobby and the restaurants, lounge, and public areas have a casual but luxurious feel and are decorated with Indian artifacts and Western-style furnishings.

Tours from the hotel get you into the park and to the Badger Pass Ski Area. There are a fully staffed children's daycamp program here and, nearby, many trailheads for walks, hikes, and mountain-bike rides through pine forests and along streamsides.

Try the **Lewis Creek National Recreation Trail,** 5 miles south of the Yosemite Gate, a 3.5-mile path through dogwood, azalea, and pines with two waterfalls and some fishing holes in Lewis Fork Creek. The lodge offers complimentary guided hikes every day and a detailed "Master Hiking" guide describing guided, self-guided, and scenic trails.

Bikes are available at the hotel. Five minutes away is a stable for guided horseback rides. You can cross-country ski right from the lodge and rent equipment here, skiing on your own or taking the guided tour.

Tenaya Lodge is the nation's first luxury resort to be classified a "green" hotel by the EPA, with environmental programs such as water conservation, outdoor lighting designed to eliminate ambient light bleed, special kitchen equipment, and recycling services.

At the end of an afternoon in the great outdoors, take a dip in the indoor or outdoor pools.

Dinner: At the **Sierra Restaurant,** in the lodge. Fresh fish, local produce, California and Northern Italian cuisines, fireplace, mountain views.

Lodging: At Marriott's Tenaya Lodge (see above). A 242-room resort hotel with two pools, a fitness salon, a sauna, steam baths, and spas.

Day 2

Morning

Breakfast: At the **Parkside Restaurant,** in the lodge. All-American breakfasts. If you decide to picnic today, the Parkside Deli will put together sandwiches, salads, and giganto brownies.

Drive or bike 7 miles on Highway 41 into the park to **Mariposa Grove** and take the tram through the grove to see the 209-foot, 300-ton **Grizzly Giant;** the **Columbia** (290 feet); and hundreds more 2,000-year-old giant sequoias. This is the largest and most impressive of three sequoia groves in the park. At several tram stops you can hop off and wander along nature trails, the best way to enjoy these magnificent beings, the largest living things on earth. A vista point, accessible by a short walk from the top of the grove, overlooks the entire Wawona basin. In the **Mariposa Grove Museum** are displays about the big trees and the flora and fauna of Yosemite. Continue to drive the main road for a few minutes until you reach the Wawona Hotel, which is located across the street from the golf course.

Lunch: At the **Wawona Hotel.** (209) 252–4848. Good American food in a Victorian-era dining room, with charming Old Yosemite touches.

Afternoon

With long verandas looking over sweeping lawns and meadows and the **Wawona Golf Course,** the **Wawona Hotel** is a National Historic Landmark and the oldest resort hotel in the state. Rooms are simple and nicely maintained. On Saturday evenings in summer, barbecues are held outdoors, with red-checked tablecloths, corn on the cob, steaks, hamburgers, and all the trimmings.

Just down the road is the **Yosemite Pioneer History Center,** a compound of historic buildings and vintage vehicles. Here costumed docents play the parts of residents from bygone days.

Stroll around **Wawona Meadow,** beginning across from the hotel, a flat route through the pines around the huge wildflower-strewn meadow, ending behind the hotel, a 3-mile round-trip. This is one of several meadows making Wawona a popular area for cross-country skiing.

A more challenging hike is to **Chilnualna Falls,** a steep, 8-mile round-trip through pines, cedars, and manzanita to a jetting avalanche of water, refreshing when you jump in the icy pool at the base of the upper falls. The trailhead is located 1.7 miles east of the main road, on Chilnaulna Falls Road.

Beaches and swimming spots are easily accessible on the south fork of the **Merced River** as it runs through Wawona. About 200 yards upstream from the covered bridge are small swimming and wading pools, the warmest waters in the park.

Dinner: At Marriott's Tenaya Lodge. Or, if an extraspecial dinner is called for, take the twenty-minute drive to Oakhurst to **Erna's Elderberry House** (see page 294).

Lodging: Marriott's Tenaya Lodge.

Day 3

Morning

Breakfast: At Marriott's Tenaya Lodge.

Five minutes from the lodge, on Highway 41, is the **Yosemite Mountain Sugar Pine Railroad** (209–683–7273), set in a lovely wooded glade. An eighty-four-ton vintage locomotive, the largest ever built for a narrow-gauge track, pulls open cars 4 miles through forestlands into **Lewis Creek Canyon.** Steam rolls out from under the great engine, black smoke belches up into the sky, and a conductor spins tales of when the railroad hauled millions of board feet of lumber out of the Sierras. From here rough-sawn boards floated in a wooden flume through a steep canyon all the way to Madera, more than 40 miles away. From June through September, a "Moonlight Special" evening train excursion ends with a steak barbecue and live music around a campfire. There's a beautiful picnic spot here, and cross-country skiing is excellent throughout the Sugar Pine area.

Lunch: **Narrow Gauge Inn,** next to the railroad station. (209) 683–7720. The Victorian era and the Old West are combined in the dining hall and Bull Moose saloon; cozy in cool weather, when logs burn in the big stone fireplaces.

Afternoon

Retrace your route back to the Bay Area.

There's More

Fresno Flats Historical Park, a mile from Oakhurst on Road 427. (209) 683–6570. Re-created Western community from the region's early timber and ranching era. Old buildings have been moved from all over the county, including jails, schools, barns, wagons, buggies, and a furnished home from the last century.

Sierra Mono Museum, at Malum Ridge Road (Road 274) and Mammoth Pool Road (Road 225), between North Fork and South Fork. (209) 877–2115. Major exhibition of American Indian artifacts and California wildlife displays.

Yosemite High Country Wilderness Tours. (209) 683–4013. Four-wheel-drive treks in the Sierra National Forest, fabulous views, knowledgeable guides, air-conditioned vehicles, snacks and deli lunch.

Southern Yosemite Mountain Guides, P.O. Box 301, Bass Lake. (800) 231–4575. Guided backpacking trips, including all equipment, in the Ansel Adams Wilderness, and Kings Canyon and Sequoia National Parks.

Nelder Grove. Ten miles north of Oakhurst on Highway 41, take Sky Ranch Road 6 miles; also accessible by vehicle from Tenaya Lodge via several miles of dirt road. One of the largest trees in the world, the Bull Buck, rests in a wilderness grove of more than a hundred specimen sequoias; a 1-mile, self-guided trail runs through the grove along the banks of Nelder Creek.

Lewis Creek National Recreation Trail, 5 miles south of the southern Yosemite Gate. A 3.5-mile trail through dogwood, azalea, pines; Corlieu and Red Rock falls; fishing in Lewis Fork Creek.

Horseback riding. Yosemite Trails Pack Station, P.O. Box 100, Fish Camp 93623. (800) 635–5807. Guided trips into Mariposa Grove and other parts of the park. Inquire at Marriott's Tenaya Lodge.

Golf. Wawona Golf Course. (209) 375–6572. Nine holes.
Boat rentals at Bass Lake. The Forks. (209) 642–3737.
Miller's Landing. (209) 642–3633.
The Pines Marina. (209) 642–3565.

Special Events

April. Oakdale PRCA Rodeo, Oakdale. (209) 847–2244. One of the state's top rodeos, a week of events, parade, dance, World Champion Cowboys.
May. Mountain Peddlers' Fair, Oakhurst. (209) 683–7766. Some 500 antiques dealers.
June. Custom and Classic Car Show, Bass Lake. (209) 642–3676. Fifties weekend, barbecue, dance.
August. Bass Lake Arts and Crafts Festival. (209) 642–3676.
August. Indian Fair Days and Pow Wow, Sierra Mono Museum, at Roads 225 and 228, North Fork. (209) 877–2115.
September. Sierra Mountaineer Days, Oakhurst. (209) 683–8492. Parade, carnival, dance.
October. Bass Lake Farmers' Market and Worlds' Best Apple Baking Contest, Bass Lake. (209) 642–3676.
December. Yosemite Pioneer Christmas. (209) 372–0265. Special programs at the Wawona Hotel, caroling, candlelight tours.

Other Recommended Restaurants and Lodgings

Oakhurst

Erna's Elderberry House Restaurant, 48688 Victoria Lane, off Highway 41. (209) 683–6800. A surprising find in this unassuming little town. European and California cuisine extraordinaire in elegant country French surroundings; lunch and dinner. Also Chateau du Sureau, Erna's out-of-this-world European-style inn, a castle with nine luxurious suites; pricey, a place for honeymoons.

Best Western Yosemite Gateway Inn, 40530 Highway 41. (209) 683–2378. Has 118 rooms in a parklike setting; mountain views; indoor and outdoor pools; some kitchens; restaurant; bar.

Fish Camp

Narrow Gauge Inn, 48571 Highway 41. (209) 683–7720. Rooms and breakfast in a wooded setting.

Karen's Bed and Breakfast Yosemite Inn, 1144 Railroad Avenue. (800) 346–1443. One mile from the park on Highway 41. Charming

country-style accommodations with TLC from Karen, plus big breakfasts; very close to the park.

Summerdale Campground, operated by the U.S. Forest Service.
(209) 683–4665. Nice, small, streamside sites.

Ahwahnee

The Homestead, 41110 Road 600. (209) 683–0495. Four very nice
adobe housekeeping cottages with a corral and barn space for horses.

Ahwahnee Resort and Country Club, 46795 Road 621, near
Oakhurst. (209) 683–3979. Quiet, tree-shaded RV sites with a swimming pool and a beautiful golf course.

Wawona

Redwoods Cottages, P.O. Box 2095 95389. (209) 375–6666. One
hundred privately owned cabins to rent.

Yosemite West

Yosemite's Four Seasons, 7519 Henness Circle, near the south entrance to the park. (800) 669–9300. Rooms, studios, homes, apartments
to rent, simple to luxurious.

Bass Lake

The Pines Resort, P.O. Box 109. 93604. (800) 350–7463. Rustic condos at the lake; tennis, sauna, hot tub.

Ducey's on the Lake, P.O. Box 329. 93604. (800) 350–7463. Luxury
suites on the lake; packages with meals at Ducey's restaurant are available.

Bass Lake Land Office, P.O. Box 349. (209) 642–3600. Cabins and
houses to rent.

For More Information

Yosemite National Park, P.O. Box 577, Yosemite, CA 95389. General information: (209) 372–0265. Reservations: (209) 252–4848. Road
and weather information: (209) 372–4605.

MISTIX, campground reservations. (800) 365–2267.

Yosemite campground reservations. (800) 436–7275.

Yosemite Deaf Services Coordinator. (209) 372–4726.

Sierra National Forest Ranger District. (209) 841–3311.

Southern Yosemite Visitor's Bureau, P.O. Box 1404, Oakhurst, CA
93644. (209) 683–INFO.

Advice: Hikers and campers should keep in mind that sudden
storms are not uncommon in Yosemite, any month of the year.
Weather changes rapidly in the Sierras, and snow can fall as early as
September.

Index

About the Author

A native Northern Californian, Karen Misuraca makes her home in California's wine country, the Napa Valley. She is the author of *Family Adventure Guide Northern California, The Best Years of Their Lives: Seniors at Work, Success Strategies for Retail Selling* and *Selling Books in the Bay Area.* Karen specializes in writing about travel, golf, subjects for seniors, and business, and is a contributor to magazines and newspapers, including *Alaska Airlines Magazine, Napa Valley Appellation, Copley News Service, Golfweek, Family Fun, Dallas Morning News,* and others.

Misuraca escapes into California's great outdoors nearly every weekend unless she is on assignment abroad. Her dog-eared passport is matched by those of her three daughters, five granddaughters, one grandson, and her companion, Michael Capp.